ALASKA CRUISE TRADE GUIDE 2024 EDITION

Table of Contents:

1. Introduction

- Purpose of the Guide

- Overview of the Alaska Cruise Industry

2. Planning an Alaska Cruise

- Choosing the Right Cruise Line

- Selecting the Itinerary

- Travel Seasons and Weather Considerations

- Booking and Reservations

3. Alaskan Ports of Call

-Juneau: Alaska's Capital City

-Skagway: Gateway to the Klondike Gold Rush

-Ketchikan: The Salmon Capital of the World

-Sitka: A Blend of History and Nature

-Anchorage: Alaska's Urban Hub

-Glacier Bay: A Natural Wonder

-Icy Strait Point: Authentic Alaskan Experience

4. Cruise Ship Amenities and Features

- *Cabin Options*

- *Onboard Entertainment*

- *Dining and Culinary Experience*

NOTE:

Embark upon an unparalleled journey as you immerse yourself in the very essence of this Alaska Cruise travel guide. Crafted not only to inform but to spark your imagination, nurture your creativity, and awaken the adventurer within you, this guide extends an invitation to step into a realm of exploration that is distinctly your own. Departing from the ordinary, you won't find accompanying images within these pages. Our firm belief rests in the idea that the true beauty of every discovery is most vividly experienced firsthand, untainted by visual interpretations or preconceived notions.

Picture every monument, each destination, and even the hidden corners of Alaska Cruise as exquisite surprises, patiently awaiting the moment to captivate and astonish you when you find yourself standing before them. We are steadfast in our commitment to preserving the thrill of that initial gaze, the sheer wonder that accompanies the revelation of something new. With this guide in hand, you stand on the precipice of an extraordinary voyage where curiosity is your sole mode of transportation, and this guide serves as your unwavering companion. Set aside any preconceived notions and allow yourself to be transported into an authentic Alaska Cruise of revelations—the enchantment of your adventure begins right here. However, keep in mind that the most enchanting images will be the ones etched by your own eyes and treasured within your heart.

In stark contrast to conventional guidebooks, this volume intentionally omits intricate maps. The reason, you may ask? We ardently believe that the most extraordinary discoveries unfurl when you let yourself lose track, allowing the very essence of each place to guide you while embracing the uncertainty of the path. Bid farewell to predetermined itineraries and meticulously laid out routes, for our aim is to empower you to navigate Alaska Cruise in your very own way, unburdened by boundaries. Allow yourself to be carried by the currents of exploration, uncovering hidden gems that remain elusive on conventional maps. Summon the courage to embrace the unknown, trusting your instincts as you boldly venture forth, prepared to be pleasantly surprised—because the magic of your journey starts now, in a realm where maps are nonexistent, and the paths unfold with each step. The most extraordinary adventures await within the uncharted folds of the unfamiliar.

Section 1: Introduction

Purpose of the Guide

The "Alaska Cruise Trade Guide 2024" serves as an indispensable resource for all stakeholders involved in the vibrant and dynamic world of the Alaska cruise industry. This comprehensive guide is meticulously crafted to provide a deep understanding of the industry's nuances, challenges, opportunities, and trends that will shape the cruise trade landscape throughout the year and beyond. With a focus on fostering informed decision-making, facilitating seamless operations, and promoting sustainable growth, this guide encapsulates the essence of the Alaska cruise trade.

At its core, the purpose of this guide is to bridge the knowledge gap and empower cruise lines, tour operators, local businesses, regulatory authorities, and enthusiasts with insights that transcend the ordinary. The Alaska cruise industry is a multi-dimensional tapestry, interwoven with diverse threads of maritime expertise, tourism dynamics, environmental stewardship, cultural appreciation, and economic prosperity. The guide recognizes this complexity and strives to unravel its intricacies, offering a holistic perspective that encourages collaboration, innovation, and responsible practices.

For cruise lines and tour operators, the guide functions as a compass guiding them through the vast Alaskan waters. It aids in curating itineraries that resonate with passengers seeking unforgettable experiences. By dissecting the unique characteristics of each port of call, the guide aids in the selection of excursions that capture the spirit of the region, from exploring majestic glaciers to immersing in indigenous cultures. Furthermore, it navigates the evolving landscape of onboard amenities and entertainment, enabling operators to craft journeys that seamlessly blend luxury, adventure, and education.

Local businesses find in this guide a blueprint for harmonious collaboration. It unveils strategies to maximize the economic benefits of the cruise industry while ensuring that the cultural and natural heritage of Alaska remains preserved for generations. By fostering partnerships that prioritize authenticity and sustainability, businesses can cater to the discerning tastes of cruise passengers, offering them a genuine taste of Alaskan life.

Regulatory authorities and policymakers discover a wealth of information that supports their stewardship of the Alaskan waters. The guide dissects environmental regulations, encouraging a proactive approach to safeguarding the delicate ecosystems that cruise ships navigate. It expounds upon best practices for waste management, emissions reduction, and wildlife protection, equipping authorities with the tools to uphold the pristine beauty that lures visitors to these shores.

Passengers embarking on an Alaskan adventure will find the guide to be an indispensable prelude to their journey. It sets their expectations by shedding light on the diverse landscapes, weather patterns, and wildlife encounters that await. Through this insight, passengers can pack appropriately, plan their activities wisely, and fully engage with the experiences that Alaska offers, making each moment aboard a ship or on land an enriching chapter in their travelogue.

In essence, the "Alaska Cruise Trade Guide 2024" transcends the conventional notion of a guidebook. It assumes the role of a facilitator, a catalyst, and an advocate. It aspires to be a cornerstone of informed decision-making, fostering collaborations that enhance the cruise experience, support local communities, and protect the natural beauty that Alaska is celebrated for. By encapsulating the spirit of exploration, education, and responsible tourism, the guide embraces the purpose of not just serving the Alaska cruise trade, but also safeguarding the very essence of the Last Frontier.

Overview of the Alaska Cruise

The Alaska cruise Industry, a dynamic and captivating realm within the broader maritime and tourism sectors, has long been a symbol of adventure, wonder, and unparalleled natural beauty. Nestled within the northwestern corner of North America, Alaska offers a pristine wilderness that has, for decades, beckoned travelers from all corners of the globe. This overview delves into the multifaceted tapestry of the Alaska cruise industry, unraveling its historical evolution, economic significance, environmental considerations, and the intricate interplay of stakeholders that shape its present and future.

The roots of the Alaska cruise industry can be traced back to the mid-20th century when intrepid travelers began to seek passage to this remote frontier. Initially, explorers and researchers ventured aboard rudimentary vessels, setting the stage for the cruise industry's birth. Over the years, as infrastructure improved and accessibility increased, cruise lines recognized the allure of Alaska's untouched landscapes. The industry's growth soared in the latter half of the 20th century, leading to the development of specialized cruise ships designed to navigate the region's icy waters while offering passengers unparalleled views of glaciers, fjords, and wildlife.

The Alaska cruise industry is not only a visual spectacle but a vital economic engine for the region. The influx of cruise passengers, coupled with their expenditures on accommodations,

dining, shopping, and excursions, injects substantial revenue into Alaskan communities. Ports of call such as Juneau, Ketchikan, and Skagway have evolved from modest settlements to bustling hubs, strategically adapting their infrastructure to accommodate ships of varying sizes. This economic impact ripples through various sectors, from tourism-related enterprises to local artisans and service providers, fostering growth and diversification.

The enchanting allure of Alaska's glaciers, towering peaks, and diverse wildlife must be harmoniously balanced with the imperative to protect and preserve the environment. Cruise lines operating in Alaska have committed to adopting stringent environmental standards, adhering to regulations that safeguard delicate ecosystems. Innovative technologies, such as advanced wastewater treatment systems and shore power connections, mitigate the impact of cruise operations on air and water quality. Furthermore, wildlife protection guidelines ensure that passengers can observe creatures like humpback whales and bald eagles without disturbing their habitats.

The Alaska cruise industry thrives within a complex web of stakeholders, each contributing to its vibrancy. Cruise lines, ranging from luxury to expedition-focused, craft itineraries that cater to diverse traveler interests. Local businesses collaborate to offer authentic experiences that reflect the region's cultural richness. Government agencies monitor compliance and facilitate sustainable practices. Indigenous communities share their traditions, stories, and art, enhancing passengers' understanding of Alaska's history and heritage. Environmental organizations and researchers work in tandem with the industry to promote responsible tourism.

Alaska's unique climate and geography influence the cruise season, typically spanning from May to September. The summer months offer extended daylight hours, allowing passengers to savor the breathtaking vistas without the cloak of darkness. However, weather fluctuations can be dramatic, ranging from sunny days that highlight the crystalline waters to sudden showers that accentuate the region's verdant landscapes. Flexibility and preparation are paramount for passengers and operators alike.

Beyond its awe-inspiring natural wonders, the Alaska cruise experience delves into the cultural fabric of the state. Native Alaskan communities share their traditions through dance, storytelling, and art, offering passengers a glimpse into millennia-old cultures that remain deeply intertwined with the land. The guide explores the significance of indigenous perspectives and the cruise industry's efforts to promote cultural sensitivity and authenticity.

As the Alaska cruise industry charts its course into the future, several key trends emerge. The demand for expedition cruises, emphasizing immersive exploration and educational experiences, is on the rise. Sustainable tourism practices are increasingly integral to the industry's ethos, with a focus on reducing emissions, conserving resources, and contributing positively to local communities. Additionally, technology is transforming the onboard

experience, from interactive wildlife observation tools to digital storytelling that enhances passengers' understanding of the landscapes they encounter.

In conclusion, the Alaska cruise industry stands as a testament to humanity's enduring curiosity and reverence for nature. It encapsulates the harmonious convergence of adventure, commerce, conservation, and culture. Through its historical evolution, economic significance, environmental considerations, and the intricate interplay of stakeholders, the Alaska cruise industry continues to evoke wonder while paving the way for a sustainable and immersive exploration of the Last Frontier.

Section 2: Planning an Alaska Cruise

Choosing the Right Cruise Line for an Alaskan Adventure: A Comprehensive Guide

Embarking on an Alaska cruise is a journey of a lifetime, a chance to explore the rugged beauty, majestic glaciers, and abundant wildlife that define this remote wilderness. Yet, amid the multitude of cruise lines offering Alaskan itineraries, selecting the perfect voyage can be a daunting task. The decision hinges on a myriad of factors, from cruise style and ship amenities to budget considerations and personal preferences. This comprehensive guide delves deep into the art of choosing the right cruise line for an Alaska cruise, equipping travelers with the insights needed to make an informed and fulfilling decision.

The first step in the selection process involves defining the type of cruise experience you desire. Alaska offers a spectrum of cruise styles, ranging from mainstream cruises on large ships to boutique expeditions on smaller vessels. Each style caters to different tastes and interests. Mainstream cruises often feature diverse onboard amenities, from entertainment options to dining choices. In contrast, expedition cruises prioritize immersive exploration and educational opportunities, taking passengers into remote regions inaccessible to larger vessels.

Alaska's charm lies in its diverse range of destinations, each with its own allure and activities. While most cruises feature popular ports like Juneau, Skagway, and Ketchikan, some itineraries delve deeper into lesser-known locales like Sitka or Wrangell. Consider the activities you're most drawn to: Are you excited about whale watching, glacier trekking, or cultural experiences? Research each port's offerings to align your interests with the destinations you'll visit.

The size of the cruise ship plays a pivotal role in your experience. Larger ships offer a wide array of onboard amenities, from multiple dining venues and entertainment options to spacious cabins and pools. Smaller ships, on the other hand, provide an intimate ambiance and greater access to remote locations. They can navigate narrow fjords and dock at ports that larger vessels can't reach. If you prioritize a personalized experience and the ability to explore hidden gems, a smaller ship might be the ideal choice.

The amenities and entertainment options offered onboard can greatly influence your overall enjoyment. Some cruise lines feature Broadway-style shows, casinos, and spa facilities, ideal for travelers seeking diverse activities without stepping ashore. Others focus on enrichment programs, offering lectures by naturalists, historians, and scientists who enhance your understanding of Alaska's ecosystems and cultures. Review the cruise line's offerings to ensure they align with your preferences.

Culinary experiences are a highlight of any cruise. Research the dining options available on board, from casual buffets to upscale specialty restaurants. Some cruise lines prioritize local and sustainable ingredients, allowing you to savor the flavors of Alaska. If you're a food enthusiast, consider a cruise that offers cooking demonstrations, wine tastings, or opportunities to dine with guest chefs.

Traveling with family or as a solo traveler requires specific considerations. Some cruise lines offer extensive kids' programs, ensuring that young travelers have a memorable and enriching experience. Solo travelers can explore cruise lines that provide activities and social opportunities for those journeying alone. Research the offerings tailored to your situation to ensure an inclusive and enjoyable adventure.

Determining your budget is a crucial aspect of selecting the right cruise line. Alaskan cruises vary widely in price, and while some luxury cruises offer all-inclusive packages, others might have additional fees for excursions, gratuities, or specialty dining. It's essential to factor in all associated costs to gauge the overall value of the cruise experience and ensure it aligns with your financial plan.

Reading reviews and seeking recommendations from experienced travelers can provide valuable insights into what each cruise line offers. Online forums, travel blogs, and social media platforms often feature firsthand accounts of Alaskan cruises, highlighting the strengths and areas for improvement of different cruise lines. Engaging with the experiences of fellow travelers can help you make an informed decision.

While research is invaluable, don't underestimate the power of your own intuition. Consider what matters most to you in a cruise experience. Are you seeking adventure, relaxation, or cultural immersion? Do you value eco-friendly practices, personalized service, or vibrant nightlife? Trusting your instincts and aligning your decision with your personal preferences will ensure a cruise that resonates with you on a deeper level.

In conclusion, choosing the right cruise line for an Alaska cruise is a nuanced endeavor that requires careful consideration of various factors. By defining your cruise style, evaluating itineraries, understanding ship sizes, examining onboard amenities, and factoring in your budget and personal preferences, you can navigate the sea of options and find the voyage that best captures the essence of Alaska's captivating landscapes and enriching experiences.

Selecting the Perfect Itinerary for Your Alaska Cruise Adventure

Embarking on an Alaska cruise is akin to setting sail into a world of breathtaking landscapes, vibrant cultures, and unparalleled natural wonders. The Last Frontier, as Alaska is often fondly called, offers a tapestry of experiences that range from glacier-carved fjords to verdant forests teeming with wildlife. As you prepare to embark on this once-in-a-lifetime journey, the choice of itinerary becomes a pivotal decision that shapes the essence of your Alaskan adventure. This comprehensive guide delves into the art of selecting the perfect itinerary for your Alaska cruise, offering insights into the diverse routes, ports of call, and excursions that weave together to create an unforgettable voyage.

Alaska's vastness necessitates dividing its cruise routes into distinct regions. Each region boasts its own unique characteristics and attractions. Southcentral Alaska showcases iconic destinations like Anchorage and the Kenai Peninsula, while Southeast Alaska encompasses the Inside Passage with its labyrinth of islands and fjords. Meanwhile, the Gulf of Alaska reveals the grandeur of glaciers and the raw beauty of coastal communities. Your first step is understanding these regions and identifying the one that resonates most with your interests.

The two primary routes for Alaska cruises are the Inside Passage and the Gulf of Alaska. The Inside Passage offers a sheltered journey through coastal waters, providing a calm and scenic route with ample opportunities for wildlife spotting and cultural experiences at ports like Juneau, Ketchikan, and Skagway. The Gulf of Alaska route, often longer and more adventurous, delves into the open waters of the Gulf, offering opportunities to witness massive glaciers calving into the sea and explore ports like Seward and Anchorage.

An Alaska cruise is not just about the ship; it's about the destinations you'll explore. Research the ports of call associated with each itinerary to ensure they align with your interests. Some offer glacier excursions, where you can witness these icy giants up close, while others emphasize cultural immersion through visits to native communities and museums. Consider what activities resonate with you—whale watching, dog sledding, hiking, or simply strolling through quaint towns—and select an itinerary that caters to your preferences.

xcursions are the heart of your Alaska cruise, offering the chance to delve into the region's tunning landscapes and cultures. From kayaking among icebergs to witnessing bears fishing for almon, these experiences are the essence of an Alaskan voyage. Review the excursion options offered at each port of call to ensure they align with your interests and activity level. Some excursions are gentle and family-friendly, while others cater to adrenaline enthusiasts and hose seeking remote wilderness.

Alaska's wildlife is legendary, with opportunities to observe humpback whales, bald eagles, sea ions, and bears in their natural habitats. Different itineraries offer varied wildlife viewing experiences, so consider the species you're most excited to encounter and select an itinerary that maximizes these opportunities. Additionally, the chance to witness glaciers calving into the ocean is a spectacle that defines an Alaska cruise; research which itineraries offer the most comprehensive glacier experiences.

Alaska cruises typically range from 7 to 14 nights, each offering a distinct experience. A longer cruise allows for deeper exploration of more ports and potentially less crowded excursions. However, a shorter cruise might better suit those with time constraints. Additionally, the cruise season spans from May to September, with each month offering unique advantages. May and September provide quieter, cooler experiences, while June, July, and August offer warmer weather and longer daylight hours.

While selecting the right itinerary is crucial, also consider the onboard experience. Some itineraries prioritize scenic cruising, offering more time at sea to appreciate Alaska's grandeur from the comfort of the ship. Others emphasize extensive port stops, allowing you to immerse yourself in the communities and landscapes at each destination. Balance your desire for both onboard relaxation and onshore exploration when evaluating itineraries.

It's essential to align your chosen itinerary with your budget. Longer cruises, itineraries with more ports, and those featuring exclusive excursions might come at a premium. While budget is a factor, remember that an Alaska cruise is a rare and transformative experience. It's often worth investing in excursions that provide immersive encounters with Alaska's natural and cultural treasures.

Ultimately, your Alaska cruise is a narrative waiting to be written. Consider your dreams and aspirations for this journey. Do you dream of kayaking past glaciers, watching orcas breach, or exploring indigenous cultures? Is witnessing the Northern Lights on your bucket list? Tailor your itinerary to include the experiences that resonate with your personal aspirations.

In conclusion, selecting the perfect itinerary for your Alaska cruise is a process that melds your interests, passions, and desires with the rich tapestry of Alaska's landscapes and cultures. By understanding the regions, choosing between the Inside Passage and the Gulf of Alaska, exploring ports of call, curating exciting excursions, and aligning your preferences with available options, you can embark on a voyage that transforms mere travel into an immersive, transformative journey into the heart of the Last Frontier.

Navigating the Seasons and Weather of Alaska: A Comprehensive Guide for Your Cruise Adventure

Alaska, the Last Frontier, is a land of boundless natural beauty, dramatic landscapes, and untamed wilderness. Embarking on an Alaskan cruise is a journey into a world that's both awe-inspiring and unpredictable. The unique climate, diverse ecosystems, and changing weather patterns make understanding the travel seasons and weather considerations of paramount importance. This comprehensive guide delves into the nuances of Alaska's seasons, helping you choose the best time for your cruise, prepare for variable weather, and make the most of your unforgettable voyage.

Alaska experiences four distinct seasons, each offering its own allure and experiences. Spring (April to May) marks the awakening of nature, with melting snow giving way to blooming flowers and migrating birds. Summer (June to August) is the peak tourist season, characterized by long daylight hours, warmer temperatures, and bustling ports of call. Fall (September to October) brings a tapestry of vibrant foliage, fewer crowds, and the possibility of witnessing the Northern Lights. Winter (November to March) blankets the landscape in snow and offers unique opportunities for winter sports and activities.

The summer months, from June to August, are the peak season for Alaskan cruises. During this time, the weather is relatively mild, and daylight hours are extended, providing ample opportunities for exploration and excursions. The vibrant atmosphere in port towns and the chance to witness iconic wildlife like humpback whales and grizzly bears make this season a favorite among travelers. However, peak season also means more crowded ports and higher demand for accommodations and excursions.

Spring and fall are considered shoulder seasons in Alaska, offering unique experiences and often more affordable options. Spring brings the renewal of the natural world, with the chance to witness the thawing landscapes and the return of migratory birds. Fall's cooler temperatures are accompanied by stunning foliage displays and the possibility of viewing the elusive

Northern Lights, especially in September and October. Shoulder seasons provide a quieter, more intimate experience, but weather conditions can be more variable.

For those seeking a unique Alaskan experience, winter offers a different kind of magic. While cruise ships are less common during this time, land-based adventures, such as aurora borealis viewing and dog sledding, take center stage. The winter months offer the opportunity to explore the state's snowy landscapes, engage in winter sports, and immerse yourself in the tranquility of Alaska's quietest season.

One of the defining features of Alaska's weather is its variability. Regardless of the season, it's wise to be prepared for sudden changes in weather. Rainfall, wind, and temperature fluctuations are common occurrences. Dressing in layers is key, allowing you to adapt to changing conditions throughout the day. A waterproof jacket, sturdy footwear, and warm clothing are essential items to pack. It's also advisable to check weather forecasts and stay informed about conditions at your ports of call.

Alaska's latitude means that its daylight hours vary significantly across seasons. During the peak of summer, especially in June and July, some areas experience the phenomenon of the "midnight sun," where the sun barely sets, providing almost continuous daylight. This extended daylight offers ample time for exploration, but it's important to bring blackout curtains if you're sensitive to light when sleeping.

Packing Essentials: What to Bring for Every Season

Regardless of the season you choose for your Alaska cruise, certain packing essentials remain consistent. These include:

1. Layered Clothing: Packing layers allows you to adapt to changing temperatures and weather conditions.

2. Waterproof Gear: A waterproof jacket, pants, and shoes are crucial for staying dry during rain or wet excursions.

3. Sturdy Footwear: Comfortable, waterproof shoes are a must for walking on uneven terrain and participating in excursions.

4. Warm Accessories: Pack gloves, scarves, hats, and thermal socks for colder days.

5. Binoculars and Camera: Capture the breathtaking landscapes and wildlife encounters with quality optics.

6. Sun Protection: Even on cloudy days, UV rays can be intense, so bring sunscreen, sunglasses, and a hat.

7. Backpack: A small daypack is useful for carrying essentials during excursions.

8. Motion Sickness Remedies: If you're prone to motion sickness, consider bringing remedies recommended by your healthcare provider.

In Alaska, weather is a dynamic and integral part of the experience. Embracing the unpredictability of weather is part of the adventure. An unexpected rain shower can enhance

the beauty of a glacier, and a sudden sunny spell can illuminate a forest in magical ways. Flexibility and adaptability are key attributes that allow you to fully immerse yourself in the ever-changing landscapes of the Last Frontier.

Local wisdom is invaluable when it comes to navigating Alaska's seasons. When in doubt, consult locals, tour guides, and cruise staff for advice on weather conditions, recommended clothing, and the best times for outdoor activities. Their insights can enrich your experience and ensure that you make the most of your time in this enchanting land.

In conclusion, understanding the travel seasons and weather considerations of Alaska is paramount for planning a successful cruise adventure. Whether you're drawn to the vibrancy of summer, the serenity of winter, or the transitional beauty of spring and fall, each season offers a unique perspective on the wonders of the Last Frontier. By packing wisely, staying informed, and embracing the spirit of adaptability, you'll embark on a journey that allows you to fully embrace the dynamic and awe-inspiring landscapes that define Alaska.

Booking and Reservations for Your Alaskan Cruise Adventure: A Comprehensive Guide

Embarking on an Alaskan cruise is an invitation to explore the Last Frontier's rugged landscapes, witness awe-inspiring wildlife, and immerse yourself in the cultures of coastal communities. As you prepare for this transformative journey, navigating the process of booking and reservations becomes a pivotal step. From selecting the right cruise line and cabin to understanding pricing structures and securing excursions, this comprehensive guide provides insights into the intricacies of booking an Alaskan cruise, ensuring a smooth and enriching experience from the moment you set sail.

Selecting the ideal cruise line sets the tone for your Alaskan adventure. Research various cruise lines and their offerings, from mainstream giants to boutique expedition operators. Consider factors such as the cruise style, onboard amenities, cultural enrichment programs, and itineraries that align with your interests. Whether you're seeking luxury, family-friendly experiences, or expedition-based adventures, choosing the right cruise line forms the foundation of your journey.

Booking your Alaskan cruise well in advance often presents a range of advantages. Many cruise lines offer early-bird discounts, allowing you to secure your preferred itinerary and cabin category at a lower cost. Additionally, booking early ensures a wider selection of cabin choices

and greater availability for excursions. As Alaskan cruises are highly sought-after, securing your spot early can be the key to unlocking a seamless and fulfilling voyage.

The type of cabin you choose greatly influences your onboard experience. Cabins range from intimate interior rooms to lavish suites with private balconies. Consider factors such as cabin location, size, view, and amenities. Balcony cabins offer breathtaking views of glaciers and wildlife from the privacy of your own space, while interior cabins are often more budget-friendly. Tailor your choice to your preferences and budget, recognizing that your cabin will be your haven throughout the voyage.

Alaskan cruise prices can vary significantly based on factors like cruise line, cabin category, itinerary, and travel season. Understanding the pricing structure is essential for budgeting. Cruise fares typically include accommodations, meals, entertainment, and basic onboard activities. However, certain amenities, specialty dining, and excursions may incur additional charges. Review the cruise line's breakdown of costs to ensure you're aware of all potential expenses.

Many cruise lines offer flexible and fixed dining options. Flexible dining allows you to dine at various times and venues, offering more adaptability in your daily schedule. Fixed dining assigns you a specific dining time and table, fostering a more consistent experience and the opportunity to build relationships with fellow passengers and staff. Consider your dining preferences and whether you prefer the flexibility to choose when and where you dine.

Most cruise lines offer specialty dining venues that provide a more intimate and diverse culinary experience. These restaurants often have a cover charge, offering a higher level of service and unique menus. Some cruise lines also offer dining packages that bundle multiple specialty dining experiences at a discounted rate. If you're a food enthusiast, these options can enhance your onboard culinary adventure.

Shore excursions are a highlight of any Alaskan cruise, offering the chance to explore glaciers, wildlife habitats, cultural sites, and thrilling activities. Research the available excursions at each port of call and prioritize those that align with your interests. Book excursions well in advance, as popular ones can fill up quickly. Keep in mind that some excursions have limited availability due to environmental restrictions, making early booking even more crucial.

Many Alaskan cruises depart from and return to major cities like Seattle, Vancouver, or Anchorage. Consider extending your journey by adding pre- or post-cruise activities to explore these cities and their surroundings. From exploring Seattle's iconic attractions to embarking on wilderness adventures in Alaska's interior, adding extra days to your trip allows you to maximize your experience beyond the cruise itself.

Booking an Alaskan cruise involves a significant financial investment. Travel insurance provides peace of mind by offering coverage in case of unexpected cancellations, trip interruptions,

medical emergencies, and other unforeseen events. Carefully review the coverage options and terms of the insurance policy to ensure that it aligns with your needs and concerns.

Ensure you have all necessary travel documents before embarking on your cruise. A valid passport is usually required, and some itineraries may necessitate additional visas or permits. Research the specific documentation required for your cruise, especially if you plan to visit ports in different countries. Verify expiration dates and allow ample time for processing any necessary documents.

Cruise lines often provide portals or apps that keep you informed about your cruise details, itinerary changes, and onboard activities. Stay engaged with these communication channels to ensure you're aware of important information, embarkation procedures, dining reservations, and entertainment schedules. Being informed enhances your cruise experience and allows you to make the most of each day.

Many travelers opt to book their Alaskan cruises through travel agents, who offer expert guidance and personalized service. Travel agents can help you navigate the myriad options, recommend suitable cruise lines, and assist with booking excursions, flights, and pre- and post-cruise activities. Their expertise ensures that your journey is tailored to your preferences and smoothly executed.

In conclusion, booking and reservations for your Alaskan cruise is a multi-faceted process that requires careful consideration of various factors. From choosing the right cruise line and cabin to understanding pricing structures, booking excursions, and arranging travel documents, each step plays a crucial role in crafting a seamless and enriching experience. By planning ahead, staying informed, and seeking expert guidance when needed, you're well on your way to embarking on a transformative journey into the heart of Alaska's captivating landscapes and cultures.

Section 3: Alaskan Ports of Call

Alaska is home to a collection of captivating ports that offer a diverse range of experiences, from encountering majestic glaciers to immersing yourself in indigenous cultures. Each port has its unique charm and attractions, making it difficult to pinpoint a single "best" port. However, I can highlight some of the most popular and renowned ports in Alaska that consistently capture the hearts of travelers:

1. Juneau: Alaska's Capital City

As the capital city of Alaska, Juneau is a bustling port nestled between mountains and the sea. It's renowned for its stunning backdrop, including the Mendenhall Glacier. Visitors can explore the glacier, go whale watching, experience dog sledding, and delve into Alaska's history and culture at local museums and galleries.

2. Skagway: Gateway to the Klondike Gold Rush

Skagway boasts a rich history tied to the Klondike Gold Rush of the late 1800s. Its well-preserved downtown area immerses visitors in the gold rush era, while the White Pass and Yukon Route Railroad offers breathtaking views of the surrounding landscapes. The town's vibrant atmosphere and unique attractions make it a must-visit port.

3. Ketchikan: The Salmon Capital of the World

Known as the "Salmon Capital of the World," Ketchikan is situated along the Inside Passage and offers opportunities for salmon fishing, as well as bear watching and exploring Native American culture. The Totem Heritage Center and Saxman Native Village are highlights for those interested in indigenous art and traditions.

4. Sitka: A Blend of History and Nature

Sitka showcases a blend of Russian and Tlingit cultures, with landmarks like the Russian Orthodox St. Michael's Cathedral and the Sitka National Historical Park. The town is surrounded by stunning natural beauty, including the Tongass National Forest and opportunities for kayaking and wildlife spotting.

5. Anchorage: Alaska's Urban Hub

While not a traditional port of call for cruise ships, Anchorage serves as a gateway to a wide range of Alaskan adventures. Visitors can explore the Anchorage Museum, embark on wildlife tours, and even catch a glimpse of the Northern Lights during the winter months.

6. Glacier Bay: A Natural Wonder

Although not a traditional port, Glacier Bay is a highlight of many Alaskan cruise itineraries. This UNESCO World Heritage Site features towering glaciers, icy fjords, and abundant marine life. Cruising through Glacier Bay offers an unparalleled opportunity to witness the raw power and beauty of Alaska's glaciers.

7. Icy Strait Point: Authentic Alaskan Experience

Icy Strait Point is owned and operated by a Native Tlingit corporation, offering visitors an authentic Alaskan experience. It features cultural exhibits, opportunities for bear watching, and a variety of adventure activities. The pristine wilderness and cultural immersion make it a standout port.

Juneau: Alaska's Capital City – Where Nature and History Unite

Nestled within the heart of the stunning Alaskan landscape, Juneau stands as a remarkable testament to the harmonious coexistence of nature's grandeur and human history. As the capital city of Alaska, Juneau holds a unique position as both a bustling urban center and a gateway to the wild beauty that defines the Last Frontier. With its awe-inspiring landscapes, captivating history, and vibrant culture, Juneau offers visitors a multifaceted experience that blends the authentic spirit of Alaska with the conveniences of modern life.

Juneau's origin story is closely intertwined with the promise of gold that lured prospectors to the region in the late 19th century. Founded during the 1880s Gold Rush, Juneau quickly transformed from a modest mining camp to a thriving town. Named after prospector Joe Juneau, the city's history is alive in its well-preserved downtown area, where historic buildings and streets offer glimpses into the past. The infamous Red Dog Saloon, with its charmingly rustic

interior and memorabilia from the Gold Rush era, stands as a testament to the city's wild and adventurous history.

One of Juneau's most iconic natural wonders is the Mendenhall Glacier, a breathtaking testament to the raw power of nature. This massive glacier, which stretches over 12 miles from its source in the Juneau Icefield, captivates visitors with its towering ice walls and stunning blue hues. The Mendenhall Glacier Visitor Center provides an educational hub, offering insights into glaciology, the local ecosystem, and the glacier's ongoing transformation. The center also serves as a launch point for hiking trails that lead to jaw-dropping viewpoints, allowing visitors to witness the glacier's majesty up close.

Juneau's strategic location along the Inside Passage offers visitors the chance to witness the mesmerizing dance of humpback whales. The nutrient-rich waters of the region attract these majestic creatures during their seasonal migrations, providing a unique opportunity for whale watching. Guided tours take visitors on boat excursions to observe these gentle giants as they breach, fluke, and glide through the water. The experience of encountering these awe-inspiring marine mammals against the backdrop of Alaska's pristine waters is truly unforgettable.

As visitors explore Juneau, they have the opportunity to engage with the rich cultural heritage of Alaska's indigenous communities. The Sealaska Heritage Institute offers a glimpse into the art, history, and traditions of the Tlingit, Haida, and Tsimshian peoples. The institute's exhibits, galleries, and totem poles are a testament to the enduring legacy of Alaska's Native cultures. Visitors can also experience the intricate artistry of indigenous crafts, from intricate beadwork to traditional regalia, reflecting the deep connection between Alaska's native communities and their land.

No visit to Juneau is complete without sampling the region's delectable culinary offerings. Fresh seafood, including succulent Alaskan king crab and locally caught salmon, takes center stage on many menus. Restaurants in Juneau pride themselves on serving locally sourced ingredients, allowing visitors to savor the authentic flavors of Alaska's waters and land. From casual seafood shacks to upscale dining establishments, Juneau's culinary scene offers a diverse array of options to satisfy every palate.

Juneau's natural playground beckons outdoor enthusiasts with a plethora of activities. Hiking trails wind through lush forests, offering opportunities to witness diverse flora and fauna. Adventurers can embark on kayaking expeditions along serene waterways, witnessing glaciers, marine life, and waterfalls along the way. For those seeking an adrenaline rush, zip-lining through the treetops or embarking on a thrilling helicopter tour are experiences that showcase Alaska's beauty from exhilarating perspectives.

Despite its historical roots and natural wonders, Juneau is a modern city that offers a range of amenities and conveniences for visitors. The city's downtown area features a vibrant array of

shops, galleries, and boutiques, where travelers can find locally crafted souvenirs, art pieces, and unique treasures. Quaint cafes, coffee shops, and eateries provide respite and nourishment after a day of exploration. The warm hospitality of Juneau's residents and the sense of community that pervades the city contribute to an inviting and welcoming atmosphere.

While summer draws the majority of visitors to Juneau, the winter months offer their own special allure. Travelers who venture to Juneau during the colder season have the opportunity to witness the mesmerizing display of the Northern Lights, or Aurora Borealis. The clear, dark nights of winter provide optimal conditions for observing this natural phenomenon, transforming the sky into a canvas of swirling colors and celestial magic.

Juneau is a shining example of responsible tourism, with a commitment to preserving its natural beauty and cultural heritage. Local organizations and businesses prioritize sustainable practices, environmental conservation, and respect for indigenous cultures. Visitors are encouraged to partake in eco-friendly activities, follow Leave No Trace principles, and engage with local communities in a culturally sensitive manner.

In conclusion, Juneau, Alaska's capital city, encapsulates the spirit of the Last Frontier through its captivating history, awe-inspiring natural wonders, vibrant cultural scene, and warm hospitality. From the glaciers that shape the landscape to the indigenous cultures that enrich the community, Juneau offers a multifaceted experience that celebrates the intertwining of human heritage and the untamed beauty of nature. Whether you're exploring the Mendenhall Glacier, embracing native traditions, or savoring local cuisine, Juneau's charm and authenticity ensure that your visit to this remarkable city will be etched in your memories forever.

Best Attractions and Activities in Juneau: A Journey into Alaska's Capital City

Juneau, Alaska's capital city, is a treasure trove of natural wonders, cultural experiences, and outdoor adventures. From witnessing towering glaciers to immersing yourself in indigenous heritage, Juneau offers a diverse array of attractions and activities that capture the essence of the Last Frontier. Whether you're drawn to the raw beauty of nature, the captivating history of the Gold Rush era, or the vibrant arts and cuisine scene, Juneau has something to offer every traveler's taste and preferences. Here are some of the best attractions and activities that make Juneau a must-visit destination:

1. Mendenhall Glacier: Glacial Majesty Unveiled

Witnessing the Mendenhall Glacier is an essential experience when visiting Juneau. The glacier's stunning blue hues and towering ice walls create a mesmerizing spectacle. The Mendenhall Glacier Visitor Center provides educational exhibits, walking trails, and viewpoints that offer breathtaking perspectives of this natural wonder.

2. Whale Watching: Encounter Marine Giants

Juneau's waters are a prime destination for whale watching. Embark on a guided boat excursion to witness the graceful movements of humpback whales as they breach and fluke. The experience of encountering these majestic marine mammals against the backdrop of Alaska's scenic coastline is truly unforgettable.

3. Tracy Arm Fjord: Glacial Splendor

Explore the stunning Tracy Arm Fjord on a boat tour. Surrounded by towering cliffs and cascading waterfalls, the fjord leads to the majestic Sawyer Glacier. The experience of sailing through this narrow passage and witnessing the grandeur of the glacier-carved landscape is a highlight for many visitors.

4. Alaska State Museum: Cultural Exploration

Immerse yourself in Alaska's rich history and indigenous cultures at the Alaska State Museum. The museum's exhibits showcase native art, artifacts, and historical displays that provide insights into the state's diverse heritage. The museum's focus on storytelling and interactive exhibits makes it an engaging educational experience.

5. Mount Roberts Tramway: Panoramic Views

Take a tram ride up Mount Roberts for panoramic views of Juneau and its surrounding landscapes. At the top, you'll find hiking trails, an informative nature center, and opportunities to spot wildlife. The observation deck offers stunning vistas of the city, the Gastineau Channel, and the distant mountains.

6. Salmon Hatchery: Aquatic Insights

Visit the Macaulay Salmon Hatchery to learn about Alaska's salmon industry and witness the different stages of salmon life cycles. The hatchery offers informative tours and exhibits, allowing visitors to gain a deeper understanding of the vital role salmon play in Alaska's ecosystems and economy.

7. Douglas Island: Outdoor Adventures

Cross the Gastineau Channel to Douglas Island and explore its hiking trails and scenic viewpoints. The island offers opportunities for nature walks, birdwatching, and tranquil moments amid the lush forests. Eaglecrest Ski Area on the island provides winter sports enthusiasts with skiing and snowboarding options during the colder months.

8. Native Heritage Center: Cultural Immersion

Experience the indigenous cultures of Alaska at the Sealaska Heritage Institute's Walter Soboleff Building. Explore exhibits, artworks, and performances that celebrate the traditions, languages, and artistry of the Tlingit, Haida, and Tsimshian peoples.

9. Alaska Brewing Company: Craft Beer Delights

For those who appreciate craft beer, a visit to the Alaska Brewing Company is a treat. Take a brewery tour to learn about the beer-making process and the company's commitment to sustainability. The tasting room allows you to sample a variety of their locally crafted brews.

10. Outdoor Adventures: Embrace the Wilderness

Juneau's surrounding wilderness offers endless outdoor activities. Hiking enthusiasts can explore trails like the Perseverance Trail, which leads to remnants of historic gold mines. Kayaking, ziplining, and helicopter tours are just a few of the adventure options that allow you to immerse yourself in Alaska's untamed beauty.

11. Local Cuisine: Savor Alaska's Flavors

Indulge in Alaskan cuisine by sampling locally caught seafood, including salmon and king crab. Juneau's dining scene offers a range of options, from waterfront seafood restaurants to cozy

cafes and bakeries. Don't miss the opportunity to savor the flavors of the region's bountiful waters and land.

12. Northern Lights: Winter's Celestial Show

Visiting Juneau during the winter months offers the chance to witness the Northern Lights, or Aurora Borealis. The clear, dark skies provide optimal conditions for observing this natural phenomenon, as vibrant hues dance across the night sky in a dazzling display.

13. Arts and Culture: Creative Expressions

Explore Juneau's arts and culture scene by visiting local galleries, studios, and theaters. The Juneau Arts & Culture Center hosts performances, exhibits, and events that showcase the talents of Alaskan artists and performers.

14. Downtown Juneau: Historic Stroll

Take a leisurely stroll through downtown Juneau's charming streets, lined with historic buildings, boutiques, and art galleries. The walkable downtown area offers a delightful blend of shopping, dining, and cultural exploration.

15. Glacier Gardens Rainforest Adventure: Floral Fantasy

Visit the Glacier Gardens Rainforest Adventure to experience a unique blend of horticulture and natural beauty. The gardens feature colorful flowers and plants creatively arranged in upturned trees, offering a whimsical and captivating sight.

In conclusion, Juneau, Alaska's capital city, beckons travelers with a plethora of attractions and activities that celebrate the region's natural wonders, cultural heritage, and adventurous spirit. From witnessing glaciers and whales to exploring indigenous traditions and indulging in local cuisine, Juneau's offerings provide a well-rounded and unforgettable Alaskan experience. Whether you're drawn to outdoor adventures, cultural immersion, or simply basking in the breathtaking scenery, Juneau invites you to embark on a journey that unveils the captivating essence of the Last Frontier.

Mendenhall Glacier: Glacial Majesty Unveiled

In the heart of Alaska's rugged landscapes, a natural marvel of immense proportions awaits those who seek the sublime beauty of the Last Frontier. The Mendenhall Glacier, a towering masterpiece of ice and time, stands as a testament to the grandeur of the natural world. Located near Juneau, Alaska's capital city, the glacier captures the imagination and stirs the soul of every visitor who gazes upon its breathtaking splendor. From its history to its ever-changing form, the Mendenhall Glacier unveils the majestic story of Earth's frozen wonders.

The Mendenhall Glacier, a 13.6-mile-long river of ice, is a product of the mighty Juneau Icefield. This colossal icefield, which stretches across approximately 1,500 square miles, is the source of multiple glaciers that descend into the valleys below. The Mendenhall Glacier's journey begins at an elevation of around 5,000 feet atop the Juneau Icefield and gracefully winds its way down into the Mendenhall Valley, where it ends at the edge of the pristine Mendenhall Lake.

One of the most awe-inspiring features of the Mendenhall Glacier is its radiant blue ice. The mesmerizing blue hues result from the density and compression of ice, which causes light to be absorbed in longer wavelengths and scattered, revealing stunning shades of blue. As sunlight filters through the ice, visitors are treated to a visual symphony of colors that range from brilliant turquoise to deep sapphire, creating an otherworldly and ethereal experience.

The Mendenhall Glacier Visitor Center stands as a gateway to the glacial wonderland. Located just a short distance from the glacier's terminus, the center serves as an educational hub that offers a deeper understanding of glaciology, the natural world, and the delicate balance of ecosystems. Interactive exhibits, informative displays, and engaging programs provide visitors with insights into the forces that shape the glacier and the environments it influences.

The Mendenhall Glacier is a living, breathing entity that undergoes continuous transformation. Like a slow-moving river, the glacier's ice flows downhill, carving its path and shaping the land as it goes. This dynamic movement results in ever-changing landscapes, from crevasses that open and close to ice caves that form and collapse. Witnessing these changes underscores the glacier's vitality and the relentless forces that shape its existence.

The Mendenhall Glacier, like many glaciers around the world, has been impacted by the effects of climate change. Over the past century, the glacier has experienced significant retreat, with its terminus moving backward at an alarming rate. This retreat serves as a stark reminder of the delicate balance between natural processes and human actions. Visitors to the Mendenhall Glacier are given the opportunity to witness the effects of climate change firsthand, fostering a greater understanding of the urgent need for environmental stewardship.

Exploring the Mendenhall Glacier is a journey into a world of ice, beauty, and adventure. Guided tours and excursions allow visitors to get up close and personal with the glacier's features, from its towering ice walls to its intricate ice formations. Adventurers can embark on glacier hikes, ice climbing experiences, and even kayak trips on the glacial lake, offering unique perspectives and unforgettable memories.

For those seeking a deeper connection with the Mendenhall Glacier's origins, a journey to the Tracy Arm Fjord is a must. This awe-inspiring fjord, accessible by boat, provides a breathtaking passage through towering cliffs, icebergs, and cascading waterfalls. The fjord culminates in a dramatic encounter with the majestic Sawyer Glacier, offering an intimate glimpse into the forces of nature that shape the glacial landscape.

As visitors are drawn to the Mendenhall Glacier's beauty, it's essential to approach exploration with the utmost respect for its delicate ecosystems. Sustainable tourism practices, such as following designated trails and respecting wildlife habitats, ensure that future generations can continue to experience the glacier's splendor. Responsible travel allows for the preservation of the glacier's majesty and the protection of the environment it embodies.

The Mendenhall Glacier is more than a physical presence; it's a living testament to the passage of time and the resilience of nature. Its towering ice walls, deep crevasses, and brilliant blue hues invite visitors to ponder the vast expanse of Earth's history. As you stand before the glacier, you're not only witnessing a frozen wonder; you're gazing into the depths of time itself, marveling at the profound mysteries that shape our planet.

In conclusion, the Mendenhall Glacier stands as a crown jewel of Alaska's natural wonders, offering a glimpse into the forces that shape our world and the delicate balance between nature's grandeur and the impacts of human activity. From its radiant blue ice to its dynamic movement and the tales it tells of climate change, the glacier's majesty serves as a poignant reminder of the need for environmental stewardship. As visitors stand before the glacier's towering presence, they're granted a rare opportunity to witness the immense power and beauty of Earth's frozen realms, leaving an indelible mark on their hearts and minds.

Whale Watching: Encounter Marine Giants

In the vast expanse of the open ocean, a breathtaking spectacle unfolds as majestic marine giants breach the surface, captivating the hearts and imagination of those fortunate enough to witness their graceful movements. Whale watching, an awe-inspiring experience that transcends age and background, offers a unique opportunity to connect with the mysteries of

the deep, uncovering the enigmatic world of these colossal creatures. From the coastal waters of Alaska to the azure expanses of the world's oceans, whale watching unveils a mesmerizing journey into the lives of marine giants that have captured our fascination for centuries.

Whales, these magnificent denizens of the seas, belong to a lineage that spans millions of years. As Earth's largest creatures, they inspire awe and reverence, reminding us of the vastness and complexity of our planet's oceans. Whales come in a myriad of species, each with its unique characteristics and behaviors, from the iconic humpbacks with their acrobatic displays to the mysterious blue whales, the largest animals to have ever lived on Earth.

One of the most thrilling aspects of whale watching is witnessing the breathtaking acrobatics of these marine giants. The sight of a humpback whale breaching, launching its massive body out of the water before crashing back with a resounding splash, is a sight that leaves an indelible impression. This behavior, believed to serve various purposes from communication to removing parasites, is a display of power and grace that fills spectators with wonder.

Whales are known for their complex vocalizations, often referred to as "songs." These intricate melodic compositions, sung by male humpback whales during mating season, have captivated researchers and enthusiasts alike. The purpose of these songs, whether to attract potential mates or establish territory, remains a subject of ongoing study. Whale watching provides a rare chance to listen to these enchanting underwater melodies through hydrophones, opening a window into the mysterious communication of the deep.

Whales are renowned for their remarkable migratory journeys that span thousands of miles. These epic migrations are driven by various factors, including the search for food, the quest for warmer waters, and the cycle of mating and birthing. Whale watching enthusiasts can witness these journeys as they unfold in different parts of the world, from the gray whales' migration along the coasts of North America to the Southern Hemisphere's krill-rich waters that attract humpbacks and blue whales.

The coastal waters of Alaska stand as a prime destination for whale watching, offering a front-row seat to the annual migrations of various whale species. The nutrient-rich waters of Alaska's Inside Passage and the Gulf of Alaska provide an abundant food source for whales, making these regions ideal feeding grounds. Visitors to Alaska are treated to the majestic sight of humpbacks, orcas, gray whales, and more as they navigate the cool, pristine waters.

Humpback whales are perhaps the most celebrated stars of Alaska's whale-watching scene. These gentle giants are known for their charismatic behaviors, including breaching, tail slapping, and bubble-net feeding—a collaborative technique used to corral fish. The sight of a humpback's massive tail arching out of the water before descending is an image that captures the essence of these marine giants.

Orcas, also known as killer whales, command both respect and fascination as apex predators of the ocean. With their distinct black and white markings and powerful presence, orcas inspire awe wherever they roam. Their complex social structures, hunting strategies, and vocalizations add to the allure of encountering these intelligent and enigmatic creatures during whale watching expeditions.

While whale watching offers a unique opportunity to witness these majestic creatures in their natural habitats, responsible practices are essential to minimize disturbances to the animals and their environments. Regulations and guidelines set by marine conservation organizations ensure that interactions are respectful and safe for both the whales and the observers. Keeping a safe distance, adhering to designated routes, and minimizing noise pollution are all crucial components of responsible whale watching.

Whale watching isn't just about witnessing incredible displays—it's also an educational opportunity that fosters a deeper understanding of marine ecosystems. Naturalists and guides often accompany whale watching tours, providing insights into the behavior, biology, and conservation status of the whales. Learning about the challenges these creatures face, from habitat degradation to climate change, inspires a greater sense of responsibility for protecting Earth's oceans.

Whale watching transcends language barriers and cultural differences, uniting people from around the world in a shared experience of wonder and awe. The collective gasps of amazement, the joyous cheers as a whale breaches, and the shared stories of encounters create connections that bridge geographical distances. The impact of witnessing these majestic beings in their natural habitat often ignites a passion for marine conservation and a commitment to safeguarding the oceans.

Whale watching not only offers a transformative experience for individuals but also contributes to the broader awareness of marine conservation. By witnessing whales' beauty and vulnerability firsthand, people become advocates for protecting these creatures and their habitats. This collective awareness has led to efforts to reduce plastic pollution, establish marine protected areas, and advocate for responsible fishing practices, all of which play a crucial role in safeguarding the oceans for future generations.

In conclusion, whale watching is a voyage into the heart of our planet's oceans, a journey that unveils the majesty, mystery, and vulnerability of marine life. From the mesmerizing displays of breaching humpbacks to the haunting melodies of whale songs, the experience is a testament to the interconnectedness of Earth's ecosystems. As we witness the splendor of these marine giants, we're reminded of our responsibility to protect the oceans and their inhabitants—a responsibility that extends beyond the water's edge and into the very fabric of our shared planet.

Tracy Arm Fjord: Glacial Splendor

In the heart of the Alaskan wilderness, a journey into the breathtaking wonders of Tracy Arm Fjord unveils a realm of towering cliffs, shimmering icebergs, and cascading waterfalls. This majestic fjord, carved by ancient glaciers, stands as a testament to the colossal forces that have shaped our planet over millennia. Located south of Juneau and accessible by boat, Tracy Arm Fjord is a hidden gem that offers intrepid explorers an opportunity to immerse themselves in the raw beauty and serene grandeur of a glacial landscape. From its awe-inspiring ice-carved features to its vibrant ecosystem, Tracy Arm Fjord stands as a testament to the sublime power of nature's artistry.

Tracy Arm Fjord is a living testament to the legacy of glacial movements that have sculpted the Earth's surface. The fjord's rugged landscapes, characterized by towering granite walls and pristine waters, are the result of millennia of glacial activity. As massive glaciers once flowed through this region, they carved deep valleys, leaving behind towering cliffs that now embrace the tranquil waters of the fjord.

At the heart of Tracy Arm Fjord's allure lie its glaciers—massive rivers of ice that have captured the imagination of explorers and adventurers for centuries. The Sawyer Glacier, the fjord's most iconic resident, is a dazzling masterpiece of blue and white. Its colossal expanse of ice, punctuated by towering seracs and crevasses, extends down to the fjord's edge, where it releases a steady procession of icebergs into the crystal-clear waters.

Calving—the dramatic process by which chunks of ice break off from the glacier's face—creates a mesmerizing spectacle in Tracy Arm Fjord. As these massive icebergs plunge into the water with thunderous roars, they create ripples that send waves coursing through the fjord. These ice sculptures in motion, ranging in size from small chunks to towering ice cathedrals, drift gracefully along the fjord's currents, reflecting the dynamic interplay between ice, water, and gravity.

The sheer cliffs of Tracy Arm Fjord are adorned with a symphony of cascading waterfalls that tumble from great heights. These ephemeral ribbons of water, born from melting glaciers and snowfields, add a sense of ethereal beauty to the rugged landscapes. The sight and sound of waterfalls streaming down moss-covered walls create a sense of tranquility and remind visitors of the constant flow of life in this seemingly frozen realm.

While the icy landscapes of Tracy Arm Fjord might appear inhospitable, the fjord teems with life both above and below the water's surface. The fjord's nutrient-rich waters support a diverse array of marine life, including seals, sea lions, and otters. Bald eagles perch majestically atop

rocky outcrops, while mountain goats gracefully navigate the fjord's steep slopes. The fjord's surroundings burst to life with vibrant wildflowers during the brief but vibrant summer months.

For the intrepid traveler seeking a closer encounter with Tracy Arm Fjord's wonders, kayaking offers a unique vantage point. Paddling across the fjord's pristine waters brings adventurers face to face with the towering glaciers and icebergs. The tranquility of kayaking allows for a deep connection with the fjord's serene grandeur and the sounds of nature that echo through the landscapes.

Tracy Arm Fjord's dramatic landscapes can be explored by boat, a journey that takes visitors on a visual expedition into the heart of glacial splendor. As vessels weave through the fjord's narrow passages, travelers are treated to breathtaking views of towering cliffs, icy blue glaciers, and mirror-like waters. The tranquil atmosphere and the gentle lapping of waves against the vessel create an experience of serenity that contrasts with the fjord's rugged terrain.

Tracy Arm Fjord also serves as a poignant reminder of the ongoing effects of climate change. The retreating glaciers of the fjord echo the global phenomenon of glacial retreat and shrinking ice sheets. Witnessing the impact of climate change on this pristine landscape underscores the urgent need for conservation efforts and sustainable practices to preserve Earth's delicate ecosystems.

Tracy Arm Fjord beckons photographers and artists alike to capture its splendor on canvas and film. The interplay of light and shadow, the vivid colors of ice against the deep blue waters, and the contrast between rugged cliffs and delicate ice formations provide endless opportunities for creative expression. The fjord's ever-changing landscapes ensure that each visit yields new perspectives and artistic inspiration.

Tracy Arm Fjord's remote location and limited accessibility contribute to its sense of serenity and tranquility. Far from the hustle and bustle of urban life, the fjord offers a sanctuary where visitors can disconnect from the world's distractions and immerse themselves in the natural rhythms of glacial landscapes. This remote tranquility allows for introspection, rejuvenation, and a profound connection with nature.

As more travelers seek the enchanting beauty of Tracy Arm Fjord, responsible tourism practices become paramount to its preservation. Guided tours and expeditions follow designated routes to minimize disturbances to the delicate ecosystems. Adhering to the principles of Leave No Trace ensures that the fjord's pristine landscapes remain untouched by human impact, allowing future generations to experience its splendor.

Tracy Arm Fjord transcends words and descriptions, offering an experience that taps into the human connection with the sublime. As visitors gaze upon the towering cliffs, navigate the icy waters, and witness the dance of calving glaciers, they are enveloped in a sense of wonder that defies explanation. The fjord's glacial splendor speaks to something primal within us, a recognition of the Earth's vastness and our place within its intricate web of life.

In conclusion, Tracy Arm Fjord stands as a masterpiece of nature's artistry—a testament to the immense power of glaciers, the beauty of rugged landscapes, and the delicate ecosystems that thrive in the presence of ice and water. As visitors embark on a journey into its depths, they're enveloped in the serenity of its waters, the majesty of its icebergs, and the timeless allure of its grandeur. Tracy Arm Fjord, a realm of glacial splendor, invites all who venture into its embrace to witness the harmonious dance of nature's elements and be forever transformed by the beauty that resides within its icy heart.

Alaska State Museum: Cultural Exploration

Nestled in the heart of Juneau, the Alaska State Museum stands as a testament to the rich tapestry of history, culture, and art that defines the Last Frontier. As a repository of Alaska's heritage, the museum offers a captivating journey through time, inviting visitors to explore the diverse stories of indigenous peoples, early settlers, and the natural wonders that shape the state. With its engaging exhibits, authentic artifacts, and immersive experiences, the Alaska State Museum serves as a portal to the past, a window into the present, and a source of inspiration for the future.

The Alaska State Museum weaves together the multifaceted story of the state, tracing its history from the early days of indigenous civilizations to the modern challenges and triumphs of the present. Each exhibit is a thread in the tapestry, contributing to the rich narrative of Alaska's evolution. From the exploration of Russian traders to the Klondike Gold Rush and the emergence of a vibrant contemporary culture, the museum paints a vivid picture of the forces that have shaped Alaska's identity.

At the heart of the Alaska State Museum lies a celebration of the indigenous peoples who have called this land home for thousands of years. Intricately carved totem poles, traditional regalia, and ancestral artifacts provide a glimpse into the rich cultural heritage of Alaska's native communities. As visitors engage with these exhibits, they embark on a journey that transcends time, connecting with the beliefs, traditions, and stories that have been passed down through generations.

The totem poles that grace the Alaska State Museum's exhibits are more than mere sculptures; they are guardians of ancestral stories and repositories of cultural significance. Each totem pole is a visual narrative, depicting the history, legends, and identity of indigenous clans. These

towering works of art serve as a bridge between the past and the present, reminding visitors of the enduring legacy of Alaska's native cultures.

Alaska's artistic traditions are a living expression of the state's unique identity. The museum's galleries showcase a diverse range of art forms, from indigenous carvings and beadwork to contemporary paintings and sculptures. These exhibits highlight the interplay between tradition and innovation, offering insights into the ways in which Alaskan artists draw inspiration from their environment, culture, and personal experiences.

Alaska's awe-inspiring landscapes are an integral part of its cultural identity. The museum's exhibits delve into the natural wonders that define the state, from towering mountains and pristine forests to the icy expanses of glaciers. Through interactive displays, visitors gain a deeper understanding of the geological forces that have shaped Alaska's terrain and the delicate ecosystems that thrive within its boundaries.

The Klondike Gold Rush of the late 19th century is a pivotal chapter in Alaska's history, marking a period of frenzied excitement and economic transformation. The museum's exhibits transport visitors back in time, allowing them to relive the experiences of prospectors who flocked to the region in search of fortune. Through photographs, artifacts, and personal stories, the Klondike Gold Rush comes to life, offering a window into the challenges and aspirations of those who participated in this historic event.

The Alaska State Museum goes beyond history and culture, embracing the scientific exploration that informs our understanding of the state's unique environment. Natural history exhibits provide insights into Alaska's diverse ecosystems, showcasing the flora and fauna that inhabit its forests, waters, and skies. From observing a replica of a coastal rainforest to exploring the world of marine life, these exhibits foster a deeper appreciation for the interconnectedness of Alaska's ecology.

The Alaska State Museum is not merely a collection of artifacts; it is a dynamic space that encourages hands-on engagement and interactive learning. Visitors of all ages can participate in activities that bring history and culture to life. From trying on traditional clothing to handling historical objects, these interactive experiences provide a deeper connection to the stories being told within the museum's walls.

Beyond its exhibits, the Alaska State Museum plays a vital role in the preservation of cultural heritage. The museum's conservation efforts ensure that artifacts are safeguarded for future generations, allowing the stories they tell to endure. By serving as a repository of cultural knowledge, the museum honors the contributions of indigenous communities and serves as a bridge between the past and the present.

The Alaska State Museum's impact extends beyond its physical space, reaching into communities across the state. Through educational programs, workshops, and outreach

initiatives, the museum fosters connections between generations, ensuring that cultural knowledge is passed down and shared. By engaging with schools, local organizations, and diverse audiences, the museum becomes a catalyst for dialogue, understanding, and cultural appreciation.

Museums hold the power to inspire, educate, and provoke thought. The Alaska State Museum's exhibits not only convey information but also invite visitors to reflect on their place within the larger narrative of Alaska's history and culture. Whether experiencing a poignant moment of empathy, marveling at artistic expression, or contemplating the resilience of indigenous communities, visitors are given the opportunity to connect with the stories that shape the world around them.

The Alaska State Museum stands as a bridge—a bridge that spans generations, cultures, and landscapes. As visitors walk through its galleries, they walk through time, traversing the eras and events that have shaped Alaska's identity. But the museum also reaches into the future, inspiring a new generation of storytellers, artists, and advocates who will continue to carry forward the legacy of Alaska's cultural richness.

In conclusion, the Alaska State Museum is a treasure trove of history, culture, and art that invites visitors to embark on a journey of exploration, understanding, and inspiration. Through its exhibits, artifacts, and interactive experiences, the museum fosters a connection between the past and the present, celebrating the diverse voices that contribute to Alaska's vibrant tapestry. As a place of learning, reflection, and cultural exchange, the Alaska State Museum illuminates the intricate threads of the state's identity and invites all who enter its doors to join in the collective story of Alaska.

Mount Roberts Tramway: Panoramic Views

Rising majestically above the charming city of Juneau, the Mount Roberts Tramway offers a gateway to an awe-inspiring world of panoramic vistas, alpine beauty, and serene wilderness. A marvel of engineering, this aerial tramway transports visitors from the bustling streets below to the tranquil heights of Mount Roberts, where breathtaking views of mountains, forests, and waterways unfold in all directions. With its blend of natural wonder and human ingenuity, the Mount Roberts Tramway provides an unforgettable experience that connects travelers with the grandeur of Alaska's landscapes.

The adventure begins as visitors step into the tram cars and embark on a vertical journey to the summit of Mount Roberts. As the tramway ascends, the city of Juneau gradually shrinks below,

revealing the expanse of the Gastineau Channel and the surrounding landscapes. The sensation of gliding through the air, with panoramic windows framing the unfolding scenery, adds a touch of exhilaration to the experience.

Upon reaching the summit, visitors are greeted by a symphony of natural beauty that spans the horizon. The Mount Roberts Tramway offers an unobstructed view of the Alaskan wilderness, with a backdrop of towering mountains, verdant forests, and shimmering waters. The vistas extend as far as the eye can see, capturing the essence of the Last Frontier's untamed landscapes.

While the grand vistas are undoubtedly captivating, the Mount Roberts Tramway also invites visitors to embrace the art of observation. The details that unfold upon closer examination—wildflowers swaying in the breeze, distant waterfalls cascading down rocky slopes, and eagles soaring overhead—paint a richer portrait of the natural world. This intersection of grandeur and intricacy provides a well-rounded experience that satisfies both the desire for panoramic views and the yearning for intimate connections with nature.

Upon arriving at the summit, visitors are presented with the opportunity to explore a network of nature trails that wind through the alpine landscape. These well-maintained paths offer a chance to immerse oneself in the serene beauty of the mountains. Whether it's a leisurely stroll among wildflowers or a more ambitious hike to higher viewpoints, the trails provide a meditative escape from the bustling world below.

Mount Roberts Tramway is more than a platform for scenic views; it's a vantage point to observe the diversity of Alaska's wildlife. Keen-eyed visitors may spot soaring bald eagles, listen to the melodic songs of songbirds, or catch a glimpse of marmots and mountain goats as they navigate the rugged terrain. The opportunity to witness these creatures in their natural habitat adds a layer of authenticity to the alpine experience.

The Mount Roberts Tramway also serves as a bridge to Alaska's indigenous heritage. At the summit, the tramway complex includes the Chilkat Theater, a venue that hosts cultural performances and presentations. Visitors have the chance to learn about the Tlingit people, their history, and their cultural traditions. These insights enrich the visit, providing a deeper understanding of the land's significance to the native communities.

The breathtaking vistas and stunning landscapes of Mount Roberts Tramway offer a haven for photographers and memory-makers. From professional photographers seeking the perfect shot to families creating lasting memories, the mountain's panoramic viewpoints provide a canvas for capturing the beauty and wonder of Alaska. The play of light and shadow, the interplay of colors, and the ever-changing dynamics of nature's elements offer endless opportunities for creative expression.

For many, the journey to Mount Roberts Tramway is more than a sightseeing excursion; it's a retreat from the hustle and bustle of everyday life. The tranquil setting and panoramic vistas create an environment conducive to contemplation, reflection, and renewal. Whether it's finding a quiet spot to soak in the scenery or engaging in a moment of mindfulness amidst nature's beauty, the tramway's summit offers a respite from the demands of the modern world.

The experience at Mount Roberts Tramway is a dynamic one, as the weather and lighting conditions continuously shape the vistas before visitors' eyes. Clouds drifting across the sky, rainbows arching over the landscape, and the play of sunlight and shadow create an ever-changing tapestry of visual delights. Each visit to the tramway offers a unique encounter with nature's elements, ensuring that no two moments are alike.

While Mount Roberts Tramway provides an unparalleled opportunity to connect with nature, it's also a reminder of the importance of environmental stewardship. The tramway's management and staff are committed to sustainable practices that minimize the impact on the surrounding ecosystem. From waste reduction initiatives to educational programs on conservation, the tramway's commitment to preserving Alaska's natural beauty is a testament to its dedication to the well-being of the land.

In a world filled with distractions and noise, the Mount Roberts Tramway offers a moment of awe—an opportunity to stand on the edge of a mountaintop and gaze out at the vast expanse of Alaska's landscapes. It's a moment that reminds us of our place within the natural world, igniting a sense of wonder and humility. The panoramic views, the serenity of the alpine urroundings, and the majesty of the mountains all conspire to create a moment that lingers in he heart and mind long after the journey has ended.

he Mount Roberts Tramway is not just a means of transportation; it's a journey into the heart f Alaska's beauty and the essence of exploration. Whether travelers seek adventure, ranquility, or a deeper connection with nature, the tramway provides a path to fulfill those spirations. From families with young children to seasoned adventurers, everyone who steps nto the tram cars embarks on a shared experience—one that celebrates the wonder of the vorld we inhabit.

n conclusion, the Mount Roberts Tramway is more than a ride to a mountaintop; it's an nvitation to explore, discover, and connect with the unparalleled beauty of Alaska's andscapes. As visitors ascend to the summit, they are transported to a realm of panoramic views, alpine tranquility, and immersive experiences that evoke a sense of wonder and appreciation for the natural world. From the exhilaration of the ascent to the serenity of the mountain's heights, the tramway provides an opportunity to embrace the grandeur of the Last Frontier and carry its essence with them long after they've descended back to the world below.

Salmon Hatchery: Aquatic Insights

In the heart of Alaska's pristine landscapes, salmon hatcheries stand as windows into the intricate world of aquatic life, offering a glimpse into the incredible journey of one of the region's most iconic inhabitants: the salmon. These facilities are not just breeding grounds for fish; they are centers of education, conservation, and scientific research that reveal the interconnectedness of ecosystems, the life cycle of salmon, and the efforts to ensure the sustainability of this vital species. Through their exhibits, tours, and conservation efforts, salmon hatcheries provide aquatic insights that foster a deeper understanding of the delicate balance between human activities and the natural world.

At the heart of every salmon hatchery is a commitment to unravel the complex life cycle of these remarkable fish. Visitors are introduced to the stages of the salmon's life, from the moment they hatch from eggs to their epic migration to the sea and their eventual return to their natal rivers for spawning. This cycle is a testament to the resilience and adaptability of salmon, who navigate diverse environments, overcome obstacles, and ensure the survival of their species.

Salmon hatcheries play a crucial role in the early stages of a salmon's life. Here, salmon eggs are carefully incubated in controlled environments to maximize their chances of survival. Visitors have the unique opportunity to witness the delicate process of caring for these eggs, observing the transformation from translucent orbs to tiny, wriggling fry. Through informative exhibits and interactive displays, hatcheries illuminate the careful balance of factors required to raise healthy salmon fry.

Salmon hatcheries serve as hubs of education and outreach, inspiring visitors of all ages to become stewards of their natural surroundings. Guided tours, workshops, and interactive programs provide insights into the ecological significance of salmon and the broader impact of their life cycle. By fostering a sense of connection with these fish and the ecosystems they inhabit, hatcheries nurture a deeper appreciation for the importance of preserving aquatic habitats.

Hatcheries are often at the forefront of efforts to safeguard the delicate balance of aquatic ecosystems. Conservation initiatives extend beyond raising salmon fry; they encompass habitat restoration, water quality management, and the protection of biodiversity. By collaborating with local communities, government agencies, and environmental organizations, hatcheries contribute to the preservation of rivers, streams, and coastal areas that support not only salmon but an entire web of life.

Salmon are more than just aquatic inhabitants; they hold cultural, spiritual, and economic significance for indigenous communities across Alaska. Salmon hatcheries honor this heritage by collaborating with native communities to promote sustainable fishing practices and preserve traditional knowledge. Through cultural exhibits, storytelling sessions, and partnerships, hatcheries bridge the gap between modern science and the ancestral wisdom of native cultures.

Salmon hatcheries are not static institutions; they are hubs of scientific innovation that contribute to the understanding of aquatic ecosystems. Through research initiatives, biologists and ecologists study salmon behavior, genetics, and interactions with their environments. Insights gained from these studies inform conservation strategies, enhance hatchery practices, and shed light on the broader implications of changes in aquatic ecosystems.

The influence of salmon hatcheries extends beyond conservation and education; they also play a pivotal role in sustaining Alaska's commercial and recreational fisheries. By bolstering salmon populations, hatcheries contribute to the availability of fish for both commercial harvests and recreational fishing, which in turn supports local economies, livelihoods, and a thriving tourism industry centered around sportfishing.

Certain salmon populations, including many wild runs, are considered endangered or threatened. Hatcheries often engage in efforts to support the rehabilitation of these imperiled populations through captive breeding and release programs. By strategically releasing young fish into their natural habitats, hatcheries bolster the numbers of struggling populations, giving them a fighting chance for survival and recovery.

One of the most poignant moments in the life cycle of salmon is their return to their natal rivers for spawning. Hatcheries witness the culmination of their efforts as salmon—bred, raised, and nurtured within their facilities—complete their journey back to the wild. The sight of adult salmon leaping up waterfalls and navigating rapids is a testament to the resilience of these creatures and the success of hatchery programs.

Salmon hatcheries have evolved into eco-tourism destinations that offer immersive experiences for visitors from around the world. Eco-tours take participants behind the scenes, showcasing the processes involved in raising and releasing salmon fry. These tours provide an opportunity for cultural exchange, where visitors can learn about indigenous traditions, connect with local communities, and witness the significance of salmon in Alaskan life.

Salmon hatcheries are a reminder that the health Of aquatic ecosystems is intrinsically linked to the well-being of human communities. As visitors explore hatchery exhibits, witness salmon releases, and learn about conservation efforts, they are invited to connect with the beauty, complexity, and fragility of the natural world. The story of salmon is a story of interconnectedness, and it calls upon us to embrace our roles as caretakers of the oceans, rivers, and streams that sustain life.

Salmon hatcheries serve as more than educational institutions; they are centers of inspiration. The journey of salmon—from eggs in a hatchery to their return as powerful swimmers—is a metaphor for resilience, adaptability, and the indomitable spirit of life. These fish face immense challenges, yet they persist, adapt, and thrive. In a world grappling with environmental changes, the story of salmon imparts valuable lessons about resilience, collaboration, and the capacity of both nature and humanity to overcome adversity.

Ultimately, the work of salmon hatcheries underscores the shared responsibility to protect and preserve aquatic ecosystems. By engaging with hatcheries, visitors become part of a collective effort to ensure the continued existence of salmon and the countless other species that rely on healthy rivers and oceans. From the hatchery to the wild waters, the journey of salmon is a call to action—a reminder that our choices and actions can shape the fate of aquatic ecosystems for generations to come.

In conclusion, salmon hatcheries are more than facilities that nurture fish; they are beacons of education, conservation, and scientific inquiry that provide valuable aquatic insights. Through their exhibits, conservation efforts, and partnerships, they illuminate the intricate web of life that exists beneath the water's surface. By fostering a deeper understanding of the salmon's journey and its significance, hatcheries inspire a collective commitment to preserving the health and beauty of aquatic ecosystems for present and future generations.

Douglas Island: Outdoor Adventures

Nestled in the embrace of Alaska's rugged coastline, Douglas Island beckons adventurers and nature enthusiasts to uncover a world of outdoor wonders. This majestic island, located just a short ferry ride from Juneau, offers a sanctuary of untamed landscapes, diverse ecosystems, and thrilling activities that cater to all levels of exploration. From towering forests to pristine shores, Douglas Island is a playground for those seeking to immerse themselves in the raw beauty and serene tranquility of the Last Frontier's wilderness.

Douglas Island boasts a network of hiking trails that wind through its lush forests and offer stunning views of the surrounding waters. For those seeking a leisurely stroll, trails such as the Perseverance Trail provide a gentle introduction to the island's natural beauty. More intrepid adventurers can tackle challenging trails that lead to panoramic viewpoints, like the Mount Jumbo Trail, where the reward for the ascent is a breathtaking vista that stretches across the Alaskan coastline.

Cycling enthusiasts find their paradise on Douglas Island, where scenic roads and trails invite bikers to explore at their own pace. The island's relatively low traffic and picturesque landscapes create an ideal setting for leisurely rides and heart-pounding challenges alike. Pedaling along the winding roads that cut through dense forests and coastal vistas provides an intimate connection with the island's diverse ecosystems.

Douglas Island's proximity to the water invites waterborne adventures that reveal a new perspective of its natural beauty. Kayakers and canoeists can glide along the tranquil waters of the Gastineau Channel, exploring hidden coves, witnessing marine wildlife, and savoring the serene ambiance that only the ocean can offer. The interplay of light on water, the salty breeze, and the occasional glimpse of marine life create an immersive experience that embodies the essence of coastal Alaska.

For fishing enthusiasts, Douglas Island is a haven of angling opportunities. The island's waters are home to a variety of fish species, including salmon, halibut, and trout. Whether casting a line from the shoreline or embarking on a chartered fishing expedition, anglers can immerse themselves in the tranquility of the ocean, anticipating the thrill of reeling in a prized catch.

Douglas Island's diverse habitats support a rich array of wildlife, both on land and in the water. Bald eagles soar overhead, their keen eyes scanning the shores for potential prey. Marine mammals, including seals and sea lions, can be spotted basking on rocky outcrops. Patient observers may even witness the majestic breach of a humpback whale as it navigates the channel. The island's natural symphony of life showcases the delicate balance that sustains these creatures in their native habitat.

For those who prefer to explore at a more relaxed pace, scenic drives around Douglas Island provide an opportunity to take in the island's beauty from the comfort of a vehicle. The East Douglas Road offers stunning views of the Gastineau Channel and the surrounding mountains. Along the way, pull-off points invite travelers to pause and soak in the vistas, capturing photographs that capture the grandeur of the Alaskan landscape.

The rugged terrain of Douglas Island presents a playground for rock climbers and boulderers. With cliffs, crags, and rocky formations dotting the landscape, adventurers can challenge themselves to scale new heights and conquer natural obstacles. Whether it's the thrill of reaching the summit or the satisfaction of solving a bouldering puzzle, rock climbing on the island combines physicality with a deep connection to the natural world.

Douglas Island is a photographer's paradise, offering an array of picturesque settings to capture with a lens. From the vibrant hues of wildflowers that carpet the landscape in summer to the ethereal play of light on water during golden hours, the island's changing moods and seasons provide endless opportunities for creative expression. Photographers can capture the essence

of Alaska's wilderness through landscapes, wildlife shots, and candid moments that tell a visual story of the island's allure.

Even in winter, Douglas Island does not lose its enchantment. Snow-covered landscapes transform the island into a winter wonderland, offering opportunities for snowshoeing, cross-country skiing, and even ice skating on frozen lakes. The serene hush of the winter woods, the glisten of snow-covered branches, and the thrill of embracing the chill create a unique outdoor experience that invites a deeper connection with nature.

Douglas Island's natural beauty serves as a backdrop for idyllic picnics and al fresco dining. Scenic viewpoints, serene beaches, and tranquil forests provide settings for enjoying a meal in the embrace of nature. Whether it's a simple picnic with locally sourced treats or a gourmet meal prepared with care, dining outdoors on the island is an opportunity to savor not only the flavors but also the sights, sounds, and scents of the Alaskan wilderness.

Douglas Island isn't just a destination; it's an open invitation to connect with the great outdoors in myriad ways. Whether seeking adrenaline-pumping adventures or moments of quiet contemplation, the island offers a canvas for outdoor enthusiasts to explore, discover, and immerse themselves in the natural rhythms of the wilderness. The island's untouched landscapes, diverse ecosystems, and breathtaking vistas provide a reminder that the beauty of

Alaska's wilderness is not to be observed from afar but to be experienced, embraced, and cherished.

In conclusion, Douglas Island is a symphony of senses—an invitation to see, hear, touch, smell, and taste the essence of Alaska's untamed landscapes. It's a place where outdoor adventures become transformative experiences, where moments of awe and connection with nature transcend the ordinary. From hiking through ancient forests to kayaking on pristine waters, each activity on the island unfolds a new chapter in the story of exploration. Through its natural beauty and the myriad outdoor pursuits it offers, Douglas Island embodies the spirit of adventure that beckons travelers to embrace the wilderness, immerse themselves in its wonders, and leave with a deeper appreciation for the magic that the natural world holds.

Native Heritage Center: Cultural Immersion

Amid the sprawling landscapes of Alaska, where mountains meet glaciers and rivers weave tales of time, lies a place of profound cultural significance—the Native Heritage Center. This immersive cultural haven stands as a testament to the rich tapestry of Alaska's indigenous peoples, offering visitors a unique opportunity to delve into the heritage, traditions, and stories

of these ancient communities. Through vibrant exhibits, engaging performances, and interactive experiences, the Native Heritage Center serves as a bridge between the past and the present, inviting all who enter to embark on a transformative journey of cultural immersion.

The Native Heritage Center transports visitors into the heart of Alaska's indigenous history—a history that predates colonization and encompasses a deep relationship with the land, the elements, and the community. Through meticulously curated exhibits, historical artifacts, and informative displays, the center breathes life into the stories of native cultures, tracing their evolution from ancestral times to the present day.

Alaska is home to a multitude of indigenous cultures, each with its own unique traditions, languages, and ways of life. The Native Heritage Center showcases the diversity of these cultures, providing insights into the distinct identities of groups such as the Athabascans, Inupiaq, Yup'ik, Tlingit, and more. Visitors have the privilege of gaining a deeper understanding of the worldviews, practices, and artistic expressions that define each culture.

One of the highlights of the Native Heritage Center is the vibrant array of cultural performances that take place within its grounds. Traditional dances, songs, and storytelling sessions serve as windows into the heart of indigenous communities. As performers don regalia adorned with intricate beadwork and vibrant colors, they share not only the beauty of their artistry but also he soul of their cultural heritage. These performances create a profound connection between he audience and the centuries-old traditions being celebrated.

he indigenous peoples of Alaska have a rich tradition of artistic expression, creating intricate works that tell stories, convey beliefs, and honor their connection to the natural world. At the Native Heritage Center, visitors have the privilege of witnessing this artistry firsthand. From intricately carved totem poles to delicate beadwork and finely crafted tools, the center's exhibits showcase the artistic legacy that has been passed down through generations.

Immersive experiences take cultural immersion to new heights at the Native Heritage Center. Through hands-on activities and interactive demonstrations, visitors can engage with indigenous practices and gain a deeper appreciation for the skills that have been honed over centuries. From participating in traditional crafts to learning about the significance of ceremonial regalia, these experiences provide a tangible connection to indigenous ways of life.

he Native Heritage Center honors the wisdom of elders—guardians of cultural knowledge who carry the stories and traditions of their ancestors. Through personal interactions, storytelling sessions, and guided tours, visitors have the privilege of engaging with these esteemed members of indigenous communities. Listening to their narratives, insights, and perspectives offers a rare opportunity to glean firsthand knowledge and wisdom.

The Native Heritage Center plays a pivotal role in the revitalization and preservation of indigenous cultures. By providing a platform for cultural expression and education, the center

ensures that traditions are passed down to future generations. Moreover, it serves as a catalyst for cultural revival, empowering native communities to reconnect with their roots, celebrate their heritage, and assert their identities in a rapidly changing world.

Among the center's immersive experiences are recreations of traditional indigenous dwellings, each offering a glimpse into the distinct ways in which native communities lived and thrived in harmony with their environments. Visitors can step inside these structures—ranging from the birch bark-covered dwellings of the Athabascans to the coastal longhouses of the Tlingit—and imagine the lives of those who once called them home.

Alaska's indigenous cultures are deeply rooted in the land and waters that have sustained them for generations. The Native Heritage Center reflects this profound bond by situating itself amid a natural setting that mirrors the environments inhabited by native communities. This alignment between the center's physical location and the cultural narratives it presents creates a seamless blend of experience and education.

The Native Heritage Center extends its impact beyond its walls by engaging with local communities, schools, and organizations. Educational programs, workshops, and outreach initiatives foster a deeper understanding of indigenous cultures and histories. By connecting with younger generations, the center ensures that cultural knowledge remains alive and relevant, bridging the gap between the past and the future.

Visiting the Native Heritage Center is not merely an exercise in tourism; it's a transformative journey of cultural sensitivity and respect. As visitors learn about the struggles and triumphs of indigenous communities, they are invited to reflect on their own roles in fostering understanding and advocating for cultural preservation. The experience fosters empathy, humility, and a deeper awareness of the challenges faced by indigenous peoples.

In essence, the Native Heritage Center is a place of connection—a space where people from all walks of life can come together to share stories, experiences, and perspectives. It's a reminder that while cultures may differ, there is a shared humanity that unites us all. Through the lens of indigenous cultures, visitors are reminded of the importance of cultural exchange, respect for diversity, and the preservation of heritage.

As visitors depart the Native Heritage Center, they carry with them more than memories; they carry the seeds of inspiration, respect, and cultural awareness. The center's impact resonates far beyond the boundaries of its physical space, as the experiences and insights gained within its walls continue to shape the way visitors perceive the world around them. The lessons of cultural immersion become catalysts for positive change, advocacy, and a deeper appreciation for the beauty of cultural diversity.

In conclusion, the Native Heritage Center stands as a beacon of cultural immersion—a place where the stories, traditions, and artistry of Alaska's indigenous peoples come to life. Through

exhibits, performances, interactive experiences, and personal connections, the center offers a transformative journey that transcends boundaries and fosters a deeper understanding of the rich tapestry of human culture. As visitors engage with indigenous heritage, they embark on a path of empathy, respect, and a commitment to preserving the cultural treasures that enrich our shared global heritage.

Alaska Brewing Company: Craft Beer Delights

In the heart of the Last Frontier, where glaciers meet mountains and untouched wilderness stretches as far as the eye can see, a different kind of treasure awaits: the Alaska Brewing Company. Nestled in the rugged landscapes of Juneau, this iconic brewery has become a beacon of craft beer excellence, embodying the spirit of innovation, adventure, and reverence for the natural world. With a commitment to quality, sustainability, and a dash of Alaskan ingenuity, the Alaska Brewing Company has carved its place in the world of craft beer as a purveyor of unique flavors and a steward of the environment.

The essence of Alaska permeates every aspect of the Alaska Brewing Company, from its recipes to its ethos. The brewery's commitment to using locally sourced ingredients reflects a deep connection to the Alaskan terroir. The pristine waters, wild berries, and indigenous grains that define the landscape find their way into the beers, creating a sensory experience that transports beer enthusiasts to the heart of the Last Frontier with every sip.

At the heart of the Alaska Brewing Company is a dedication to the art and science of brewing. Each batch of beer is crafted with meticulous attention to detail, from selecting the finest malts and hops to the precise timing of fermentation. The result is a range of beers that showcase not only traditional styles but also innovative twists that celebrate the spirit of exploration and experimentation.

The Alaska Brewing Company boasts a diverse portfolio of beers that cater to a wide range of palates. From rich stouts that evoke the depth of an Alaskan winter to crisp lagers that mirror the clarity of glacial waters, each beer is a journey through the flavors of the state. The company's commitment to both classic styles and contemporary innovations ensures that there's something for every beer enthusiast to savor.

Beyond crafting exceptional beer, the Alaska Brewing Company is a trailblazer in sustainability and environmental stewardship. The brewery's commitment to minimizing its carbon footprint is evident in every facet of its operations. The pioneering use of a carbon recapture system,

fueled by spent grain and other brewery byproducts, showcases a commitment to sustainable practices that goes beyond the brewing process itself.

The Alaska Brewing Company isn't just a place for brewing; it's a space for community engagement and connection. The brewery's events, festivals, and gatherings serve as opportunities for locals and visitors alike to come together, share stories, and celebrate the unique culture of Alaska. The company's commitment to community goes beyond the glass, fostering a sense of belonging that echoes the warm spirit of Alaskan hospitality.

An integral part of the Alaska Brewing Company's identity is its distinctive label artistry. Each label is a canvas that tells a visual story—a reflection of the beer's character, the inspiration behind its creation, and the spirit of the Alaskan landscapes that inspired it. The labels themselves become works of art, inviting beer enthusiasts to appreciate the visual beauty that complements the flavors within.

Visiting the Alaska Brewing Company is more than just a tasting experience; it's a journey into the heart of brewing excellence. Guided tours offer visitors the chance to explore the brewery's inner workings, witness the brewing process, and gain insights into the craftsmanship that goes into each batch of beer. The tours provide a behind-the-scenes look at the commitment to quality and innovation that defines the company.

The Alaska Brewing Company is also dedicated to cultivating a deeper appreciation for craft beer. Educational initiatives, tasting events, and workshops invite beer enthusiasts to learn about the brewing process, the nuances of different styles, and the art of pairing beer with food. Through these experiences, visitors gain a deeper understanding of the complexities and subtleties that make each beer unique.

The Alaska Brewing Company embodies the spirit of adventure that defines the Last Frontier. Whether it's the thrill of discovering a new beer style or embarking on an outdoor expedition, the company's ethos encourages a sense of exploration and curiosity. The rugged landscapes, the untamed beauty, and the ever-present sense of wonder find their reflection in the diverse array of beers that the brewery offers.

For craft beer enthusiasts, the Alaska Brewing Company is more than a brewery; it's a destination. Beer lovers from around the world pilgrimage to Juneau to sample the flavors, experience the brewery's culture, and connect with fellow aficionados. The brewery's place in the craft beer landscape has transformed it into a hub of camaraderie, where the love for beer and the spirit of adventure intersect.

As the Alaska Brewing Company continues to evolve and innovate, it remains rooted in a legacy of excellence that spans decades. With every beer brewed, every label designed, and every interaction with the community, the company pays homage to the tradition of craft brewing

while embracing the possibilities of the future. Its legacy is one of fostering a deep appreciation for beer, a love for the land, and a commitment to making a positive impact.

In conclusion, the Alaska Brewing Company offers more than just craft beer; it offers a sip of the Alaskan spirit. Through its dedication to craftsmanship, innovation, sustainability, and community, the brewery has become a symbol of the state's rich culture and natural beauty. Every beer tells a story—an invitation to explore the rugged landscapes, embrace the adventurous spirit, and savor the flavors that define Alaska. The Alaska Brewing Company isn't just a brewery; it's a journey of the senses, a celebration of the outdoors, and a toast to the indomitable spirit that makes the Last Frontier truly extraordinary.

Outdoor Adventures: Embrace the Wilderness

In a world that is becoming increasingly urbanized and technology-driven, the call of the wild remains a powerful and irresistible draw. The allure of outdoor adventures, where untamed landscapes, fresh air, and the thrill of the unknown await, speaks to a primal instinct within us—an instinct to explore, connect with nature, and find solace in the great outdoors. Whether scaling towering peaks, navigating winding rivers, or simply basking in the tranquility of a forest, outdoor adventures offer a profound opportunity to embrace the wilderness and forge a deeper connection with the natural world.

Outdoor adventures are a manifestation of the human spirit's quest for challenge and discovery. These endeavors encourage individuals to step outside their comfort zones and embrace the unknown, pushing the boundaries of physical and mental limitations. Scaling a challenging rock face, embarking on a multi-day hike, or navigating white-water rapids require not only physical prowess but also mental resilience, adaptability, and a willingness to confront the unexpected.

In a world filled with noise, screens, and fast-paced living, the simplicity of nature provides a refuge for the weary soul. Outdoor adventures offer a chance to disconnect from the digital realm and reconnect with the natural world. The sound of rustling leaves, the scent of pine trees, and the sensation of wind on the skin provide a sensory symphony that rejuvenates the senses and nourishes the spirit. It's a reminder that, at our core, we are a part of the ecosystem, intricately woven into the fabric of the Earth.

Every outdoor adventure holds the promise of discovery—a hidden waterfall, a secluded beach, or a panoramic vista that takes the breath away. The thrill of exploration fuels the desire to traverse new terrains, revealing landscapes that are often untouched by human presence. It's

the joy of stumbling upon the extraordinary in the ordinary, as each step unveils the beauty and diversity of the natural world.

Outdoor adventures are as much about embracing challenges as they are about reveling in triumphs. Mother Nature has a way of testing our resilience, presenting us with unpredictable weather, rugged terrain, and unexpected obstacles. Overcoming these challenges fosters a sense of accomplishment, self-reliance, and an appreciation for adaptability—a set of skills that extend beyond the adventure itself and into various aspects of life.

In a world dominated by distractions and multitasking, outdoor adventures demand a return to mindful presence. The act of hiking a trail, paddling a river, or camping under the stars requires a focused awareness of the immediate surroundings. This immersion in the present moment fosters a deep connection with the environment and allows individuals to experience the world with heightened senses, unburdened by the worries of the past or the uncertainties of the future.

Outdoor adventures are a classroom without walls, offering lessons in ecology, geology, navigation, and survival. Whether identifying plant species, understanding weather patterns, or reading the topography of the land, adventurers engage in continuous learning. This spirit of curiosity encourages individuals to see the world through a lens of wonder, fostering a lifelong commitment to expanding their knowledge of the natural world.

Engaging in outdoor activities is inherently beneficial to physical health. Hiking, biking, kayaking, and other adventures provide cardiovascular exercise, strengthen muscles, and improve overall fitness. The natural variability of terrains also challenges the body to adapt, enhancing balance, coordination, and flexibility. Outdoor adventures offer a holistic approach to well-being, nourishing both body and mind.

As individuals immerse themselves in the beauty of the outdoors, they become acutely aware of the importance of preserving these landscapes for future generations. Outdoor adventures often foster a sense of environmental stewardship, inspiring individuals to take action to protect and conserve natural habitats. This advocacy extends beyond personal experiences and influences behaviors that contribute to the preservation of the wilderness.

Outdoor adventures have a unique way of fostering connections and deepening relationships. Whether embarking on a solo journey or partaking in group expeditions, shared experiences in the wilderness create bonds that are often forged in adversity and triumph. Stories shared around campfires, challenges overcome, and the simple joys of being in nature together contribute to the creation of lasting memories and friendships.

The wilderness has a way of stripping away distractions and allowing for moments of introspection and contemplation. The stillness of a mountain summit, the rhythm of a river's flow, and the solitude of a forest path provide the ideal backdrop for introspective thought.

Outdoor adventures offer individuals the space to ponder life's questions, gain perspective, and find solace in the midst of nature's grandeur.

For many indigenous cultures, outdoor adventures are not just recreational pursuits but integral aspects of their way of life. Learning from these communities can deepen one's understanding of the symbiotic relationship between humans and nature. Whether it's following ancient trails, practicing sustainable land use, or honoring rituals that celebrate the Earth, outdoor adventures provide an opportunity to connect with and learn from indigenous wisdom.

Outdoor adventurers often become advocates for preserving the wilderness they cherish. As they experience the beauty, fragility, and transformative power of the natural world, they feel compelled to protect it. These individuals champion conservation efforts, support sustainable practices, and engage in initiatives that ensure the landscapes they explored will be preserved for future generations.

In conclusion, outdoor adventures are not isolated experiences but an ongoing journey that spans a lifetime. They beckon us to step outside, engage with nature, and embrace the wilderness with open arms and an open heart. These adventures offer more than a fleeting escape—they provide the tools for personal growth, the gift of connection, and the inspiration to be stewards of the Earth. Whether hiking through mountains, kayaking along rugged coastlines, or camping under starlit skies, the call of the wild remains an invitation to explore, discover, and truly live in harmony with the untamed world around us.

Local Cuisine: Savor Alaska's Flavors

The culinary landscape of a region is a reflection of its history, culture, and geography. Nowhere is this more evident than in Alaska, where the local cuisine embodies the essence of the Last Frontier. From the icy waters of the Pacific Ocean to the rich soils that yield wild berries and game, Alaska's flavors are as diverse and abundant as its landscapes. Embracing the treasures of the land and sea, Alaska's cuisine offers a unique culinary journey that celebrates tradition, sustainability, and the rich tapestry of cultural influences.

Alaska's history is woven with the threads of various cultures, each contributing its own distinct flavors and culinary practices. Indigenous traditions, Russian influences, and the influx of settlers from across the globe have all left their mark on Alaska's cuisine. This fusion of traditions is reflected in dishes that draw from the bounty of the sea, the land, and the forests—a true melting pot of flavors that mirrors the state's diverse population.

Alaska's coastal location makes seafood a centerpiece of its cuisine. From succulent Alaskan king crab to tender halibut and wild salmon, the ocean provides a cornucopia of delicacies that grace the tables of locals and visitors alike. The freshness and quality of Alaskan seafood are unparalleled, with each dish offering a taste of the briny waters that surround the state.

For centuries, indigenous communities in Alaska have relied on the land for sustenance, and this connection to the wild remains a cornerstone of local cuisine. Moose, caribou, and reindeer provide lean and flavorful meat, often prepared in stews, roasts, or smoked preparations. Wild berries, such as blueberries and lingonberries, are foraged from the forests and find their way into jams, desserts, and sauces, adding a burst of natural sweetness to dishes.

Alaska's short but intense growing season yields a vibrant array of berries and plants that thrive in the northern climate. Wild raspberries, cloudberries, and salmonberries flourish in the summer, while spruce tips and fireweed blossoms are harvested to create unique flavor profiles in beverages and dishes. These indigenous ingredients provide a connection to the land and a glimpse into the natural rhythms of the region.

Alaska's commitment to sustainability is deeply ingrained in its culinary practices. Whether it's adhering to fishing quotas to protect marine life or practicing ethical hunting to maintain animal populations, the local cuisine is guided by a profound respect for the resources that sustain it. This dedication to responsible consumption ensures that future generations can continue to savor the bounty of the land and sea.

Alaska's seafood offerings are a testament to the state's coastal riches. The art of preparing seafood has been passed down through generations, resulting in dishes that are both simple and exquisite. Alaskan king crab, with its succulent meat and sweet flavor, is often enjoyed simply steamed or with a dash of melted butter. Halibut, prized for its firm texture, takes center stage in dishes ranging from grilled fillets to fish tacos.

Of all the seafood treasures Alaska offers, perhaps none is as iconic as wild salmon. The five species of salmon—sockeye, king, coho, pink, and chum—journey from the open ocean to the rivers of Alaska to spawn, traversing epic distances that define their flavor and texture. Whether enjoyed smoked, grilled, cured, or poached, salmon is a symbol of the state's natural bounty and a testament to the delicate balance of its ecosystems.

Alaska's indigenous communities have preserved their culinary heritage for generations, passing down recipes and techniques that celebrate the bounty of the land and sea. Dishes such as "fry bread," a deep-fried dough enjoyed with savory or sweet toppings, and "akutaq," a traditional dessert made with whipped animal fat, berries, and sometimes fish, provide a window into the culinary traditions that have sustained communities for centuries.

Alaska's history is entwined with Russian colonial influence, which left an indelible mark on the cuisine. Dishes like borscht, a hearty beet soup often served with sour cream, and piroshki,

savory pastries filled with ingredients like meat, cabbage, or potatoes, reflect the blending of Russian flavors with local ingredients. These dishes pay homage to a time when the Russian presence left a culinary legacy that endures to this day.

While tradition is a cornerstone of Alaska's culinary identity, modern interpretations and innovative techniques have also found their way into local cuisine. Chefs and home cooks alike draw inspiration from global trends while maintaining a deep connection to Alaska's flavors. This blend of tradition and innovation results in dishes that honor the past while embracing the excitement of culinary exploration.

Alaska's culinary landscape extends beyond the plate to the glass, with a burgeoning craft beverage scene that offers a diverse range of flavors. Local breweries and distilleries create unique beers, spirits, and cocktails that showcase the state's ingredients and entrepreneurial spirit. Visitors can raise a glass of Alaskan-brewed beer, sip on handcrafted spirits, or enjoy cocktails that incorporate indigenous botanicals.

In Alaska, dining is an opportunity to embark on a cultural journey that transcends borders. The local cuisine reflects the global influences that have shaped the state, allowing diners to savor flavors from around the world without leaving its shores. Thai curry, Mexican tacos, Japanese sushi, and Mediterranean-inspired dishes are all part of Alaska's culinary tapestry, reflecting the diverse communities that call the state home.

For travelers, exploring Alaska's cuisine is a journey of its own—an opportunity to savor not only the flavors but also the stories and cultural richness that define the state. Farmers' markets, food festivals, and farm-to-table experiences allow visitors to engage with local producers and learn about the origins of their meals. Culinary tourism in Alaska goes beyond the plate, inviting travelers to connect with the communities that create the dishes they enjoy.

The changing seasons in Alaska influence the culinary calendar, with each time of year offering its own unique ingredients and flavors. Spring brings the delicate emergence of edible plants, while summer's long days yield berries and fresh catches from the sea. Fall is a time of abundance, with root vegetables and game making their appearance, while winter calls for hearty stews and preserved delicacies.

In conclusion, Alaska's local cuisine is a tapestry woven from the threads of tradition, cultural exchange, and the bounties of the land and sea. It's a reflection of the state's history, a celebration of its diversity, and a testament to its commitment to sustainability. Every dish tells a story, whether it's a recipe passed down through generations, a modern interpretation

Northern Lights: Winter's Celestial Show

In the heart of the Arctic and subarctic regions, where winter nights stretch long and the skies remain cloaked in darkness, a celestial phenomenon takes center stage—the Northern Lights, also known as the Aurora Borealis. This awe-inspiring natural light display paints the night sky with vibrant hues of green, pink, purple, and blue, captivating those fortunate enough to witness its elusive beauty. The Northern Lights are more than just a breathtaking spectacle; they are a testament to the intricate dance between Earth and the cosmos, a source of wonder and inspiration that has captivated human imagination for centuries.

The Northern Lights result from a mesmerizing interplay of particles and energy between the sun and Earth. This cosmic ballet begins with the sun emitting charged particles known as solar wind. These particles travel through space and collide with Earth's magnetic field, creating a stunning reaction in the atmosphere. As the charged particles interact with gases like oxygen and nitrogen, they release energy in the form of light, illuminating the night sky in a mesmerizing display.

Earth's magnetic field plays a crucial role in the creation of the Northern Lights. This invisible shield surrounds the planet, deflecting the majority of the solar wind's charged particles away from the surface. However, near the magnetic poles, particularly in regions such as Alaska and northern Canada, the magnetic field lines converge, creating openings through which the solar wind can enter the atmosphere. This interaction is what causes the Northern Lights to be most commonly observed in these high-latitude areas.

The Northern Lights are intrinsically linked to the winter months, when the longer nights provide the perfect backdrop for their luminous display. In polar regions, where the sun barely rises above the horizon during the winter solstice, the prolonged darkness allows the Northern Lights to take center stage. It's during these months that enthusiasts from around the world venture northward to catch a glimpse of this celestial marvel.

The hues of the Northern Lights are a result of the type of gas particles that are interacting with the solar wind's charged particles. Oxygen molecules typically emit green and red light when excited, creating the iconic greenish hue often associated with the auroras. Meanwhile, nitrogen molecules contribute to the rarer purples and blues that occasionally grace the display. The varying colors and intensities add to the ethereal quality of the spectacle.

The Northern Lights have captivated humanity's imagination for centuries, inspiring myths, legends, and cultural narratives across different cultures. The lights' ethereal nature and mysterious origins have given rise to stories of celestial deities, spirits, and otherworldly visitors.

Even in modern times, the allure of the Northern Lights continues to draw adventurers, photographers, and dreamers to the Arctic's frozen landscapes.

Advancements in photography have allowed the Northern Lights to be immortalized in breathtaking images that convey their dynamic beauty. Long-exposure photography captures the dance of light across the night sky, revealing intricate patterns and hues that often go unnoticed by the naked eye. These photographs not only serve as stunning visuals but also as a testament to the power of nature's artistic prowess.

While the Northern Lights may inspire wonder and awe, they are also a subject of scientific investigation. Studying the auroras provides valuable insights into Earth's magnetosphere, the interaction between solar wind and Earth's atmosphere, and the role of charged particles in shaping our planet's environment. Space agencies and research institutions around the world collaborate to unravel the mysteries of this celestial phenomenon.

For many, witnessing the Northern Lights is a bucket-list experience—a journey into the Arctic wilderness to catch a glimpse of the cosmic spectacle. Aurora chasing involves venturing to remote locations with optimal viewing conditions and minimal light pollution. Travelers often brave freezing temperatures and long nights in the hope of witnessing the lights' ephemeral dance across the heavens.

Alaska stands as one of the premier destinations for experiencing the Northern Lights. Its location within the Arctic Circle, coupled with its vast expanses of wilderness, offers prime viewing conditions. Towns like Fairbanks and Anchorage provide accessible launching points for aurora chasers, while more remote regions like Denali National Park offer a unique blend of celestial wonder and untamed landscapes.

In indigenous cultures that inhabit the northern reaches of the world, the Northern Lights hold deep cultural and spiritual significance. These communities have their own interpretations and narratives surrounding the lights, often associating them with ancestral spirits, cosmic stories, and guiding lights. The Northern Lights are a reminder of the intricate relationship between culture, nature, and the cosmos.

Witnessing the Northern Lights is a multi-sensory experience that goes beyond sight alone. The crispness of the Arctic air, the hush of a snowy landscape, and the silence that envelops the night create a symphony of sensations that enhance the magic of the moment. As the lights shimmer and dance, they become part of a larger sensory tapestry that etches the memory deep into the soul.

The Northern Lights remind us of the vastness of the universe and our place within it. As humans gaze upward, transfixed by the cosmic light show, a sense of humility takes hold. In the face of the universe's grandeur, we are reminded of the beauty and mystery that reside beyond our daily concerns, encouraging us to embrace the unknown and savor the wonder of existence.

As climate change continues to shape the planet, there are concerns about the future visibility of the Northern Lights. The interplay between solar activity, Earth's magnetic field, and atmospheric conditions means that changes in any of these factors could affect the frequency and intensity of the auroras. Efforts to address climate change and protect the Arctic's unique ecosystems are crucial to ensuring that future generations can continue to witness this celestial spectacle.

In conclusion, the Northern Lights are a testament to the universe's capacity for beauty and wonder. These cosmic lights that dance across the night sky are a source of inspiration, contemplation, and awe. They remind us of the dynamic relationship between Earth and space, the mysteries that continue to captivate our imagination, and the importance of preserving the natural world. As each luminous display unfolds, it leaves an indelible mark on the hearts of those who witness it—a cosmic legacy that transcends time and connects us to the mysteries of the cosmos.

Arts and Culture: Creative Expressions

In the heart of Alaska's breathtaking landscapes and vibrant communities lies a rich tapestry of arts and culture that speaks to the state's diverse history, indigenous heritage, and modern creative spirit. From traditional forms of expression that have been passed down through generations to contemporary artistic movements that reflect the changing times, Alaska's arts and culture scene offers a glimpse into the soul of the Last Frontier. Through visual arts, performing arts, literature, music, and more, Alaskans weave stories, celebrate traditions, and explore the ever-evolving facets of human expression.

Alaska's visual arts are a reflection of the state's landscapes, history, and cultural diversity. Indigenous artists draw on centuries-old traditions to create intricate carvings, sculptures, and intricate beadwork that honor their heritage. Landscape painters capture the rugged beauty of the wilderness on canvas, translating the colors, textures, and vastness of Alaska onto two-dimensional surfaces. The northern light's ephemeral dance finds its way onto palettes, resulting in breathtaking depictions of the Aurora Borealis that transport viewers to the heart of the Arctic night.

Sculpture, particularly in the form of intricate woodcarvings, holds a special place in Alaska's artistic heritage. Indigenous artists, such as those of the Tlingit, Haida, and Yup'ik cultures, are renowned for their skill in transforming wood and other materials into elaborate totem poles, masks, and figures. These sculptures are more than mere art—they are vessels of storytelling, conveying myths, legends, and cultural narratives that have been cherished for generations.

Alaska's literary scene is a tapestry of voices that reflect the diverse experiences of its inhabitants. Indigenous writers weave oral traditions into written narratives that preserve cultural wisdom and ancestral stories. Non-fiction works delve into the challenges and triumphs of life in the North, offering insights into the resilience and adaptability required to thrive in this unique environment. Poets capture the essence of the wilderness, using words to convey the awe-inspiring landscapes and the emotions they evoke.

Alaska's performing arts scene encompasses a wide range of expressions, from indigenous dances that pay homage to ancestral spirits to contemporary theater productions that tackle ressing social issues. Native dance troupes share traditional stories through movement and song, preserving cultural heritage while inspiring new generations. Modern theater companies bring stories to life, often drawing inspiration from local experiences and universal themes that resonate with audiences.

Music in Alaska is as diverse as the people who call the state home. From indigenous drumming and chanting to folk ballads that celebrate life in the North, the musical landscape is a harmonious blend of cultural influences. Traditional instruments like drums and flutes coexist with modern sounds, as Alaskans find new ways to express their connection to the land and their communities. Festivals and gatherings celebrate music's power to unite and uplift, offering a platform for both established artists and emerging talents.

Alaska's arts and culture scene is characterized by the hands-on craftsmanship that infuses everyday objects with artistic flair. Handmade crafts, such as woven baskets, intricately beaded jewelry, and finely stitched garments, showcase the attention to detail and cultural significance that accompanies each creation. Indigenous artists use natural materials to fashion functional items that embody traditional aesthetics, all while celebrating the connection between art and daily life.

Throughout the year, Alaskans come together to celebrate their cultural heritage and artistic expression through festivals and gatherings. These events provide a platform for artists to showcase their work, while also inviting the community to engage with creative endeavors. Indigenous festivals honor traditions, with dance, music, and art at the center of the celebrations. Contemporary arts festivals bring together artists working in various mediums, fostering cross-cultural exchange and artistic dialogue.

Dance plays a central role in Alaska's indigenous cultures, with each dance telling a story that reflects the values, experiences, and history of the community. Traditional dances are performed at gatherings, ceremonies, and celebrations, providing a means of passing down cultural knowledge and honoring ancestral spirits. The rhythmic movements and vibrant regalia of these dances are a testament to the enduring strength of indigenous traditions in the face of modernity.

Alaska's culinary arts are a unique blend of history, geography, and cultural exchange. Indigenous ingredients, such as salmon, game, and wild berries, form the foundation of traditional dishes that celebrate the land's bounty. Contemporary chefs draw on these ingredients while also incorporating global influences to create a fusion of flavors that mirrors Alaska's diverse population. Food festivals and events showcase the culinary creativity that thrives in the Last Frontier.

Alaska's cities are hubs of creative energy, with urban artistry adding a modern layer to the state's cultural landscape. Street art, murals, and public installations transform walls and spaces into canvases that engage and provoke thought. Local galleries and art spaces provide platforms for emerging artists to showcase their work, fostering a sense of community and dialogue around contemporary artistic expression.

Preserving cultural traditions while embracing innovation is a delicate balancing act in Alaska's arts and culture scene. Indigenous artists work tirelessly to ensure that traditional practices are passed down to future generations, honoring their cultural legacy. At the same time, contemporary artists explore new mediums, experiment with technology, and engage with contemporary themes that speak to the evolving nature of life in the North.

Alaska's arts and culture scene serves as a gateway to understanding the state's history, people and landscapes. Visitors and locals alike have the opportunity to engage with the stories, aesthetics, and perspectives that shape the Alaskan identity. Museums, galleries, and cultural centers offer immersive experiences that illuminate the connection between art, culture, and the land.

In conclusion, Alaska's arts and culture scene is a testament to the power of creative expression to shape identity, foster connections, and honor tradition. Through visual arts, literature, music, dance, and culinary arts, Alaskans tell stories, celebrate heritage, and explore the complexities of the human experience. In a state where the wilderness and the communities coexist, the arts serve as a bridge between the natural world and the intricate web of human narratives that make Alaska truly unique.

Downtown Juneau: Historic Stroll

Nestled between towering mountains and the shimmering waters of the Gastineau Channel, Downtown Juneau beckons visitors with its historic charm, vibrant culture, and breathtaking natural beauty. As the capital city of Alaska, Juneau's downtown area is not only a political hub but also a cultural heart where the state's history and modern life intersect. From historic

landmarks and architectural treasures to local boutiques and bustling markets, a stroll through Downtown Juneau offers a captivating journey through time and a vibrant snapshot of the state's dynamic spirit.

Downtown Juneau is steeped in history, and its streets are lined with landmarks that offer glimpses into the city's storied past. The Alaska State Capitol, an elegant structure with neoclassical architecture, stands as a symbol of the state's political significance. Nearby, the Governor's Mansion showcases a blend of Colonial Revival and Arts and Crafts styles, offering a glimpse into the lives of Alaska's leaders.

St. Nicholas Russian Orthodox Church, adorned with onion domes and intricate woodwork, is a testament to the Russian heritage that once shaped the region. The church's historic graveyard is a resting place for many early settlers, providing a connection to the pioneers who forged the city's foundation.

Downtown Juneau's cultural offerings extend beyond its historic architecture to a rich array of galleries, museums, and cultural centers. The Juneau-Douglas City Museum delves into the city's history through exhibits that explore the Gold Rush era, indigenous heritage, and the challenges of life in Alaska's rugged landscapes. The Alaska State Museum, with its comprehensive collection of artifacts, artwork, and interactive displays, offers a deeper understanding of the state's diverse cultures and natural wonders.

Galleries featuring local artists' work showcase the creative spirit of the community, with paintings, sculptures, and crafts that capture the essence of Alaska's landscapes and cultures. These cultural spaces invite visitors to engage with the artistic expressions that define the region's identity.

Exploring Downtown Juneau's streets is a treat for shoppers seeking unique treasures. The district is dotted with boutiques, gift shops, and craft stores that offer everything from hand-carved totem poles and intricate beadwork to locally made jewelry and clothing. Visitors have the opportunity to take home a piece of Alaska's creative spirit, supporting local artisans and celebrating the craftsmanship that defines the region.

South Franklin Street is a bustling thoroughfare in Downtown Juneau, known for its historic buildings, vibrant shops, and panoramic views of the Gastineau Channel. This district has witnessed the evolution of the city, from its Gold Rush days to its modern renaissance. Walking along South Franklin Street is a journey through time, where storefronts that once housed miners' provisions now host boutiques, cafes, and galleries.

The Red Dog Saloon, a legendary establishment, stands as a living relic of the Gold Rush era. Its sawdust floors, historic memorabilia, and live music capture the spirit of Juneau's wild and storied past. The saloon's enduring popularity makes it a must-visit destination for those seeking a taste of the city's lively entertainment scene.

Downtown Juneau's proximity to the water adds an extra layer of charm to its historic ambiance. The waterfront along the Gastineau Channel offers breathtaking views of the surrounding mountains, including the iconic Mount Juneau and Mount Roberts. As cruise ships dock along the waterfront, the city's marine heritage is on full display, with bustling harbors, seaplane docks, and fishing vessels that remind visitors of Alaska's reliance on the sea.

Strolling along the waterfront promenade allows visitors to watch seaplanes take off and land, witness the changing tides, and even catch a glimpse of sea lions frolicking in the channel. This connection to the water underscores the integral role that maritime industries have played in the city's development.

Downtown Juneau's culinary scene is a testament to Alaska's diverse flavors and ingredients. Restaurants, cafes, and eateries serve up a fusion of global cuisines with locally sourced ingredients that showcase the state's bounty. Fresh seafood, including salmon, crab, and halibut, takes center stage on many menus, offering a taste of the Alaskan waters.

For those seeking a taste of local culture, salmon bakes and seafood feasts are popular dining experiences that combine delicious flavors with the traditions of the region. Downtown's eateries not only tantalize the taste buds but also offer the opportunity to connect with the local community and its culinary passions.

Downtown Juneau serves as a gateway to Alaska's indigenous cultures, with cultural centers and galleries that celebrate the heritage of the region's native communities. The Sealaska Heritage Institute showcases indigenous art, dance, and language through exhibitions, performances, and educational programs. Visitors can explore intricate carvings, learn about traditional practices, and gain insights into the cultural significance of art in indigenous communities.

Juneau's proximity to indigenous villages also offers opportunities for cultural exchanges and guided tours that provide a deeper understanding of the traditions and ways of life of Alaska's native peoples.

Throughout the year, Downtown Juneau comes alive with community celebrations that showcase the city's spirit and cultural diversity. Festivals, parades, and events bring locals and visitors together to celebrate everything from the winter solstice and Native American heritage to the state's vibrant arts scene. These gatherings offer a chance to immerse oneself in the local culture, experience traditional performances, and engage with the community's creativity and camaraderie.

Downtown Juneau is not only a destination in itself but also a gateway to the wilderness and adventure that define Alaska. The nearby Mount Roberts Tramway whisks visitors to breathtaking vistas where they can take in panoramic views of the surrounding landscapes. The Mendenhall Glacier, just a short drive from downtown, offers an opportunity to witness the awe-inspiring beauty of glacial formations and their impact on the environment.

As a central hub for transportation and activities, Downtown Juneau serves as the perfect launchpad for exploring the region's natural wonders, from whale watching and glacier hiking to kayaking and wildlife viewing.

In conclusion, Downtown Juneau is more than a collection of historic buildings and picturesque streets; it is a living legacy that embodies the spirit of Alaska's capital city. Through its landmarks, cultural institutions, local businesses, and community gatherings, the downtown district encapsulates the history, culture, and vibrant energy of the Last Frontier. As visitors stroll along its streets, they immerse themselves in the city's past, present, and the ever-evolving future that defines this charming and dynamic urban center.

Glacier Gardens Rainforest Adventure: Floral Fantasy

Nestled on the outskirts of Juneau, Alaska, lies a botanical wonderland that is as enchanting as it is unique—Glacier Gardens Rainforest Adventure. This hidden gem offers visitors a glimpse into the lush and diverse ecosystem of the temperate rainforest while showcasing the artistry of nature and the creativity of human hands. With its stunning upside-down hanging gardens, vibrant floral displays, and immersive rainforest experience, Glacier Gardens Rainforest Adventure is a floral fantasy that invites guests to step into a world of natural beauty, horticultural innovation, and ecological wonder.

Glacier Gardens Rainforest Adventure provides a captivating portal into the heart of the temperate rainforest—an ecosystem known for its high levels of rainfall, abundant plant life, and distinct biodiversity. This unique environment, characterized by towering trees, moss-covered rocks, and a verdant understory, is brought to life within the gardens' carefully curated spaces.

Visitors have the opportunity to explore the rainforest's various layers, from the towering canopy where birds and insects flutter, to the understory where ferns and mosses create a lush carpet beneath ancient trees. The gardens offer an immersive experience that educates and inspires, highlighting the importance of rainforests in global ecosystems.

One of the most iconic features of Glacier Gardens Rainforest Adventure is the innovative hanging gardens—a botanical marvel that transforms discarded tree stumps into vibrant planters suspended in midair. These hanging gardens are created by upending trees that have been toppled by storms or logging, transforming their root systems into beautiful planters for a stunning array of flowers and foliage.

The sight of colorful petunias, fuchsias, and other blooms cascading from the suspended tree stumps is both whimsical and awe-inspiring. This imaginative approach to gardening not only repurposes natural resources but also showcases the resilience of the rainforest's flora.

Beyond the hanging gardens, Glacier Gardens Rainforest Adventure features a meticulously designed landscape adorned with a stunning array of floral sculptures and arrangements. The gardens are a canvas where nature's palette and human creativity converge, resulting in living works of art that showcase the harmony between the wild and the cultivated.

Floral sculptures take various forms, from intricate wreaths and floral arches to whimsical animals and intricate patterns. The colors and textures of the flowers create a breathtaking mosaic that changes with the seasons, offering a different experience for each visit.

The centerpiece of Glacier Gardens Rainforest Adventure is the serene and reflective Mendenhall Lake, which lies at the base of the gardens. This tranquil body of water enhances the enchanting atmosphere of the rainforest experience, offering mirror-like reflections of the surrounding flora and the towering trees.

Visitors can take leisurely walks along the lake's shore, immersing themselves in the sights and sounds of the rainforest. The juxtaposition of the hanging gardens, the vibrant floral displays, and the serene lake creates a sensory-rich environment that engages the spirit and nurtures a deep appreciation for the natural world.

Exploring Glacier Gardens Rainforest Adventure is an opportunity for education and discovery. Guided tours led by knowledgeable naturalists provide insights into the rainforest's ecology, the unique hanging garden technique, and the importance of preserving this delicate ecosystem. Guests gain an understanding of the interconnectedness of plants, animals, and the environment, fostering a sense of stewardship and respect for the natural world.

The gardens at Glacier Gardens Rainforest Adventure showcase an array of plant species, both indigenous to Alaska and sourced from around the world. The unique climate and soil conditions of the rainforest provide an ideal habitat for a diverse range of flora. From native ferns, mosses, and wildflowers to exotic blooms, every corner of the gardens is a canvas of color and texture that highlights the beauty of plant life.

One of the joys of visiting Glacier Gardens Rainforest Adventure is experiencing the ever-changing landscape that mirrors the seasons. Spring brings a burst of color as the gardens come alive with the vibrant blooms of azaleas, rhododendrons, and other flowering plants. In summer, the canopy of leaves provides shade and shelter, creating a cool and inviting sanctuary for visitors.

As fall arrives, the rainforest transforms into a tapestry of gold, red, and orange hues as deciduous trees shed their leaves. Even in winter, the gardens take on a tranquil beauty, with

evergreen trees standing as sentinels and the reflection of snow-capped mountains shimmering on the lake's surface.

Glacier Gardens Rainforest Adventure is more than a botanical spectacle—it's a testament to the power of restoration and renewal. The gardens were born out of a commitment to rehabilitate logged lands, restoring them to their natural state while also creating a space for horticultural exploration and appreciation. The transformation from a logging site to a flourishing rainforest sanctuary serves as a reminder of nature's resilience and the potential for positive human impact on the environment.

Alaska's indigenous communities have deep connections to the land and its resources. Glacier Gardens Rainforest Adventure acknowledges and celebrates this heritage, integrating indigenous cultural elements into the visitor experience. Native plants and traditional practices are interwoven with the gardens' narrative, fostering a sense of cultural exchange and respect for the knowledge passed down through generations.

In conclusion, Glacier Gardens Rainforest Adventure is a floral fantasy that offers an immersive journey into the heart of the temperate rainforest. Through its hanging gardens, intricate floral sculptures, and captivating landscapes, the gardens celebrate the beauty and complexity of the natural world. As visitors wander through the lush foliage, reflect by the serene lake, and learn about the rainforest's ecology, they are invited to connect with the environment, embrace the wonder of horticultural innovation, and leave with a renewed appreciation for the delicate balance that sustains our planet.

Skagway: Gateway to the Klondike Gold Rush

Tucked away in the southeastern corner of Alaska, Skagway stands as a living testament to a pivotal era in the history of the Last Frontier—the Klondike Gold Rush. A picturesque town nestled between majestic mountains and the serene waters of the Inside Passage, Skagway boasts a rich history that harks back to the late 19th century when prospectors from around the world flocked to its shores in search of gold. Today, Skagway's charming streets, well-preserved buildings, and vibrant atmosphere continue to captivate visitors, offering a window into the past and a gateway to an array of awe-inspiring Alaskan experiences.

The Klondike Gold Rush, often dubbed the "Last Great Gold Rush," was sparked in 1896 when gold was discovered in the Yukon Territory of Canada. The allure of striking it rich drew a wave of adventurers, known as stampeders, to traverse treacherous terrain and endure harsh conditions in their quest for gold. Skagway emerged as a primary gateway to the gold fields due to its location along the preferred route—the Chilkoot Trail. Stampeders disembarked here, traversed the White Pass, and embarked on an arduous journey that tested their mettle and determination.

Skagway, once a humble Tlingit fishing camp, rapidly transformed into a bustling boomtown during the gold rush days. The town's waterfront was a hub of activity, with wharves, saloons, dance halls, and supply stores catering to the needs of prospectors. At the peak of the gold rush, Skagway's population surged to around 20,000—an astonishing number considering the remote location and the hardships of the journey ahead.

Today, visitors can step back in time by strolling through the charming historic district. Many of the buildings have been meticulously preserved, offering glimpses of the past. The Red Onion Saloon, once a raucous establishment frequented by miners, now operates as a museum and restaurant, allowing guests to experience a taste of the town's colorful history.

One of the most iconic experiences in Skagway is the White Pass and Yukon Route Railroad—a marvel of engineering that retraces the path once taken by stampeders during the gold rush. The narrow-gauge railway winds through stunning landscapes, offering panoramic views of mountains, glaciers, and deep valleys. The train journey provides not only a breathtaking ride but also a historical narrative that brings to life the challenges faced by those who traversed these lands seeking their fortunes.

For those seeking an immersive experience, the Chilkoot Trail offers the opportunity to retrace the steps of the stampeders. This historic trail, once a grueling route for miners laden with heavy packs of supplies, leads adventurers through rugged terrain and dense forests. The hike is a physically demanding endeavor that provides a profound sense of connection to the past, offering a glimpse into the hardships faced by those who embarked on this journey over a century ago.

Skagway's authenticity as a gold rush town is evident in the relics that remain scattered throughout the landscape. From rusting train tracks to abandoned cabins, these remnants serve as poignant reminders of the challenges and dreams that converged in this remote outpost. The Gold Rush Cemetery is a particularly poignant site, where the final resting places of stampeders tell stories of lives lost in pursuit of fortune.

Beyond its gold rush legacy, Skagway is enriched by its Tlingit heritage. The indigenous Tlingit people have inhabited these lands for generations, and their cultural influence is woven into the fabric of the town. Visitors have the opportunity to engage with Tlingit culture through traditional performances, totem pole carving demonstrations, and interactions with community members.

While Skagway's historical significance is a major draw, the town also serves as a launchpad for a variety of outdoor adventures. From hiking and wildlife viewing to kayaking and helicopter tours, the surrounding wilderness offers a playground for nature enthusiasts. The nearby Tongass National Forest, the largest national forest in the United States, provides a pristine backdrop for exploration.

Skagway's sense of community and vibrant spirit are palpable to all who visit. Despite its relatively small population, the town exudes warmth and hospitality. Locals embrace their town's history and are eager to share stories, insights, and recommendations with visitors. From artisans and storytellers to business owners and guides, the people of Skagway play an essential role in shaping the visitor experience.

Skagway's significance as a historical and cultural destination is not lost on its residents. The town's commitment to preserving its past is evident through its carefully maintained buildings, museums, and interpretive programs. By sharing the stories of the gold rush and the people who shaped its history, Skagway ensures that its legacy endures for generations to come.

In conclusion, Skagway stands as a living link to an era of adventure, determination, and dreams that defined the Klondike Gold Rush. Its well-preserved history, iconic railroad, captivating landscapes, and warm community invite visitors to step back in time and immerse themselves in the spirit of exploration that once thrived in these rugged lands. Whether you're drawn to the tales of stampeders or the allure of Alaskan wilderness, Skagway offers a gateway to an unforgettable journey through both the past and the present.

Attractions and Activities

Skagway, the gateway to the Klondike Gold Rush, is a treasure trove of attractions and activities that offer a captivating blend of history, natural beauty, and adventure. From immersing yourself in the town's gold rush heritage to exploring the stunning landscapes that surround it, Skagway has something for every traveler. Here are some of the best attractions and activities that make Skagway a must-visit destination:

1. White Pass and Yukon Route Railroad: A Scenic Journey

Embark on a breathtaking journey aboard the White Pass and Yukon Route Railroad. This historic narrow-gauge railway takes you through rugged mountain terrain, offering panoramic views of snow-capped peaks, lush valleys, and tumbling waterfalls. As you wind your way along the same route once traversed by gold rush stampeders, you'll be treated to an unforgettable visual narrative of Skagway's past and present.

2. Historic Skagway: A Walk Through Time

Stroll through Skagway's charming historic district, where well-preserved buildings and boardwalks transport you back to the gold rush era. The Red Onion Saloon, a former brothel turned museum and restaurant, offers guided tours that reveal the town's colorful past. The Trail of '98 Museum and the Mascot Saloon provide further insights into Skagway's history.

3. Chilkoot Trail Hike: Reliving the Stampeders' Journey

For an immersive experience, embark on a hike along the Chilkoot Trail—a historic route once taken by gold rush stampeders. This challenging trail takes you through dense forests, past old cabins, and up steep inclines, offering a glimpse into the hardships faced by those seeking gold. While a full hike requires preparation, shorter hikes are available for those looking to experience a portion of the trail.

4. Klondike Gold Rush National Historical Park: Learning and Exploration

The Klondike Gold Rush National Historical Park is dedicated to preserving and interpreting the history of the gold rush. The visitor center features exhibits, films, and ranger-led programs that provide insights into the challenges and triumphs of stampeders. Guided walking tours of the town delve into its past, showcasing historic buildings and sharing stories of those who once walked its streets.

5. Outdoor Adventures: Nature's Playground

Surrounded by pristine wilderness, Skagway offers numerous opportunities for outdoor adventures. Hiking trails wind through forests and meadows, leading to stunning vistas and viewpoints. Wildlife enthusiasts can take guided tours to spot bears, eagles, and other native creatures. Additionally, kayaking and fishing excursions allow you to explore the surrounding waters and take in the breathtaking landscapes.

6. Gold Panning: Strike It Rich (or Not)

Channel your inner prospector and try your hand at gold panning. Many attractions in Skagway offer visitors the chance to pan for gold, providing a hands-on experience that connects you to the town's gold rush heritage. Even if you don't strike it rich, the thrill of finding a glimmering speck of gold in your pan is an unforgettable experience.

7. Scenic Flights: A Bird's-Eye View

For a truly awe-inspiring perspective of Skagway's landscapes, consider taking a scenic flightseeing tour. Board a small plane or helicopter and soar over glaciers, fjords, and mountain ranges. These flights offer unparalleled views and the chance to witness the grandeur of Alaska's wilderness from above.

8. Skagway Brewing Company: Local Flavors

After a day of exploration, unwind at the Skagway Brewing Company. This historic brewery offers a variety of locally brewed beers, as well as delicious pub fare. It's an excellent place to relax, mingle with fellow travelers, and savor the flavors of Skagway.

9. Shopping and Souvenirs: Take a Piece of Skagway Home

Skagway's shops and boutiques offer an array of unique souvenirs, from locally crafted jewelry to Native Alaskan art. Be sure to explore the local galleries and gift shops to find treasures that encapsulate the spirit of your Skagway adventure.

10. Icy Strait Point Excursions: Beyond Skagway

While not in Skagway itself, nearby Icy Strait Point offers a range of excursions that can be reached by boat. Zip line through the treetops, go whale watching, or explore Tlingit culture through authentic experiences. Icy Strait Point provides an additional layer of adventure just a short journey away.

In conclusion, Skagway's attractions and activities offer a dynamic blend of history, adventure, and natural beauty that captivates travelers from all walks of life. Whether you're delving into the town's gold rush legacy, hiking the Chilkoot Trail, or soaking in the stunning landscapes, Skagway invites you to experience the essence of the Klondike Gold Rush era while embracing the spirit of modern exploration.

The White Pass and Yukon Route Railroad: A Scenic Journey through History and Wilderness

Nestled amidst the rugged landscapes of Alaska's southeastern corner lies a railroad that weaves together tales of adventure, determination, and natural beauty—the White Pass and Yukon Route Railroad. This historic narrow-gauge railway, often referred to as the "Scenic Railway of the World," offers passengers a mesmerizing journey through stunning mountain ranges, lush valleys, and pristine wilderness. As you climb aboard the vintage railcars and wind your way along the tracks, you'll be transported not only through breathtaking scenery but also back in time to an era when the promise of gold lured intrepid prospectors to these remote lands.

The White Pass and Yukon Route Railroad's story is intertwined with that of the Klondike Gold Rush—a monumental event that shaped the history of Alaska and Canada's Yukon Territory. The late 19th century saw a stampede of fortune-seekers rushing to the gold fields, with the route through Skagway and the White Pass as a primary gateway. The demand for transportation led to the construction of this narrow-gauge railway, which provided a lifeline for prospectors, as well as a connection between the ports of Skagway, Alaska, and Whitehorse, Yukon.

The construction of the White Pass and Yukon Route Railroad was a remarkable feat of engineering, considering the rugged terrain and challenging conditions. The railway spans 110 miles of track, with a substantial portion winding its way through the heart of the Coast Mountains. As the train ascends nearly 3,000 feet in just 20 miles, passengers are treated to a remarkable demonstration of engineering ingenuity, as the tracks curve, loop, and bridge their way through the landscape.

As you board the vintage railcars at the Skagway depot, the sense of embarking on a journey through time and nature becomes palpable. The train's whistle echoes across the mountains, signaling the start of an adventure that promises both sensory delights and historical insights. The railcars themselves, many of which are painstakingly restored originals, evoke a sense of nostalgia that transports passengers to a bygone era.

As the journey begins, the train hugs the coastline, offering panoramic views of the deep blue waters of the Inside Passage. Snow-capped peaks rise dramatically in the distance, creating a backdrop that seems almost surreal in its grandeur. The tracks follow the path of the Klondike Highway, a reminder of the challenges faced by those who once journeyed on foot. The route passes by scenic highlights like Bridal Veil Falls and Dead Horse Gulch, each with its own story to tell.

s the train ascends further into the mountains, the scenery undergoes a transformation. erdant forests give way to alpine tundra, and the air becomes crisp and invigorating. At the ummit of the White Pass, passengers are treated to an extraordinary sight—the sweeping istas of the Canadian wilderness stretching as far as the eye can see. The view from the bservation platform is a photographer's dream, capturing the rugged beauty that has drawn dventurers for generations.

hroughout the journey, onboard narration provides historical context and tales of the gold ush era. Passengers gain insights into the challenges faced by stampeders who navigated this ery route, as well as the engineering feats that made the railway possible. These narratives reathe life into the landscapes, allowing travelers to envision the struggles and triumphs of hose who came before.

he White Pass and Yukon Route Railroad offers a variety of excursions that provide deeper exploration of the region's history and wilderness. One such excursion takes passengers to the historic town of Bennett, where stampeders once gathered to prepare for their arduous ourney. Today, the remains of this ghost town tell a story of the gold rush's impact. Other excursions include stops at Carcross, a charming village with vibrant indigenous culture, and Emerald Lake, known for its striking turquoise waters.

The White Pass and Yukon Route Railroad's allure extends throughout the year, with each season offering its unique charm. Spring ushers in a colorful tapestry of wildflowers, summer brings the vibrant green of alpine meadows, fall paints the landscape with warm hues, and winter blankets the route in a layer of pristine snow. The changing seasons ensure that each ourney is a new and exhilarating experience.

The White Pass and Yukon Route Railroad, much like Skagway itself, is committed to preserving ts historical legacy and minimizing its environmental impact. The railway has been designated an International Historic Civil Engineering Landmark, a testament to its significance. Additionally, efforts are made to maintain the authenticity of the experience, from the carefully restored railcars to the respectful approach to the region's delicate ecosystems.

In conclusion, the White Pass and Yukon Route Railroad is more than just a scenic journey—it's a voyage through history, a celebration of engineering ingenuity, and an opportunity to connect with the raw beauty of Alaska's wilderness. As you traverse the tracks that once echoed with the footsteps of gold rush stampeders, you'll find yourself immersed in a sensory adventure that evokes the spirit of exploration and captures the essence of a defining

Historic Skagway: A Walk Through Time

Nestled along the coastline of southeastern Alaska, Skagway stands as a living testament to a bygone era—an era defined by the Klondike Gold Rush and the spirit of adventure that echoed through its rugged landscapes. As you step onto its historic streets, you're transported back to time when gold rush stampeders and pioneers roamed these boardwalks, seeking fortune and new beginning. Historic Skagway is more than just a tourist destination; it's a journey through time that unveils the tales of those who once walked these streets and the enduring legacy the left behind.

The origins of Skagway can be traced back to the Klondike Gold Rush of the late 19th century. The discovery of gold in the Yukon Territory sparked a frenzy that drew hopeful prospectors from all corners of the world. Skagway emerged as a critical gateway to the gold fields, as it provided access to the Chilkoot Trail—a treacherous path that led to the riches of the Klondike. The town's strategic location at the head of the Lynn Canal made it an ideal port for those embarking on the journey.

Skagway's historic district is a living canvas that preserves the essence of the gold rush era. Strolling through these streets is like stepping into a time capsule, where well-preserved buildings, wooden boardwalks, and vintage signs evoke a sense of nostalgia. The architecture reflects a variety of influences, from frontier style to Victorian elegance, creating a harmonious blend of structures that tells a collective story.

One of the most iconic buildings in the district is the Red Onion Saloon—a former brothel that now operates as a museum and restaurant. The Red Onion offers guided tours that peel back the layers of its history, sharing stories of the women who worked there and the clientele who frequented its halls. The saloon's décor, including the original bar and vintage furnishings, transports visitors back to the raucous days of the gold rush.

The Trail of '98 Museum immerses visitors in the trials and tribulations faced by gold rush stampeders. Through exhibits, artifacts, and interactive displays, the museum provides insights into the challenges of traversing the treacherous Chilkoot Trail and the perils of the journey. Items like old sleds, prospecting tools, and personal belongings tell the intimate stories of those who sought their fortunes in the Klondike.

The Mascot Saloon, another gem of Skagway's historic district, stands as a tribute to the town's vibrant past. This iconic building, with its characteristic false front, was once a popular watering hole for miners and townsfolk alike. Today, it serves as a living history museum, capturing the essence of a time when the saloon was the heart of the community—a place for camaraderie, celebration, and the exchange of tales from the trail.

For those seeking a more immersive experience, the Chilkoot Trail offers an opportunity to follow in the footsteps of gold rush stampeders. This historic route was once a grueling path that prospectors navigated with heavy loads of supplies. Hiking a portion of the trail provides a visceral connection to the challenges faced by those who embarked on this arduous journey. Interpretive signs along the trail offer insights into the trials and triumphs of the stampeders.

The Alaskan Hotel and Bar, a National Historic Landmark, is another testament to Skagway's storied past. Constructed in 1898, the hotel has weathered the years and stands as the oldest operating hotel in Alaska. The establishment's ornate façade and vintage décor provide a glimpse into the elegance and grandeur that gold rush-era Skagway once exuded.

Broadway Street, the main thoroughfare of Skagway, is a living testament to the town's enduring history. As you stroll down this iconic street, you'll pass by historic buildings that have been lovingly preserved and repurposed. Today, these structures house an array of shops, boutiques, restaurants, and galleries, creating a vibrant blend of the past and the present.

Skagway's commitment to preserving its history extends beyond its buildings. Local characters, dressed in period attire, can often be found roaming the streets and engaging with visitors, sharing stories of the past and bringing historical figures to life. Additionally, the National Park Service offers ranger-led interpretive programs that delve into the town's gold rush heritage, offering an educational and immersive experience.

While the gold rush era is undeniably central to Skagway's identity, the town's cultural heritage is also enriched by its Tlingit roots. Skagway is home to a vibrant indigenous community that embraces its heritage and shares it with visitors through cultural performances, art galleries, and interactive experiences. This cultural blend adds depth to the town's narrative and highlights the diversity of its history.

Skagway's commitment to preserving its historic district is evident in the meticulous restoration and maintenance of its buildings. Efforts are made to retain the authenticity of the structures, from the architecture to the furnishings, ensuring that visitors can immerse themselves in a genuine representation of the past. This dedication to preservation ensures that the legacy of the gold rush era continues to resonate with generations to come.

In conclusion, Historic Skagway is more than just a collection of buildings; it's a living storybook that invites visitors to step back in time and walk in the footsteps of those who shaped its history. From the raucous days of the Red Onion Saloon to the quiet echoes along the Chilkoot Trail, every corner of Skagway's historic district carries the weight of its past. As you explore its streets, you'll find yourself captivated by the tales of gold rush stampeders, pioneers, and adventurers who left an indelible mark on this remarkable town.

Chilkoot Trail Hike: Reliving the Stampeders' Journey

In the heart of the rugged Alaskan wilderness, a historic trail winds its way through dense forests, steep inclines, and breathtaking vistas. The Chilkoot Trail, often referred to as the "Trail of '98," stands as a living monument to the Klondike Gold Rush—an era of boundless ambition and unparalleled determination. This trail, which once witnessed the footfalls of intrepid prospectors seeking their fortunes in the Yukon Territory, now offers modern-day adventurers the chance to retrace their steps and relive the challenges and triumphs of the stampeders' journey.

The Chilkoot Trail's origins can be traced back to the Klondike Gold Rush of the late 19th century. When gold was discovered in the Yukon Territory of Canada, a frenzied rush of prospectors from around the world descended upon the area, eager to stake their claims. The Chilkoot Trail, which connected the tidewater of the Lynn Canal in Skagway, Alaska, to the shores of Bennett Lake in Canada, quickly emerged as a critical route to the gold fields. Stampeders faced the grueling task of hauling their supplies—including heavy loads of food, equipment, and tools—up the treacherous path.

As modern-day hikers set foot on the Chilkoot Trail, they embark on a journey that mirrors the challenges faced by gold rush stampeders. The trail covers approximately 33 miles (53 kilometers) of rugged terrain, crossing through dense forests, steep mountain passes, and frigid waters. The trail's elevation gain of over 3,500 feet (1,070 meters) serves as a reminder of the relentless uphill battle that stampeders endured.

Hikers must carry their own supplies, much like the prospectors of the past. While modern backpacks and lightweight gear have replaced the heavy loads of the gold rush era, the experience still offers a glimpse into the physical demands and mental fortitude required to navigate the trail.

One of the most iconic landmarks along the Chilkoot Trail is Chilkoot Pass, a mountain pass that marked the transition between the United States and Canada. For gold rush stampeders, reaching Chilkoot Pass was a moment of triumph—a testament to their determination and tenacity. Today, as hikers crest the pass, they are met with a sense of accomplishment and a view that stretches across the rugged landscapes, offering a panoramic reward for their efforts.

Throughout the trail, historical markers and remnants of the gold rush era offer glimpses into the lives of those who once walked this path. Rusting equipment, abandoned cabins, and relics of the past serve as poignant reminders of the challenges and dreams that converged on the Chilkoot Trail. Interpretive signs share stories of stampeders' experiences, offering hikers a deeper connection to the history that surrounds them.

The "Golden Stairs" section of the trail is infamous for its grueling ascent—a steep and relentless climb that challenged the stamina and resolve of stampeders. This section, characterized by wooden steps that helped stampeders navigate the treacherous incline, is a visceral reminder of the hurdles faced by those who sought their fortunes on the trail. For modern hikers, conquering the Golden Stairs evokes a sense of respect for the perseverance of those who came before.

Modern hikers on the Chilkoot Trail have the opportunity to camp at designated sites along the route, offering a chance to experience the wilderness in its raw form. As the sun sets and darkness falls, the trail's history seems to come alive in the sounds of the forest and the rustling of leaves. The silence of the night is a reminder of the solitude and camaraderie that stampeders must have felt as they rested after a day of arduous travel.

While the Chilkoot Trail is renowned for its challenges, it also offers an array of scenic rewards. Hikers traverse diverse landscapes, from dense forests and alpine meadows to pristine lakes and river crossings. The beauty of the trail serves as a counterpoint to its difficulty, offering moments of respite and awe-inspiring vistas that provide solace to the weary.

As hikers emerge from the Chilkoot Pass and reach Bennett Lake, they arrive at the end of the Chilkoot Trail—a point of convergence for modern adventure and historical legacy. Here, they can reflect on the experiences of the stampeders who continued their journey to the gold fields of the Yukon. The remains of old structures and remnants of the past offer a tangible connection to the stories that unfolded in this remote wilderness.

The Chilkoot Trail is more than just a physical challenge; it's an opportunity to connect with history and gain a profound understanding of the stampeders' lives. As hikers push themselves beyond their comfort zones, they gain insights into the sacrifices, aspirations, and determination that defined the gold rush era. This shared experience fosters a sense of camaraderie among modern adventurers, mirroring the bonds that were formed among stampeders facing a common goal.

The Chilkoot Trail's significance as a historical landmark is carefully preserved by the National Park Service of the United States and Parks Canada. Efforts are made to protect the trail's delicate ecosystem, while interpretive programs and markers ensure that the stories of the past are passed down to future generations. The Chilkoot Trail remains a living testament to the indomitable spirit of those who pursued their dreams in the face of adversity.

In conclusion, the Chilkoot Trail offers more than just a physical challenge; it offers a transformative journey that transports hikers through time and history. As modern-day adventurers walk in the footsteps of gold rush stampeders, they gain a deeper appreciation for the sacrifices and triumphs of those who sought their fortunes in the Yukon's rugged landscapes. The Chilkoot Trail serves as a bridge between the past and the present, inviting hikers to relive the epic tale of the Klondike Gold Rush while forging their own enduring memories along the trail.

Klondike Gold Rush National Historical Park: Learning and Exploration

Nestled within the dramatic landscapes of Alaska and the Yukon Territory, the Klondike Gold Rush National Historical Park stands as a testament to an era that shaped the history of the North American frontier—the Klondike Gold Rush of the late 19th century. Encompassing sites in Skagway, Alaska, and Seattle, Washington, this national park offers a window into the trials, triumphs, and tales of the gold rush stampeders who journeyed to the Yukon in pursuit of fortune. From immersive exhibits to guided tours, the park invites visitors to explore the past, learn about the human spirit, and discover the enduring legacy of an unprecedented era.

The Klondike Gold Rush National Historical Park encompasses several sites in Skagway, a town that played a pivotal role in the gold rush era. As the primary gateway to the gold fields, Skagway served as the launchpad for thousands of stampeders who embarked on a journey of unparalleled challenges and aspirations. The park's Skagway Visitor Center serves as the epicenter of exploration, offering a starting point for visitors to delve into the history and stories that shaped the Klondike Gold Rush.

The Skagway Visitor Center offers a wealth of interactive exhibits that immerse visitors in the gold rush experience. From life-sized replicas of gold rush scenes to multimedia presentations, the exhibits provide a sensory journey into the lives of the stampeders. Visitors can visualize the treacherous conditions of the Chilkoot Trail, step into a prospector's tent, and even test their skills at gold panning—an activity that resonates with the pursuit of fortune that drew people to the region over a century ago.

The park's ranger-led programs offer a unique opportunity to connect with history through guided tours, talks, and demonstrations. Rangers, dressed in period attire, share stories of the stampeders' experiences, providing insights into the challenges they faced and the determination that fueled their journey. Whether it's a guided walk through historic Skagway or a presentation on the art of storytelling during the gold rush, these programs bring history to life and foster a deep appreciation for the human spirit of adventure.

As part of the park's Skagway offerings, visitors have the chance to stroll through the historic district—a living canvas that preserves the architecture, atmosphere, and allure of the gold rush era. Walking along the wooden boardwalks, exploring the iconic buildings, and soaking in the mbiance of the past provide an authentic connection to the town's history. The buildings nemselves serve as storytellers, each with its own narrative to share.

he Klondike Gold Rush National Historical Park extends beyond Skagway to include a portion f the Chilkoot Trail—a trail once traversed by gold rush stampeders on their arduous journey. nterpretive signs along the trail provide insights into the experiences of the prospectors who aced the daunting task of hauling their supplies up the steep slopes. Walking a portion of the rail offers a firsthand glimpse into the hardships and determination that defined the gold rush ra.

he park's Seattle Unit offers a different perspective on the gold rush, focusing on the hubbub f activity that surrounded the departure of stampeders from the United States. The historic Cadillac Hotel building, located in the Pioneer Square Historic District, houses exhibits that xplore the frenzy and excitement that gripped Seattle as news of the gold discovery spread. The exhibits delve into the stories of those who sought to profit from the gold rush, including utfitters, journalists, and entrepreneurs.

Central to the park's mission is the preservation and sharing of historical records, photographs, nd artifacts related to the gold rush era. The Klondike Gold Rush National Historical Park's archives and collections are a treasure trove of primary sources that offer valuable insights into he experiences of stampeders and the broader historical context. Researchers and enthusiasts like can explore these resources to uncover the stories and details that shaped the gold rush narrative.

While the Klondike Gold Rush is undeniably the focal point of the park's narrative, it also embraces the rich cultural heritage of the region. The park collaborates with indigenous communities to share their stories and perspectives, fostering a more inclusive understanding of the history. Programs and exhibits highlight the contributions of indigenous peoples and offer insights into their traditional ways of life, enhancing the park's portrayal of the era.

The Klondike Gold Rush National Historical Park serves as a bridge between the past and the present, connecting modern visitors with the resilience, determination, and dreams of those who embarked on the gold rush journey. By exploring the challenges and aspirations of the stampeders, visitors gain a deeper appreciation for the human spirit that drove them to undertake a treacherous and uncertain expedition.

The park's educational initiatives extend beyond its physical sites. Educational programs and resources engage students and learners of all ages in the stories and history of the gold rush. The lessons learned from the challenges faced by the stampeders—perseverance, adaptability, and the pursuit of dreams—remain relevant in today's world, making the park a living classroom that imparts timeless values.

Central to the Klondike Gold Rush National Historical Park's mission is the preservation of its sites and resources for future generations. The park's commitment to stewardship ensures that the stories of the gold rush continue to resonate with visitors for years to come. Efforts to conserve historic buildings, maintain trails, and protect fragile ecosystems ensure that the legacy of the Klondike Gold Rush endures.

In conclusion, the Klondike Gold Rush National Historical Park is more than a collection of exhibits and historic sites; it's a gateway to an era that captured the imagination and spirit of adventurers from around the world. Through immersive experiences, ranger-led programs, and preservation efforts, the park offers a unique opportunity to step into the shoes of the gold rush stampeders, explore their challenges and dreams, and gain a deeper understanding of the forces that shaped the history of the North American frontier.

Outdoor Adventures: Nature's Playground in Alaska's Wilderness

Alaska, often referred to as the "Last Frontier," boasts a landscape of unparalleled beauty and diversity. From towering mountains to pristine fjords, dense forests to vast glaciers, the state's wilderness is a playground for outdoor enthusiasts and nature lovers alike. Whether you're seeking thrilling activities, serene landscapes, or a chance to connect with the natural world, Alaska offers a wide range of outdoor adventures that cater to every level of experience and interest. In this exploration of Alaska's wilderness, we'll delve into the exhilarating activities and breathtaking vistas that make outdoor adventures in the state an unforgettable experience.

Alaska's wilderness is characterized by its grandeur, with landscapes that evoke both awe and inspiration. Vast expanses of untouched nature, teeming with wildlife and dramatic features, beckon adventurers to explore their mysteries. From the towering peaks of the Alaska Range to the winding waterways of the Inside Passage, the state's natural beauty is a canvas that invites outdoor enthusiasts to embark on a journey of discovery.

Alaska's network of hiking trails offers a diverse range of options, catering to both casual walkers and seasoned hikers. Whether you're seeking a leisurely stroll through alpine meadows or a challenging ascent up a mountain peak, the state's trails provide opportunities for exploration at various levels. Trails like the Crow Pass Trail and the Harding Icefield Trail offer breathtaking views of glaciers, while the Kesugi Ridge Trail provides panoramic vistas of Denali and the surrounding wilderness.

Alaska's wilderness is a haven for wildlife, offering opportunities to observe animals in their natural habitats. From grizzly bears to bald eagles, moose to wolves, the state's fauna is as diverse as its landscapes. Wildlife viewing tours and excursions provide a chance to witness these creatures in action, while maintaining a respectful distance to ensure the animals' well-being. The Alaska Wildlife Conservation Center, for example, offers a safe space for injured and orphaned animals to thrive and educates visitors about the state's wildlife.

The coastal waters of Alaska are a prime destination for whale watching. The state's marine environment is home to a variety of whale species, including humpback whales, orcas, and gray whales. Tours and cruises take visitors on journeys to witness these majestic creatures breaching, feeding, and socializing. The Inside Passage and Kenai Fjords National Park are renowned for their opportunities to spot whales, creating unforgettable moments in nature.

Exploring Alaska's waterways by kayak or canoe is a serene and immersive way to connect with the environment. Paddling through tranquil bays, fjords, and rivers offers a unique perspective on the landscape and its inhabitants. Glacier kayaking excursions provide the chance to glide through icy waters and witness the ethereal beauty of glaciers up close. Paddling along the shores of Prince William Sound or Lake Clark offers tranquility and the opportunity to spot wildlife.

Alaska's glaciers are among the most iconic features of its wilderness. Glacier tours and hikes take adventurers onto the frozen landscapes, allowing them to witness the immense ice formations and their ever-changing contours. The Mendenhall Glacier near Juneau and the Matanuska Glacier are popular destinations for guided glacier hikes, offering insight into the unique geology and history of these frozen giants.

Dog sledding, a traditional mode of transportation for Alaska's indigenous peoples, is also a thrilling adventure for visitors. Guided dog sledding tours provide the opportunity to experience the teamwork and camaraderie between mushers and their teams of sled dogs. Whether you're racing across snowy trails or gliding through tranquil forests, dog sledding offers an authentic connection to Alaska's history and spirit of adventure.

Alaska's rivers, lakes, and coastal waters offer some of the world's best fishing opportunities. The state is known for its salmon runs, with species like king salmon, sockeye salmon, and coho salmon drawing anglers from around the globe. Fishing trips range from guided excursions on remote rivers to charter fishing expeditions in the open ocean. Whether you're an experienced angler seeking a trophy catch or a novice eager to learn, Alaska's fishing experiences are unmatched.

For those seeking an immersive wilderness experience, camping and wilderness lodges provide opportunities to disconnect from the modern world and embrace the rhythms of nature. Remote lodges offer a blend of rustic charm and comfort, allowing visitors to explore the wilderness by day and relax in cozy accommodations by night. Camping in Alaska's national parks and forests allows for a direct connection to the land, with the sounds of nature and star-filled skies as companions.

Alaska's landscapes are a haven for photographers and artists, providing a canvas of dramatic scenery and ever-changing light. The play of sunlight on glaciers, the dance of the Northern Lights in the winter sky, and the reflections on still lakes offer endless opportunities for creative expression. Whether you're an amateur with a smartphone or a professional with sophisticated gear, Alaska's wilderness is an inspiring muse that sparks the imagination.

As visitors engage in outdoor adventures in Alaska's wilderness, it's important to approach these experiences with a sense of environmental stewardship. Respecting wildlife habitats, adhering to Leave No Trace principles, and following responsible tourism practices are essential to preserving the state's natural beauty for future generations. Organizations and tour operators often emphasize the importance of minimizing impact and contributing to the conservation efforts that safeguard Alaska's wilderness.

In conclusion, Alaska's wilderness serves as a playground of adventure, offering a diverse range of outdoor experiences that tap into the heart of nature's beauty and power. From hiking trails that lead to mountain vistas, to encountering wildlife in their habitats, to paddling through pristine waters, every outdoor adventure in Alaska is an opportunity to connect with the landscape and embrace the spirit of exploration. With its untouched landscapes and abundance of opportunities, Alaska invites outdoor enthusiasts to forge their own paths of discovery and create memories that will last a lifetime.

Gold Panning: Strike It Rich (or Not) in the Spirit of Adventure

The allure of gold has captivated human imagination for centuries, from the ancient civilizations of Egypt to the modern-day prospectors who still seek the precious metal. One of the quintessential images associated with gold discovery is that of a prospector bent over a riverbed, carefully panning for gold. This timeless activity, known as gold panning, conjures images of adventure, excitement, and the thrill of striking it rich. In the context of modern recreational and educational pursuits, gold panning offers individuals the chance to connect with history, nature, and the pursuit of a rare and valuable treasure. In this exploration of gold panning, we delve into its history, techniques, and the unique experiences it offers to those who venture to sift through the sands in search of fortune.

The gold rush era, characterized by frenzied quests for riches, was marked by the discovery of gold in various corners of the world. From California to Alaska, Australia to South Africa, the mere whisper of gold led to massive migrations and historic events. The Klondike Gold Rush of the late 19th century, in particular, drew prospectors from all walks of life to the remote Yukon Territory in Canada. The quest for gold captured the collective imagination, inspiring adventurers to brave harsh conditions and undertake perilous journeys.

At the heart of the gold rush was the act of gold panning—a relatively simple method of extracting gold particles from riverbeds and sediments. The process involves filling a shallow pan with sediment-rich material from a water source, then swirling and agitating the pan to allow lighter materials to be washed away. Over time, with careful technique, gold particles settle to the bottom of the pan, revealing their gleaming presence.

Modern gold panning is a recreational and educational activity that allows individuals to step into the shoes of the prospectors who once roamed the wilderness in search of riches. While the chance of striking it rich may be slim, the experience offers a tangible connection to history and the opportunity to engage in a tradition that stretches back centuries. Gold panning becomes more than just an activity; it becomes a means of channeling the spirit of adventure and exploration that defined the gold rush era.

While gold panning may appear straightforward, mastering the technique requires practice and finesse. Prospectors must carefully control the angle and movement of the pan to ensure that heavier materials—such as gold—settle to the bottom. Separating out unwanted materials while preserving the precious metal requires a delicate touch. Aspiring gold panners often learn from experienced guides who teach the subtleties of the process and provide valuable insights into identifying the telltale glint of gold.

Basic gold panning equipment includes a shallow pan, a classifier to sift out larger rocks, and a vial or container to collect the recovered gold. While the equipment is relatively simple, the right gear can greatly enhance the gold panning experience. Modern pans are designed to optimize gold recovery, and specialized tools like snuffer bottles aid in the delicate task of transferring recovered gold without loss.

Gold panning opportunities are available in various regions around the world, each with its unique history and potential for finding gold. Alaska, with its rich gold rush heritage, remains a popular destination for modern-day prospectors. Streams and rivers that once echoed with the sounds of gold panning during the Klondike Gold Rush now offer enthusiasts the chance to try their luck. The Cariboo region in British Columbia, Canada, is another renowned location where hopeful panners can relive the excitement of the gold rush era.

For many, gold panning is less about striking it rich and more about the joy of spending time outdoors and engaging in a historical pursuit. Families, school groups, and individuals of all ages participate in gold panning experiences offered by tour operators, national parks, and educational institutions. These experiences often include demonstrations of gold panning techniques, historical narratives, and the opportunity to uncover the glittering treasures hidden in the sand.

As with any outdoor activity, responsible practices are essential to protect the environment and ensure that the experience remains enjoyable for all. Regulations and guidelines may vary by location, but the principles of Leave No Trace—minimizing impact, respecting wildlife, and preserving the landscape—are universally important. Modern gold panners are mindful of their surroundings, ensuring that their pursuit of adventure does not harm the natural habitats they explore.

While the ultimate goal of gold panning is to find the elusive treasure, the true value of the experience extends beyond the glimmer of gold. The thrill of discovery—whether it's a tiny flake or a gleaming nugget—evokes a rush of excitement that transcends monetary value. Gold panners often describe the emotional connection they feel when they spot that first glint in their pan—the connection to history, nature, and the indomitable human spirit.

Gold panning also serves as a catalyst for connecting with the natural world. Enthusiasts find themselves immersed in the tranquility of riverside settings, attuned to the sounds of flowing water, rustling leaves, and the calls of birds. The experience of gold panning encourages a deep appreciation for the intricate web of ecosystems that support life and sustain the natural world.

As more individuals engage in gold panning as a recreational activity, there is a growing appreciation for its historical and cultural significance. Organizations, national parks, and tour operators work to preserve the history of the gold rush era and educate participants about the challenges and triumphs of the prospectors who once roamed the wilderness. Gold panning experiences often include storytelling, sharing tales of adventure and hardship that further enrich the experience.

In conclusion, gold panning is more than a mere activity—it's an adventure that taps into the spirit of exploration and connects individuals with history, nature, and the timeless pursuit of treasure. Whether participants strike it rich or not, the experience offers a chance to engage in a tradition that spans centuries, evoking the thrill of the gold rush era while fostering a deeper connection to the world around us. Gold panning serves as a reminder that adventure, discovery, and the pursuit of dreams are timeless aspects of the human experience.

Scenic Flights: A Bird's-Eye View of Nature's Grandeur

Imagine soaring above the world, leaving behind the constraints of gravity and stepping into a realm where the landscape unfolds beneath you like a breathtaking tapestry. Scenic flights offer a unique opportunity to experience the world from a different perspective—a bird's-eye view that unveils nature's grandeur in all its glory. From towering mountains to winding rivers, dense forests to azure coastlines, scenic flights offer a perspective that words often struggle to capture. In this exploration of scenic flights, we take to the skies to discover the beauty, wonder, and profound sense of awe that these experiences provide.

The act of flight has long been a human fascination, a testament to our desire to transcend our earthly limitations and explore the unknown. From the earliest hot air balloon rides to the modern marvel of aviation, the ability to take to the skies has opened up new vistas and realms of possibility. Scenic flights build upon this fascination, offering individuals the chance to view the world below from an angle that few have the privilege to witness.

The world's most iconic landscapes take on a whole new dimension when viewed from above. Scenic flights reveal the sheer magnitude of natural wonders—be it the vast expanse of the Grand Canyon, the intricate patterns of the Great Barrier Reef, or the sweeping curves of the Norwegian fjords. These vistas, often too expansive to fully grasp from the ground, become tangible and awe-inspiring when observed from a bird's-eye perspective.

Mountains, with their towering majesty and rugged beauty, are particularly captivating when viewed from above. Scenic flights over mountain ranges offer a glimpse into the geological forces that shaped these landscapes. Peaks rise like majestic sentinels, valleys wind their way like intricate mazes, and glaciers glisten like frozen rivers. The Andes, the Rockies, the Himalayas—each range takes on a unique character when seen from the sky.

The meeting point of land and sea is a dynamic and ever-changing landscape, and scenic flights provide a front-row seat to this natural drama. Coastal flights showcase the interplay between cliffs and beaches, waves and tides. From the rugged coastlines of Ireland to the coral-fringed atolls of the Maldives, the beauty of these transitions is heightened when viewed from above.

The changing angle of the sun throughout the day brings about a mesmerizing play of light and shadow on the landscape. Scenic flights at different times of the day offer unique perspectives, each with its own magical quality. Witnessing a sunrise from the sky, with the first rays of light painting the world in hues of gold and orange, is a moment that imprints itself on memory.

The vantage point of a scenic flight offers a unique perspective on the natural world's most awe-inspiring events. The Great Migration in Africa, where vast herds of wildebeest traverse the

plains, takes on a new dimension when seen from above. The patterns and movements of thes migrations become tangible, revealing the scale of the phenomenon and the rhythms of life in the animal kingdom.

Some of the world's most pristine and inaccessible wilderness areas can only truly be appreciated from the air. Remote islands, inaccessible mountain valleys, and untouched rainforests unveil their secrets as the aircraft soars overhead. Scenic flights become a gateway to exploration, offering glimpses of places that few have the opportunity to visit on foot.

Glaciers, with their massive ice formations and ethereal blue hues, are a sight to behold from any angle. However, viewing glaciers from above provides a sense of scale and grandeur that is unparalleled. From the glaciers of Alaska to the icefields of Patagonia, these frozen wonders take on an almost otherworldly quality when seen from the sky.

Scenic flights over urban areas offer a different kind of visual feast. The organized chaos of city streets, the interplay of buildings and green spaces, and the juxtaposition of human activity against the backdrop of nature create a compelling visual narrative. City skylines and architectural landmarks reveal themselves as intricate pieces of a larger puzzle when viewed from above.

Scenic flights invite contemplation and reflection. As individuals look down upon the world below, there is a sense of disconnect from the everyday, allowing for a broader perspective on life and the universe. The experience fosters a deep sense of wonder, a reminder of the vastness of the planet and the interconnectedness of all its elements.

Scenic flights are a playground for photographers and artists, offering a canvas of endless possibilities. The challenge of capturing the vastness, colors, and textures of the landscape from above pushes creative boundaries. The resulting images often become visual testaments to the beauty of the Earth and the artistry of those who capture it.

While the beauty of the landscape is undeniable, scenic flights also highlight the fragility of our planet. The effects of climate change, deforestation, and human activity become more evident when viewed from above. The experience serves as a reminder of the importance of environmental stewardship and responsible practices to preserve these natural wonders for future generations.

In the end, the essence of a scenic flight is the sense of awe and inspiration it evokes. The beauty of nature, the marvel of creation, and the boundless horizons of the world become tangible and personal. Scenic flights offer a gift—an opportunity to witness the world with fresh eyes, to embrace the wonder that surrounds us, and to carry that sense of amazement into our daily lives.

In conclusion, scenic flights transcend mere sightseeing; they provide an experience that touches the soul and stirs the imagination. The opportunity to view the world from a bird's-eye perspective offers a renewed appreciation for the Earth's beauty, complexity, and interconnectedness. Whether soaring over mountains, coastlines, or urban landscapes, scenic flights offer a chance to step into a realm of wonder and discovery—a realm where the beauty of nature's grandeur unfolds beneath the wings of the aircraft, revealing a tapestry of awe-inspiring vistas.

Skagway Brewing Company: Crafting Local Flavors and Community Spirit

In the heart of the picturesque town of Skagway, Alaska, where history meets wilderness and the rugged charm of the frontier still lingers, there lies a unique establishment that captures the essence of the region. The Skagway Brewing Company, with its rich blend of craft beer, local flavors, and community spirit, stands as a testament to the art of creating not just beverages, but experiences that embody the soul of a place. From the clinking of glasses to the stories that flow as freely as the beer, the Skagway Brewing Company weaves together the elements of craftsmanship, community, and Alaska's vibrant culture.

The story of Skagway Brewing Company is deeply intertwined with the history of Skagway itself. This small town, which once served as a gateway to the Klondike Gold Rush, retains much of its 19th-century charm and character. Founded in 1897, Skagway became a bustling hub as stampeders from around the world converged in search of gold. The Skagway Brewing Company pays homage to this legacy, blending the nostalgia of the gold rush era with modern craft brewing techniques.

At the heart of Skagway Brewing Company's allure lies the craftsmanship that goes into each and every brew. From hop selection to fermentation, the process is a delicate dance of science and art. The brewery's team of dedicated brewers take pride in crafting a diverse range of beers, each with its own unique flavor profile and character. Whether it's a hop-forward IPA, a smooth amber ale, or a rich stout, each brew tells a story of ingredients, technique, and inspiration.

One of the defining features of Skagway Brewing Company is its commitment to using local ingredients to infuse their brews with the flavors of Alaska. Situated in a state known for its pristine waters, the brewery sources glacier-fed water, a key component in the creation of its beers. In addition to water, the brewery incorporates Alaskan-grown barley, hops, and other

locally-sourced ingredients, resulting in beverages that are uniquely tied to the land they call home.

Skagway Brewing Company's taproom offers a journey through a diverse array of brews that cater to a wide range of palates. The iconic Spruce Tip Blonde Ale, made with handpicked spruce tips, offers a refreshing and subtly piney taste of the Alaskan wilderness. The Chilkoot Trail IPA pays homage to the historic trail that stampeders traversed during the gold rush, boasting a bold hop character that mirrors the rugged journey. Meanwhile, the Prospector Pale Ale and the seasonal releases provide further exploration of flavors that reflect the changing seasons and local ingredients.

Skagway Brewing Company is not only a haven for beer enthusiasts, but also a destination for those seeking a culinary adventure. The brewery's on-site restaurant offers a carefully crafted menu that pairs delectable dishes with the brewery's signature brews. From hearty pub fare to seafood delicacies, the menu showcases locally sourced ingredients and an imaginative approach to flavors. The art of beer and food pairing is taken to new heights, creating a symphony of tastes that delight the senses.

Visitors to Skagway Brewing Company have the opportunity to go beyond the tasting room and take a peek behind the scenes with guided brewery tours. These tours offer a fascinating journey into the brewing process, from the mashing of grains to the fermentation and bottling stages. Guests gain insights into the art and science of craft brewing, as well as the history and culture that shape the brewery's identity.

Skagway Brewing Company is more than just a brewery; it's a gathering place where locals and travelers come together to share stories, laughter, and camaraderie. The brewery's warm and welcoming atmosphere invites visitors to relax, unwind, and connect with the spirit of the town. Live music events, trivia nights, and community gatherings foster a sense of belonging, making the brewery a cornerstone of Skagway's social fabric.

In a region known for its pristine landscapes, Skagway Brewing Company is dedicated to environmental stewardship. The brewery implements sustainable practices to minimize its ecological footprint, from energy-efficient brewing processes to waste reduction initiatives. By respecting the land and resources that contribute to their craft, the brewery embodies a commitment to preserving the natural beauty of Alaska for future generations.

For those who want to take a piece of Skagway Brewing Company's essence home, the brewery offers a range of merchandise that captures its spirit. From branded glassware to clothing adorned with the brewery's iconic logo, these souvenirs serve as tangible reminders of the experience and memories created within its walls.

As Skagway Brewing Company continues to thrive and evolve, it remains grounded in its roots while looking toward the future. The brewery's legacy intertwines with the town's history, and

its commitment to craftsmanship, community, and local flavors ensures that it will remain a beloved institution for years to come. Just as the Klondike Gold Rush era left an indelible mark on Skagway, the Skagway Brewing Company leaves its own mark through the experiences and connections it fosters.

In the heart of Skagway, where history's echoes intertwine with the present, the Skagway Brewing Company stands as a celebration of craftsmanship, community, and the flavors of Alaska. With every sip of their handcrafted brews, visitors and locals alike partake in a journey through the landscapes, stories, and spirit that define the Last Frontier. From the first foamy pour to the last lingering taste, Skagway Brewing Company offers not just beer, but a sensory experience that captures the essence of a town, a region, and a way of life.

Shopping and Souvenirs: Capturing the Essence of Skagway to Cherish Forever

Skagway, a picturesque town nestled in the heart of the Alaskan wilderness, is a place of rich history, natural beauty, and vibrant culture. As visitors explore its charming streets, they are met with a variety of shops and boutiques offering an array of treasures that capture the essence of this unique destination. From locally crafted art pieces to Alaskan delicacies, shopping in Skagway is not merely a commercial experience—it's an opportunity to take a piece of the town's spirit home and cherish it forever. In this exploration of shopping and souvenirs in Skagway, we delve into the diverse offerings that allow visitors to create lasting memories of their Alaskan adventure.

Shopping for souvenirs is more than a transaction; it's a journey of discovery. Skagway's shops are a treasure trove of items that reflect the town's history, culture, and natural beauty. The experience of souvenir hunting becomes an opportunity to connect with the spirit of the destination, to find objects that tell a story and evoke the memories of the trip long after it's over.

One of the most captivating aspects of shopping in Skagway is the opportunity to acquire unique pieces of art created by local artisans. From hand-carved totem poles that pay homage to indigenous cultures to intricate jewelry made from Alaska's native stones, each piece is a work of art that embodies the region's creative spirit. These items offer more than a physical keepsake; they carry the passion and craftsmanship of the artists who call this wild landscape home.

Skagway is situated in a region rich with indigenous heritage, and shopping here provides a chance to connect with this cultural legacy. Visitors can find native crafts that encompass the traditions and stories of the Tlingit people, who have inhabited the area for generations. From intricate beadwork to woven baskets, these crafts celebrate the artistry and history of the indigenous communities.

The allure of precious gemstones, reflective of Alaska's geological wonders, draws many shoppers seeking unique jewelry pieces. Local jewelers showcase a range of designs that incorporate Alaskan gemstones like jade, gold nuggets, and Alaskan diamonds. These pieces not only embody the natural beauty of the region but also serve as wearable reminders of the adventure taken in Skagway's surroundings.

Souvenirs need not be limited to physical objects; they can also be delectable flavors that encapsulate the essence of a place. Skagway offers an abundance of Alaskan delicacies that visitors can bring home to savor. Wild-caught smoked salmon, local jams and preserves made from berries harvested in the wilderness, and reindeer sausage are just a few examples of culinary delights that allow travelers to relive their Alaskan experience through taste.

Skagway's rich history as a gateway to the Klondike Gold Rush is reflected in its shops through historical keepsakes. Replicas of antique maps, vintage-style posters, and artifacts that harken back to the era of the gold rush provide a tangible link to the past. These items offer a glimpse into the town's transformative history, allowing visitors to carry a piece of Skagway's heritage with them.

Skagway's proximity to the great outdoors makes it a hub for adventure enthusiasts. Shoppers can find a wide range of outdoor gear, from sturdy hiking boots to weatherproof jackets, that are essential for exploring the Alaskan wilderness. These practical souvenirs serve as reminders of the adventures undertaken during the visit and inspire future journeys into the wild.

For those seeking to infuse their homes with a touch of Skagway's charm, the shops offer a variety of home décor items that capture the spirit of the town. Cozy blankets inspired by the region's landscapes, locally crafted ceramics, and wooden furnishings reminiscent of the frontier era are among the offerings that allow visitors to recreate the ambiance of Skagway within their own living spaces.

ashion enthusiasts can also find pieces that embrace the rugged and distinctive style of Alaska. From cozy knitwear that fends off the chill to outerwear that withstands the elements, the clothing boutiques of Skagway offer an opportunity to dress in Alaskan style while carrying the memories of the trip wherever you go.

For those who prefer to immerse themselves in the stories and history of a destination, Skagway's bookstores provide a selection of literature that delves into the town's past and its

natural wonders. Historical accounts of the gold rush, field guides to local flora and fauna, and works by Alaskan authors offer a deeper understanding of the region's allure.

In line with the growing awareness of ethical consumerism, many shops in Skagway prioritize sustainability and support local communities. Handmade items, eco-friendly products, and fair-trade goods offer shoppers the opportunity to make conscious choices that have a positive impact on the environment and the local economy.

Beyond the physical items themselves, souvenirs hold the power to evoke emotions, memories, and connections to a place. The act of choosing a souvenir, whether it's a handcrafted art piece or a jar of locally made jam, is a personal journey that encapsulates the experiences and moments that define a trip. Each time a souvenir is admired, worn, tasted, or displayed, it has the potential to transport the traveler back to Skagway's landscapes, people, and atmosphere.

In the end, shopping and souvenirs in Skagway are about more than acquiring objects—they're about capturing the essence of a place and weaving it into the fabric of one's own story. Each item becomes a thread in a tapestry of memories, a tangible reminder of the beauty, wonder, and discoveries made during the journey. Whether it's a handcrafted piece of art, a savory taste of Alaska, or a piece of jewelry that sparkles like the northern lights, the souvenirs of Skagway offer a timeless connection to a destination that has left an indelible mark on the heart and soul.

In conclusion, shopping and souvenirs in Skagway transcend mere commercial transactions; they are opportunities to connect with the town's history, culture, and natural beauty. The items acquired serve as tangible mementos of the adventure, the people, and the experiences that define the journey through Skagway's landscapes and streets. Whether it's a locally crafted art piece, a piece of indigenous heritage, or a taste of Alaskan flavors, the souvenirs of Skagway allow travelers to carry a piece of the town's essence with them, cherishing it forever.

Icy Strait Point Excursions: Embarking on Unforgettable Adventures Beyond Skagway

Nestled in the heart of the pristine Alaskan wilderness, Icy Strait Point beckons travelers with the promise of awe-inspiring landscapes, rich cultural experiences, and thrilling adventures that go far beyond the ordinary. Situated just a stone's throw away from Skagway, this unique destination serves as a gateway to some of the most remarkable excursions and activities that the Last Frontier has to offer. From exploring ancient traditions to encountering the wonders of nature, Icy Strait Point excursions promise unforgettable journeys that reveal the true spirit of

Alaska. In this exploration of Icy Strait Point excursions, we delve into the diverse array of activities that allow visitors to embark on once-in-a-lifetime adventures beyond Skagway's borders.

Icy Strait Point, with its untamed landscapes and unspoiled beauty, stands as a testament to the raw power of nature. The site's name itself evokes images of icy waters, towering mountains, and pristine forests. It's a place where the modern world intersects with the wild, creating an environment that invites exploration and promises unparalleled experiences.

For those seeking an adrenaline rush and a unique perspective on the Alaskan wilderness, ziplining through the treetops is an exhilarating excursion that's hard to match. The Icy Strait Point Zipline offers a breathtaking journey high above the forest floor, allowing participants to soar like eagles over lush landscapes and glimpses of the ocean below. The rush of wind, the panoramic views, and the feeling of freedom combine to create an adventure that's as heart-pounding as it is awe-inspiring.

The icy waters surrounding Icy Strait Point are home to some of the world's most magnificent marine creatures. Whale watching excursions here offer the chance to witness the awe-inspiring spectacle of humpback whales breaching and fluking against the backdrop of snow-capped mountains. The experience of being in close proximity to these gentle giants of the sea leaves a lasting impression, fostering a deep appreciation for the delicate balance of the marine ecosystem.

Icy Strait Point's connection to the indigenous Tlingit culture is a cornerstone of its identity. Cultural excursions offer visitors the opportunity to immerse themselves in the traditions, artistry, and storytelling of the Tlingit people. From guided walks through ancestral sites to interactive demonstrations of traditional crafts, these excursions provide a window into a rich cultural heritage that spans generations.

Alaska is known for its diverse and unique wildlife, and Icy Strait Point is no exception. Bear watching excursions offer participants the chance to observe these majestic creatures in their natural habitat. Whether it's the iconic grizzly bear or the elusive black bear, witnessing them forage, fish, and play in the wild offers a humbling and unforgettable encounter with nature's untamed beauty.

The waters surrounding Icy Strait Point are teeming with an abundance of marine life, making it a prime location for fishing enthusiasts. Whether casting a line for salmon, halibut, or other prized catches, fishing excursions provide the thrill of reeling in a trophy catch while soaking in the stunning Alaskan scenery.

Exploring the Alaskan wilderness from the water's edge is an experience like no other. Kayaking excursions allow participants to paddle through tranquil bays, glide past towering icebergs, and navigate pristine waterways. The serenity of kayaking offers a unique perspective on the landscape and wildlife, creating a sense of intimacy with the environment.

The temperate rainforests of Alaska are a lush and vibrant ecosystem, and Icy Strait Point offers excursions that allow visitors to delve into their depths. Guided rainforest walks unveil a world of towering trees, moss-covered landscapes, and the gentle melody of nature. These excursions provide a connection to the rhythms of the natural world and the importance of preserving these delicate ecosystems.

Food is a gateway to culture, and Icy Strait Point's culinary excursions provide a chance to savor the flavors of Alaska while learning about the region's history. From sampling freshly caught seafood to experiencing traditional Tlingit dishes, these excursions celebrate the bounty of the land and sea while offering insight into the culinary traditions that have shaped the region.

For those who seek to maximize their Alaskan adventure, combo excursions offer the best of both worlds. Combining activities such as ziplining, wildlife watching, and cultural experiences, these excursions provide a comprehensive snapshot of Icy Strait Point's offerings. Whether it's a day filled with exploration or a combination of relaxation and adventure, these packages offer a well-rounded and immersive experience.

As the allure of Icy Strait Point's excursions draws more visitors, a commitment to responsible tourism becomes paramount. Excursion operators and guides prioritize environmental stewardship, ensuring that interactions with wildlife are respectful and that the delicate ecosystems are preserved for generations to come. Many excursions also provide educational components that raise awareness about the importance of conservation.

Beyond the thrills and discoveries that excursions offer, they create lasting memories that become an integral part of a traveler's narrative. The rush of ziplining, the awe of whale watching, and the moments shared with local guides and fellow adventurers become stories that are retold and cherished for years to come. The spirit of adventure and exploration lives on through these memories, inspiring further journeys and a deeper connection to the natural world.

In conclusion, Icy Strait Point excursions offer a gateway to unforgettable adventures that go beyond the confines of Skagway's borders. From heart-pounding ziplining experiences to serene kayak journeys, each excursion provides a unique perspective on the Alaskan wilderness, culture, and wildlife. Through these activities, travelers not only gain a deeper understanding of the region's beauty but also create lasting memories that become an integral part of their journey. Icy Strait Point excursions embody the very essence of exploration, inviting visitors to embark on journeys of discovery that reflect the spirit of Alaska itself—an untamed, awe-inspiring, and unforgettable landscape.

Ketchikan: The Salmon Capital of the World

Nestled in the heart of the stunning Inside Passage of Alaska, Ketchikan emerges as a unique gem that captivates visitors with its rich history, vibrant culture, and breathtaking natural beauty. Often referred to as the "Salmon Capital of the World," Ketchikan is renowned for its thriving salmon fishing industry, its lush landscapes, and its deep connection to indigenous cultures. As you step ashore in this charming port, you're welcomed into a world where towering totem poles stand as silent storytellers, pristine waters teem with life, and the echoes of Alaska's past resonate through the streets.

The history of Ketchikan is steeped in the traditions of its indigenous inhabitants, the Tlingit people. For centuries, they thrived in harmony with the land and sea, relying on the bounties of nature for sustenance and inspiration. The arrival of European explorers and later, American settlers, marked a significant turning point in Ketchikan's evolution. The discovery of gold and the burgeoning fishing industry drew people from all walks of life, transforming Ketchikan from a small Tlingit village to a bustling frontier town.

At the heart of Ketchikan's identity lies its deep connection to salmon. The town's title as the "Salmon Capital of the World" is well-deserved, as the surrounding waters are a veritable haven for five species of Pacific salmon: chinook (king), coho (silver), sockeye (red), pink, and chum. These fish embark on epic migrations, returning to their birthplace in Ketchikan's rivers and streams to spawn, perpetuating the cycle of life. The importance of salmon isn't just economic—it's cultural, environmental, and integral to the town's identity.

Ketchikan's fishing industry forms the backbone of its economy and culture. Its historic roots in salmon canneries date back to the late 1800s, when the area became a hub for processing the abundant salmon catches. Today, you can still witness the bustling activity of fishing vessels returning to port with their precious cargo. Salmon fishing excursions are a popular attraction for visitors, offering the chance to experience the thrill of angling for these iconic fish while surrounded by Alaska's stunning scenery.

Ketchikan's rich indigenous heritage is embodied in its towering totem poles. Totem poles are an intricate art form that tells stories of ancestral legends, clan histories, and cultural traditions. The Totem Heritage Center in Ketchikan is a treasure trove of these masterpieces, with meticulously restored and preserved totem poles that provide insight into the Tlingit, Haida, and Tsimshian cultures. Visitors can delve into the history and significance of totem carving, gaining a deeper appreciation for the artistry and spiritual connections embedded within each pole.

Saxman Native Village offers a deeper immersion into the indigenous cultures that have shaped Ketchikan's identity. This living cultural village showcases traditional Tlingit art, dance, and craftsmanship. Visitors have the opportunity to witness captivating performances, interact with local artisans, and gain insights into the daily lives of Alaska's indigenous peoples. Saxman is a testament to the resilience of these cultures, providing an authentic and educational experience that fosters cross-cultural understanding.

Beyond its cultural riches, Ketchikan's natural wonders are equally mesmerizing. The town is enveloped by the Tongass National Forest, the largest national forest in the United States. This temperate rainforest is a haven for diverse flora and fauna, including bald eagles, black bears, and Sitka black-tailed deer. Nature enthusiasts can explore trails, embark on wildlife-watching tours, or simply bask in the tranquility of the verdant landscapes.

Ketchikan offers a multitude of outdoor adventures, catering to visitors of all ages and interests. Kayaking through pristine waters, zip-lining through lush canopies, or embarking on a seaplane flightseeing tour that showcases the grandeur of the Misty Fjords National Monument—there's no shortage of exhilarating experiences. These activities provide a unique perspective on Ketchikan's landscapes, allowing you to see the town and its surrounding wilderness from new heights and angles.

As Ketchikan continues to evolve, it remains committed to preserving its essence—the delicate balance between its natural wonders and its cultural heritage. Conservation efforts work hand in hand with tourism, ensuring that the town's natural beauty and indigenous traditions endure for generations to come. Ketchikan serves as a model of how communities can harmonize economic development with environmental stewardship and cultural preservation.

Ketchikan's allure is undeniable. Its picturesque waterfront, the rhythmic pull of tides, the stories whispered by totem poles, and the aroma of freshly caught salmon—all these elements contribute to a sensory symphony that lingers long after you've departed. Ketchikan invites you to be more than a visitor; it invites you to be a participant in its ongoing narrative, a story woven from threads of history, culture, and the enduring spirit of Alaska's wilderness. Whether you're exploring the town's heritage, casting a line into the salmon-rich waters, or simply gazing at the horizon, Ketchikan leaves an indelible mark on your journey through the remarkable landscapes of the Last Frontier.

Attractions and Activities

Ketchikan, known as the "Salmon Capital of the World," is a treasure trove of attractions and activities that showcase its rich cultural heritage, stunning natural beauty, and vibrant fishing industry. From exploring indigenous art to embarking on outdoor adventures, there's something for every type of traveler. Here are some of the best attractions and activities to experience in Ketchikan:

1. Totem Heritage Center: Immersion in Indigenous Art

The Totem Heritage Center is a must-visit attraction for anyone interested in the art and culture of the Tlingit, Haida, and Tsimshian peoples. This center houses a remarkable collection of totem poles, some of which are over a century old. The totem poles are meticulously restored and provide insights into the stories, history, and traditions of Alaska's indigenous communities.

2. Saxman Native Village: Cultural Experience

Saxman Native Village offers an immersive cultural experience where you can witness indigenous dances, explore traditional longhouses, and interact with local artisans. The village features the largest collection of totem poles in the world, providing a fascinating glimpse into the artistry and spirituality of native cultures.

3. Creek Street: Historic Waterfront District

Creek Street is a picturesque waterfront district with a colorful history. Once a red-light district, it's now a charming area with wooden boardwalks, historic buildings, and boutique shops.

xplore the galleries, boutiques, and local eateries, and don't miss the opportunity to take a
:roll on the iconic Married Man's Trail.

Alaska Rainforest Sanctuary: Nature and Wildlife

his sanctuary offers guided tours that allow you to explore the lush Tongass National Forest.
Walk along well-maintained trails through old-growth rainforests, and keep an eye out for
vildlife such as bald eagles, bears, and deer. The sanctuary provides an educational experience
bout the region's ecosystem and wildlife.

Fishing Excursions: Salmon and More

iven its reputation as the "Salmon Capital," no visit to Ketchikan is complete without a fishing
xcursion. Join a guided fishing tour to try your hand at catching salmon or halibut in the
bundant waters. Whether you're an experienced angler or a beginner, the thrill of reeling in a
rized catch is a memorable experience.

5. Misty Fjords National Monument: Scenic Flightseeing

:mbark on a flightseeing tour to the Misty Fjords National Monument, a breathtaking
vilderness area of fjords, cliffs, and waterfalls. Witness the grandeur of this remote landscape
rom above, and perhaps even touch down on a pristine alpine lake. This aerial perspective
offers an unparalleled view of Alaska's natural beauty.

7. Wildlife Watching: Eagles and Bears

Ketchikan is a paradise for wildlife enthusiasts. Join guided wildlife tours to spot bald eagles
soaring overhead and black bears foraging along the shoreline. Some tours take you to prime
ocations for wildlife viewing and photography, providing you with a unique opportunity to
witness Alaska's diverse fauna up close.

8. Kayaking Adventures: Coastal Exploration

Explore the serene waters around Ketchikan by kayak. Paddle through picturesque fjords, glide
past lush forests, and experience the tranquil beauty of the coastline. Guided kayaking tours
are available for all skill levels, allowing you to connect with nature and marvel at the stunning
landscapes.

9. Great Alaskan Lumberjack Show: Entertaining Performance

Experience Ketchikan's logging history through an entertaining and action-packed lumberjack show. Watch as professional lumberjacks compete in feats of strength, agility, and skill, all set against the backdrop of Alaska's timber industry heritage. This family-friendly show offers a m of entertainment and education.

10. Tongass Historical Museum: Local History

Delve into Ketchikan's history at the Tongass Historical Museum. The exhibits explore the town's diverse heritage, from indigenous cultures to the fishing industry and beyond. The museum's artifacts, photographs, and interactive displays provide a comprehensive look at Ketchikan's past.

11. Whale-Watching Tours: Marine Marvels

Ketchikan's coastal waters are home to a diverse range of marine life, including humpback whales, orcas, sea lions, and porpoises. Join a guided whale-watching tour to witness these magnificent creatures in their natural habitat. Knowledgeable guides provide insights into the behaviors and conservation efforts of these marine marvels.

In conclusion, Ketchikan, the "Salmon Capital of the World," is a destination that offers a dynamic blend of cultural immersion, natural exploration, and outdoor adventures. From experiencing indigenous art and traditions to fishing for prized catches, kayaking along serene waters, and witnessing the majesty of wildlife, Ketchikan provides a multitude of attractions and activities that cater to diverse interests. Whether you're drawn to history, nature, culture, or a mix of everything Alaska has to offer, Ketchikan's allure ensures an enriching and unforgettable experience for every traveler.

Totem Heritage Center: Immersion in Indigenous Art

Deep within the heart of Ketchikan, Alaska lies a place where the artistry of indigenous peoples is not only preserved but celebrated—the Totem Heritage Center. This remarkable center stands as a testament to the cultural vibrancy and artistic legacy of the Tlingit, Haida, and Tsimshian communities that have called this land home for centuries. As you step into the center's hallowed halls, you're transported into a world where intricately carved totem poles serve as storytellers, connecting the past with the present and offering a window into the rich heritage of Alaska's native cultures.

The Totem Heritage Center is more than a museum; it's a sanctuary for the preservation and celebration of indigenous art, culture, and history. Established in 1976, this center was born out of a recognition that the totem poles, which once graced the villages of Alaska's native peoples, were rapidly deteriorating due to exposure to the elements. The center's founders sought to

protect these invaluable artifacts and create a space where their significance could be shared with the world.

At the heart of the Totem Heritage Center's mission lies its collection of totem poles—magnificent pieces of art that encapsulate the stories, traditions, and spirituality of native communities. The center houses over 30 unrestored totem poles, each telling a unique narrative through its intricate carvings and designs. Some totem poles date back to the 19th century, their weathered surfaces reflecting the passage of time and the enduring spirit of the cultures they represent.

One of the center's most remarkable aspects is its commitment to restoration. Skilled carvers and artisans work tirelessly to restore totem poles that have fallen victim to the ravages of time. The process is both an art and a science, involving meticulous research, documentation, and craftsmanship. The goal isn't merely to repair; it's to breathe new life into these pieces of history while retaining their authenticity.

Totem poles are more than static sculptures; they are vessels of cultural expression. Each carving, symbol, and figure on a totem pole carries layers of meaning that reflect the ancestral lineage, clan affiliations, and stories of the people who crafted them. These totem poles served as markers of identity, community, and spiritual connection. As you explore the Totem Heritage Center, you're invited to decode these symbols, to understand the dances of ravens, the tales of bears, and the wisdom of ancestors embedded within each piece.

The Totem Heritage Center isn't just a repository of art; it's a hub of education and cultural engagement. Guided tours lead visitors through the center, offering insights into the history of totem poles, the significance of their carvings, and the life stories they tell. Knowledgeable guides bridge the gap between ancient traditions and modern understanding, creating a bridge of cultural appreciation.

While the totem poles take center stage, the Totem Heritage Center offers a holistic experience that delves into various aspects of indigenous culture. Exhibits feature an array of artifacts, including baskets, regalia, and tools, providing a comprehensive look into the daily lives and spiritual practices of Alaska's native communities. The center doesn't shy away from addressing the complex history of colonization and the resilience of indigenous peoples, fostering a deeper understanding of the challenges they've faced and continue to overcome.

The artistry displayed at the Totem Heritage Center transcends the confines of the past—it's a living tradition that continues to inspire. The center hosts workshops, demonstrations, and events that celebrate the craftsmanship of indigenous artisans. Visitors have the opportunity to witness the transformation of raw materials into stunning pieces of art, connecting with the creative process that has defined native cultures for generations.

The Totem Heritage Center serves as a bridge between generations. It honors the contributions of past carvers while nurturing the talents of aspiring artists. The center's impact extends beyond its walls, as it fosters cultural continuation and encourages native youth to explore their artistic heritage. The annual Carving Legacy Project, for instance, brings young artists together to learn traditional carving techniques from master carvers, ensuring that the legacy of totem pole carving remains vibrant.

As you immerse yourself in the Totem Heritage Center, you're invited to weave your own story into the tapestry of indigenous art and culture. The center isn't a static museum; it's a living dialogue between the past and the present, between cultures and individuals. The totem poles that stand tall within its walls are not mere artifacts; they're conduits of wisdom, vessels of memory, and carriers of the human experience.

In conclusion, the Totem Heritage Center in Ketchikan offers a profound journey into the heart of indigenous art and culture. Through its meticulously restored totem poles, interactive exhibits, and commitment to education, the center provides a unique window into the diverse and vibrant heritage of Alaska's native communities. As you explore the center's galleries and immerse yourself in its stories, you're invited to embark on a voyage of understanding, appreciation, and connection with the rich tapestry of Alaska's cultural legacy.

Saxman Native Village: Cultural Experience

Nestled along the picturesque coastline of Ketchikan, Alaska, lies a place that carries the echoes of centuries past—the Saxman Native Village. This cultural haven stands as a testament to the enduring traditions and rich heritage of the indigenous Tlingit community. As you step into this vibrant village, you're transported into a world where art, history, and spirituality intertwine, inviting you to embrace the essence of Alaska's native cultures.

Saxman Native Village is more than a tourist destination; it's a gateway to the heart of Tlingit culture. Established in 1894, the village serves as a living tribute to the resilience of native communities in the face of change. While it welcomes visitors from around the world, it remains an active and thriving community that proudly carries forward the traditions of its ancestors.

The village is renowned for its remarkable collection of totem poles, each a masterpiece of artistry and symbolism. Totem poles are integral to indigenous cultures, serving as visual narratives that tell stories of lineage, legends, and spiritual beliefs. As you stroll through Saxman Native Village, you're enveloped by the towering totem poles that stand sentinel, inviting you to delve into the stories they tell and the wisdom they carry.

One of the highlights of a visit to Saxman Native Village is the opportunity to witness authentic Tlingit performances. Traditional songs and dances provide a window into the cultural expressions that have shaped generations. Dressed in regalia adorned with intricate designs and vibrant colors, dancers move to the rhythm of drums and chants, conveying stories of creation, connection, and celebration. Through these performances, visitors gain a deeper understanding of the profound spiritual connection between indigenous people and the natural world.

Saxman Native Village is a haven for artisans whose hands bring life to the traditions of their ancestors. The carving shed hums with the sound of tools shaping cedar into intricate designs, transforming raw wood into exquisite pieces of art. Master carvers pass down their knowledge and techniques to younger generations, ensuring that the art of totem pole carving remains vibrant and alive.

For those who yearn to be more than observers, Saxman Native Village offers interactive workshops that provide hands-on experiences in indigenous arts and crafts. Guided by skilled artisans, visitors can try their hand at carving, weaving, and other traditional practices. These workshops bridge the gap between cultures, inviting visitors to participate in the creative processes that have defined native communities for centuries.

Saxman Native Village features traditional longhouses that offer a glimpse into the daily lives of indigenous peoples. These communal structures were central to community gatherings, ceremonies, and storytelling. Visitors can step inside and imagine the warmth of fires, the sounds of laughter, and the sharing of wisdom that once filled these spaces.

The Totem Park within Saxman Native Village serves as an outdoor gallery where the totem poles come to life against the backdrop of lush landscapes. The park features a diverse collection of totem poles, each with its own story to tell. As you wander through the park, you're invited to reflect on the intricate carvings, the symbolism, and the enduring connections that bind past and present.

Saxman Native Village isn't merely a place for cultural immersion; it's a bridge of understanding between cultures. The village's mission extends beyond showcasing indigenous traditions; it's about fostering appreciation, respect, and cross-cultural dialogue. Visitors have the opportunity to engage with Tlingit artisans, to ask questions, and to gain insights into the challenges and triumphs of native communities.

Saxman Native Village is a testament to the ongoing journey of preserving heritage while nurturing the potential of the future. It honors the legacy of ancestors while empowering new generations to carry forth the torch of indigenous culture. The village's impact reaches beyond its boundaries, as it serves as an educational resource for schools and communities, ensuring that the tapestry of Tlingit traditions remains vibrant and alive.

As you bid farewell to Saxman Native Village, you carry with you not just the memories of vibrant performances, intricate carvings, and the beauty of the totem poles. You carry with you a piece of a tapestry woven with the threads of unity, diversity, and the interconnectedness of all cultures. Saxman Native Village isn't just a cultural experience; it's an invitation to step into a shared narrative that celebrates the beauty of humanity's varied expressions.

In conclusion, Saxman Native Village is a cultural treasure that invites visitors to step into the heart of Tlingit traditions and heritage. From the majestic totem poles that tell stories of generations to the vibrant performances that bridge past and present, the village offers a profound immersion into indigenous art, spirituality, and community. As you explore this living village, you're invited to be more than a spectator; you're invited to be a participant in a timeless exchange of cultures, a journey that enriches your understanding and connection with the rich tapestry of human experience.

Creek Street: Historic Waterfront District

Nestled along the banks of Ketchikan Creek in Alaska, Creek Street stands as a living testament to the storied history and vibrant spirit of a bygone era. This historic waterfront district, perched above the gentle rush of the creek's waters, weaves together tales of pioneers, ishermen, and a community that thrived amidst the challenges of the rugged Alaskan frontier. As you step onto the weathered wooden boardwalks and meander through the charming buildings that line the creek's edge, you're transported back in time, experiencing the heart and soul of Ketchikan's colorful past.

Creek Street's history is deeply intertwined with the gold rush fever that swept through Alaska in the late 19th century. What began as a bustling hub of commerce and enterprise transformed into a red-light district as the gold rush attracted an influx of fortune seekers. The quaint buildings that now line Creek Street once housed bordellos, saloons, and other establishments that catered to the needs and desires of the men who flocked to the area.

Walking down Creek Street today is like stepping into a vintage postcard. The buildings, with their colorful facades and ornate details, exude a quaint charm that harks back to a simpler time. The wooden boardwalks, worn smooth by the footfalls of generations, tell tales of countless individuals who traversed these planks in pursuit of dreams and adventures. The creek below provides a soothing soundtrack as it murmurs and dances on its journey to the sea.

One of the most iconic structures on Creek Street is Dolly's House, a former brothel turned museum that offers a fascinating glimpse into the district's history. Preserved much as it was

during the early 20th century, Dolly's House takes visitors on a guided tour that delves into the life and times of Dolly Arthur, a madam who played a significant role in the area's history. The museum's rooms are adorned with period furnishings and memorabilia, providing a vivid portrayal of the district's colorful past.

Creek Street's history is enriched by the presence of the Married Man's Trail, a wooden boardwalk that winds through the forest above the district. This trail was used by patrons of Creek Street's bordellos who sought a discreet path to avoid being seen by prying eyes. Today, the trail offers visitors a scenic walk through the lush Alaskan wilderness, offering both history and natural beauty.

While Creek Street is steeped in history, it also embraces the present with a delightful mix of art galleries, boutiques, and shops that cater to modern tastes. Visitors can peruse local artwork, handmade crafts, and souvenirs that capture the essence of Ketchikan's unique character. The juxtaposition of contemporary offerings against the backdrop of historic architecture creates a dynamic and charming atmosphere.

Creek Street isn't merely a relic frozen in time; it's a living canvas that breathes life into history. Interpretive displays and plaques along the boardwalk provide insights into the district's past, shedding light on the stories of the women who lived and worked there, the challenges they faced, and the resilience that defined their lives. These narratives ensure that the human experiences that unfolded on Creek Street continue to resonate with visitors today.

Beyond its historic allure, Creek Street offers breathtaking views that make it a photographer's paradise. The creek itself, flanked by lush vegetation, provides a picturesque backdrop. As the sun casts its golden glow on the water, the scene transforms into a canvas of natural beauty. The quaint buildings, the rushing waters, and the verdant landscapes create a tableau that captures the essence of Alaska's rugged and captivating landscapes.

While Creek Street's past is colorful and sometimes controversial, its evolution into a place of reflection and cultural appreciation speaks to the resilience of communities in embracing their history. Today, visitors can explore the district's galleries, museums, and shops, learning about the lives that once unfolded along these wooden walkways. They can reflect on the stories of pioneers, the dreams of prospectors, and the determination of those who carved a life in the heart of the wilderness.

Creek Street is more than a historic district; it's a journey through time that invites visitors to step into the shoes of those who came before. It's a place where tales of triumph, struggle, and everyday life merge to create a tapestry of human experiences. It's a testament to the tenacity of communities that weathered storms and challenges, leaving behind a legacy that continues to enrich the fabric of Ketchikan's identity.

In conclusion, Creek Street is a treasure trove of history and charm that beckons travelers to explore its wooden boardwalks, gaze upon its colorful facades, and immerse themselves in the stories that have shaped its character. From its gold rush origins to its transformation into a place of cultural significance, Creek Street offers a glimpse into the heart and soul of Ketchikan's past. As you wander through its streets and listen to the whispers of history carried by the creek's gentle flow, you're invited to be part of a timeless journey that celebrates the human spirit and the enduring connection between past and present.

Alaska Rainforest Sanctuary: Nature and Wildlife

Amidst the rugged landscapes and pristine wilderness of Ketchikan, Alaska, lies a sanctuary that offers a captivating window into the natural world—the Alaska Rainforest Sanctuary. This enchanting haven is a tribute to the rich biodiversity and fragile ecosystems that define the temperate rainforests of the Pacific Northwest. As you step into this lush paradise, you're enveloped by the symphony of nature's melodies, the whisper of leaves, and the gentle embrace of a world teeming with life.

The Alaska Rainforest Sanctuary is situated within the Tongass National Forest, a sprawling expanse of verdant beauty that stands as the largest national forest in the United States. This temperate rainforest is a mosaic of towering Sitka spruce, western hemlock, and red cedar trees, their lush canopies creating a tapestry that stretches as far as the eye can see. The sanctuary's trails wind through this majestic forest, inviting visitors to immerse themselves in the serenity and vitality of nature.

One of the highlights of the Alaska Rainforest Sanctuary is its guided tours, led by knowledgeable naturalists who serve as interpreters of the ecosystem's wonders. These tours are a journey of discovery, offering insights into the intricate relationships between plants, animals, and the environment. From the moss-draped branches to the delicate undergrowth, every facet of the rainforest tells a story of interconnectedness.

Central to the Alaska Rainforest Sanctuary is a salmon stream that winds its way through the heart of the sanctuary. This stream is a lifeline, a vital artery that sustains countless species and shapes the ecosystem. During the salmon's annual migration, the stream becomes a theater of life and death, as the fish struggle upstream to spawn, providing sustenance to bears, eagles, and other predators. Witnessing this cycle is a humbling reminder of the delicate balance that characterizes nature's web.

The Alaska Rainforest Sanctuary is a haven for wildlife enthusiasts and birdwatchers. The forest comes alive with a symphony of species, from bald eagles soaring overhead to black bears foraging for food along the stream's banks. The sanctuary's guided tours provide opportunities to spot and learn about these charismatic creatures, offering a rare glimpse into their natural habitats and behaviors.

One of the most remarkable aspects of the Alaska Rainforest Sanctuary is its illustration of the circle of life. The interconnectedness of predators and prey is on full display as you observe eagles perched in lofty trees, their keen eyes scanning the water for fish, while bears comb the shores in search of a feast. This dance of survival and symbiosis reminds visitors of the delicate harmony that sustains the rainforest ecosystem.

Beyond its beauty, the Alaska Rainforest Sanctuary carries profound educational significance. The guided tours serve as a platform for environmental education, fostering an understanding of the delicate balance that exists within the rainforest ecosystem. This awareness is crucial for fostering a sense of stewardship and inspiring visitors to actively contribute to the conservation of these precious natural habitats.

The rainforest's vibrant tapestry extends beyond its towering trees and flowing streams. The sanctuary's trails wind through a carpet of lush undergrowth, where ferns, mosses, and wildflowers thrive in the dappled sunlight. This understorey is a world of its own, housing myriad species that contribute to the rainforest's remarkable biodiversity.

While the forest floor is alive with activity, the canopy above harbors secrets of its own. Towering trees create a vertical world that's home to species like marbled murrelets, a rare seabird that nests high in the branches. Exploring the canopy through guided tours provides a unique perspective on the rainforest's intricate layers of life.

The Alaska Rainforest Sanctuary is more than a snapshot of nature's beauty—it's a journey through time. As you walk the sanctuary's trails, you're retracing the steps of indigenous peoples who lived in harmony with this land for millennia. You're experiencing the same natural wonders that have inspired awe in generations of explorers, artists, and conservationists.

The Alaska Rainforest Sanctuary's mission extends beyond offering visitors a glimpse of nature's splendor. The sanctuary is committed to conservation and sustainable practices that ensure the integrity of the rainforest for future generations. By raising awareness and promoting responsible interactions with the environment, the sanctuary serves as a model for how ecotourism can coexist harmoniously with nature.

In the embrace of the Alaska Rainforest Sanctuary, you're invited to become a part of nature's symphony. The rustling leaves, the rush of water, the distant calls of birds—all merge to create a chorus that resonates with the rhythms of the earth. This sanctuary is more than a destination;

it's a sanctuary for the soul, a place to reconnect with the wilderness and rediscover the wonders that have captivated humanity for eons.

In conclusion, the Alaska Rainforest Sanctuary is a sanctuary for the senses and the spirit. It offers a profound journey into the heart of nature, where towering trees, babbling streams, and a multitude of species come together in a symphony of life. The guided tours, educational significance, and commitment to conservation ensure that the sanctuary not only preserves the rainforest's beauty but also fosters a deep appreciation for the delicate balance that sustains our planet. As you explore its trails and bask in the beauty of its landscapes, you're reminded of the interconnectedness of all living things and the magic that lies within the heart of the wild.

Fishing Excursions: Salmon and More

In the pristine waters off the coast of Alaska, a world of adventure and excitement awaits fishing enthusiasts—a realm where the thrill of the catch is matched only by the breathtaking beauty of the surroundings. Fishing excursions in Alaska are not just a hobby; they're a way of life, deeply ingrained in the cultural fabric of the region. From reeling in prized salmon to encountering other species that call these waters home, a fishing excursion in Alaska offers a unique blend of sport, nature, and the pursuit of the ultimate catch.

Alaska's fishing legacy is intrinsically tied to salmon, a species that holds cultural, economic, and ecological significance. With five species of Pacific salmon—chinook (king), coho (silver), sockeye (red), pink, and chum—these waters offer a veritable bounty for anglers. The annual salmon runs, during which fish return to their natal streams to spawn, are a phenomenon that draws anglers from around the world, seeking the exhilaration of tangling with these iconic fish.

For fishing enthusiasts, the heart-pounding thrill of the catch is an experience like no other. The battle between angler and fish is a test of skill, strength, and strategy. Reeling in a salmon, feeling its powerful pull, witnessing its acrobatic leaps, and savoring the satisfaction of a successful catch is a moment that's etched into memory. Whether it's the elusive chinook or the fierce coho, each species offers its own unique challenge and reward.

Fishing in Alaska is more than a sport; it's an art form that requires knowledge, patience, and respect for the environment. Expert guides lead fishing excursions, sharing their wisdom about the behaviors of fish, the best techniques for different species, and the importance of ethical angling practices. From choosing the right bait to mastering the art of casting, fishing in these waters is a chance to deepen your connection with nature and hone your angling skills.

While salmon steal the spotlight, Alaska's waters are home to an array of other fish species that offer equally exciting fishing opportunities. Halibut, for instance, is a prized quarry known for its size and strength. Embarking on a halibut fishing excursion means battling with a powerful fish that can weigh hundreds of pounds. The thrill of reeling in a halibut, as it puts up a formidable fight, is a testament to the rugged beauty of Alaska's marine world.

Fishing excursions in Alaska offer more than the chance to catch fish; they're a journey into the heart of some of the most pristine and remote wilderness areas on the planet. These waters are surrounded by breathtaking landscapes—majestic mountains, rugged coastlines, and tranquil fjords. The experience of fishing against this backdrop is a reminder of the beauty and fragility of nature.

Alaska's fishing industry is closely intertwined with the principles of eco-tourism and conservation. Responsible angling practices are emphasized, with guides educating anglers about catch-and-release methods, sustainable fishing practices, and the importance of preserving fish populations for future generations. Fishing excursions provide an opportunity not only to enjoy the thrill of the catch but also to contribute to the conservation of Alaska's aquatic ecosystems.

Fishing is deeply embedded in the culture of Alaska's native communities. For indigenous peoples, fishing has been a way of life for generations, providing sustenance, livelihood, and a spiritual connection to the land and sea. Participating in a fishing excursion allows visitors to engage with this cultural legacy, gaining insights into the traditions, stories, and customs that revolve around the bounty of Alaska's waters.

While the catch is undoubtedly a highlight, fishing excursions in Alaska offer much more than the moment of reeling in a fish. It's the camaraderie between anglers, the anticipation of the bite, the moments of reflection while surrounded by nature's beauty, and the shared stories that become part of the journey. It's the thrill of spotting marine life such as whales, seals, and seabirds, creating a holistic experience that goes beyond the fish on the line.

The memories forged during a fishing excursion in Alaska are indelible. Whether it's the rush of adrenaline when a fish strikes, the laughter shared with fellow anglers, or the sense of awe at the rugged landscapes, these moments become cherished memories that linger long after the excursion ends. Each cast, each tug on the line, becomes a chapter in a story of adventure and connection with the wild.

Fishing excursions in Alaska offer more than the opportunity to catch fish; they provide a profound connection with nature. As you cast your line into the pristine waters, you become a part of the ebb and flow of the ecosystem. You witness the cycles of life, the dance of predator and prey, and the unending rhythm of the ocean. It's a chance to step away from the bustle of modern life and immerse yourself in the timeless serenity of the natural world.

Alaska's waters are a realm of exploration and discovery, where each fishing excursion holds the promise of something new. Whether it's encountering a species you've never caught before, witnessing the majestic breach of a whale, or simply marveling at the vastness of the ocean, these excursions evoke the spirit of the explorers who once navigated these same waters. It's a reminder that, even in an age of technology, there are still untamed frontiers waiting to be explored.

In conclusion, fishing excursions in Alaska are a harmonious blend of sport, nature, and cultural immersion. From the pursuit of iconic salmon species to the thrill of battling with powerful halibut, these excursions offer a unique opportunity to connect with the wilderness and challenge oneself in a pristine marine environment. Beyond the catch, the memories forged and the lessons learned contribute to a deeper appreciation for the natural world and the delicate balance that sustains it. Whether you're an experienced angler or a novice, embarking on a fishing excursion in Alaska is an invitation to embrace adventure, forge connections, and create stories that will be shared for generations to come.

Misty Fjords National Monument: Scenic Flightseeing

In the remote and untouched corners of southeastern Alaska lies a realm of breathtaking beauty that seems almost surreal—Misty Fjords National Monument. This awe-inspiring natural wonder is a testament to the grandeur of Mother Nature's artistic prowess, a landscape carved by ice and time into a masterpiece of towering cliffs, cascading waterfalls, pristine lakes, and mist-shrouded fjords. While the monument's rugged terrain may challenge even the most intrepid explorers, one of the most enchanting ways to experience its splendor is through scenic flightseeing—a journey that unveils a tapestry of natural marvels that few are fortunate enough to witness.

Misty Fjords National Monument is a landscape that seems to emerge from the realm of dreams. Towering granite cliffs rise majestically from the tranquil waters, shrouded in ethereal mists that lend an air of mystery to the scene. These cliffs, sculpted by ancient glaciers and the passage of time, evoke a sense of awe and reverence, as if paying homage to the forces that shaped them. As the sun's rays play upon the surfaces, the fjords come alive with a kaleidoscope of colors that dance upon the water and illuminate the landscape.

At the heart of Misty Fjords are its namesake fjords—deep, narrow inlets flanked by sheer cliffs that plunge into the water. These geological wonders are a testament to the power of ice, as ancient glaciers carved these chasms through the rugged mountains. From above, the fjords create a maze-like labyrinth that winds through the landscape, offering a glimpse into the Earth's geological history and the relentless forces of nature.

As you soar above Misty Fjords, the sky seems to weep with beauty, as countless waterfalls cascade from great heights into the fjords below. These ribbons of silver create a symphony of sound and motion that adds to the sensory experience of flightseeing. Some waterfalls tumble gently, their mist catching the light like a delicate veil, while others thunder and roar with an unbridled force that serves as a reminder of nature's unfathomable power.

Misty Fjords National Monument is not just a landscape of rock and water—it's a sanctuary for wildlife that thrives in this remote corner of Alaska. As you take to the skies, you might spot the majestic wingspan of bald eagles soaring overhead, their keen eyes surveying the land below. Brown bears might amble along the shores in search of sustenance, while seals bask on rocky outcroppings, their sleek forms glistening in the sunlight. The flightseeing experience offers a unique vantage point to witness these creatures in their natural habitat.

Scenic flightseeing is not just a mode of transportation; it's a journey that provides an unparalleled perspective on the grandeur of Misty Fjords. From the air, you're treated to a panoramic view that encapsulates the vastness and intricacy of the landscape. The fjords stretch out like intricate veins, the forests become a mosaic of green, and the waterfalls resemble delicate brushstrokes on a canvas. The aerial perspective allows you to appreciate the monument's scale, its delicate balance, and the harmonious interplay of its elements.

For photographers, Misty Fjords is a playground of inspiration and creativity. The interplay of light and shadow, the ever-changing weather that paints the skies with drama, and the reflection of the landscape upon the water—all offer endless opportunities to capture images that are nothing short of breathtaking. The challenge lies not in finding a worthy subject but in selecting from the multitude of stunning vistas that unfold with each passing moment.

Many flightseeing experiences in Misty Fjords are accompanied by knowledgeable guides who provide insights into the geological, ecological, and cultural significance of the landscape. These guides share stories of the Tlingit people who have inhabited these lands for centuries, the explorers who marveled at its beauty, and the conservation efforts that safeguard its pristine nature. This guided interpretation enriches the flightseeing experience, turning it into a journey of discovery and connection.

While the fjords and cliffs of Misty Fjords are a testament to nature's grandeur, flightseeing also offers moments of quiet intimacy. The serenity of the landscape, the tranquility of the fjords, and the sensation of gliding through the air create a space for reflection and contemplation. As you absorb the breathtaking vistas, you might find yourself transported to a place of stillness, where the worries of the world below fade into insignificance.

The choice to experience Misty Fjords through flightseeing is also a choice to preserve its pristine beauty. By exploring from the air, you minimize your impact on the fragile ecosystems that thrive within the monument. This form of ecotourism allows visitors to appreciate the landscape's majesty while ensuring that its delicate balance remains undisturbed.

Describing the experience of flightseeing in Misty Fjords with mere words falls short of capturing its true essence. It's a sensory symphony—a visual feast, an auditory tapestry, and an emotional connection with nature's wonders. It's a journey that transcends language, inviting you to be a participant in a moment of pure awe and wonder. It's a reminder that, in a world filled with noise and distractions, there are still places where the soul can find solace and inspiration.

In conclusion, scenic flightseeing over Misty Fjords National Monument is a privilege that grants a glimpse into a world of extraordinary beauty. It's an opportunity to witness the majesty of fjords, waterfalls, and wildlife from a perspective that few have the chance to experience. Beyond the aesthetic pleasures, flightseeing in Misty Fjords offers a space for reflection, contemplation, and a deep appreciation for the natural wonders that shape our planet. As you soar above this otherworldly landscape, you become part of a narrative that celebrates the awe-inspiring power and beauty of the natural world.

Wildlife Watching: Eagles and Bears

In the rugged and untamed wilderness of Alaska, a spectacular world of wildlife awaits those who venture into its embrace. From the majestic sweep of eagles in the sky to the lumbering grace of bears along the shores, Alaska's diverse landscapes provide a haven for some of the most iconic and awe-inspiring creatures on the planet. Wildlife watching in Alaska is not just an activity; it's a profound connection with the natural world, a chance to witness these magnificent animals in their natural habitats and to glimpse the beauty and complexity of life in the wild.

Alaska is often referred to as the "Eagle's Domain," and for good reason. The bald eagle, a symbol of strength, freedom, and national pride, finds its realm in these pristine landscapes. With its striking white head, powerful beak, and impressive wingspan, the bald eagle commands attention as it soars high above the land and water. In Alaska, witnessing the flight of an eagle is like observing a living embodiment of the wild spirit that defines the region.

Observing eagles in flight is a privilege that connects observers with the beauty of flight and the mastery of aerial navigation. Eagles are skilled at using thermal updrafts to effortlessly glide

through the skies, their keen eyesight scanning the terrain below for potential prey. The sight of eagles riding the currents with elegance and ease is a reminder of the intricacies of nature's design and the harmony that exists in the world of birds.

One of the most astonishing spectacles in Alaska's wildlife repertoire is the eagle feeding frenzy. During salmon runs, when these iconic fish return to their spawning grounds, eagles gather in large numbers along the rivers and streams. As salmon leap and splash, eagles swoop down with precision, snatching fish from the water's surface. The sight of dozens of eagles converging in a display of primal energy and instinct is a sight that leaves observers in awe.

Alaska is also home to another iconic creature—the bear. Brown bears and black bears roam the forests, mountains, and coastal areas of the state, embodying the majesty and mystery of the wilderness. These creatures, both powerful and elusive, offer a glimpse into the rhythms of life in the wild, reminding us of the delicate balance that sustains ecosystems.

Brown bears, also known as grizzly bears, are the epitome of Alaska's wilderness. With their hulking size and distinctive hump, these creatures are a testament to nature's ability to shape formidable predators. Observing a brown bear in its natural habitat is a privilege that grants insight into their behavior, from foraging along the shores for clams to fishing for salmon during the annual runs. Their methodical and deliberate movements reveal a wisdom honed by generations of survival in the wild.

Black bears, while smaller than their brown counterparts, are equally captivating. Their inky fur and often shy demeanor lend an air of mystery to their presence. Black bears are known for their versatility in diet, ranging from foraging for berries and plants to hunting small mammals. Spotting a black bear amidst the lush undergrowth or along a riverbank is a reminder of the dynamic nature of Alaska's ecosystems and the intricate web of life that exists within them.

In the Kodiak Archipelago, a subspecies of brown bear reigns supreme—the Kodiak bear. Known for their immense size and power, Kodiak bears are some of the largest terrestrial carnivores on the planet. These giants of the coast are expert fishers, patrolling the shores during salmon runs and demonstrating a formidable presence that commands respect. Observing a Kodiak bear in its natural habitat is a rare and humbling experience that underscores the true wildness of Alaska's landscapes.

The privilege of observing eagles and bears in the wild comes with a responsibility to engage in ethical wildlife watching. Respecting the animals' space, avoiding disruption of their behaviors, and adhering to guidelines set by experts and local authorities are essential components of responsible wildlife viewing. This approach ensures that our presence does not negatively impact the creatures we seek to admire and learn from.

Watching eagles and bears in their natural habitats provides a profound lesson in adaptation. These creatures have evolved to thrive in the harsh and ever-changing environments of Alaska.

The bald eagle's keen eyesight, the bear's ability to forage and hibernate, and their strategies for survival are a testament to the intricate balance between animal and environment. Witnessing their behaviors and interactions offers a deeper understanding of the delicate dance that defines life in the wild.

Wildlife watching in Alaska is more than just glimpsing creatures from a distance; it's an immersion in the untamed and unpredictable world of nature. It's about feeling the rush of emotion as an eagle soars overhead, capturing the intensity of a bear's gaze as it searches for food, and recognizing the vulnerability and strength of life in the wilderness. It's an invitation to step beyond the boundaries of human existence and connect with the primal rhythms of the Earth.

As you watch eagles and bears in their natural habitats, you become part of a symphony of life that reverberates through the ages. You witness the never-ending cycle of birth, survival, and death—a cycle that shapes the ecosystems of Alaska and reminds us of the interconnectedness of all living things. The eagle's flight, the bear's hunt, and the unfolding drama of the natural world become a chapter in a narrative that spans millennia.

The moments spent observing eagles and bears become treasures of memory. The silent gaze exchanged with a bear along the shore, the exhilaration of witnessing an eagle's catch, and the intimacy of these interactions become etched in the heart. These memories are more than snapshots; they're a reminder of the raw beauty and inherent value of the natural world.

In conclusion, wildlife watching in Alaska is an invitation to step into the heart of the wild. Observing eagles and bears in their natural habitats is an experience that transcends mere observation; it's a connection with the primal forces that define life on Earth. As you witness the majesty of eagles in flight and the prowess of bears along the shores, you're reminded of the fragile beauty and intricate balance of the ecosystems that make Alaska a haven for these iconic creatures. Through ethical and responsible wildlife watching, you become a participant in a narrative that celebrates the untamed spirit of the wilderness and the enduring wonder of the natural world.

Kayaking Adventures: Coastal Exploration

Amidst the pristine waters of Alaska's coastline, a world of adventure and tranquility beckons those who are willing to paddle into its embrace. Kayaking adventures along Alaska's coast offer a unique and intimate way to explore the rugged landscapes, abundant wildlife, and breathtaking vistas that define this remote region. From the serenity of gliding through glassy fjords to the exhilaration of navigating tidal currents, kayaking in Alaska is an experience that immerses adventurers in the heart of nature's grandeur and offers a profound connection with the wild.

Kayaking along Alaska's coastline is an invitation to uncover the magic that lies beyond the horizon. As you paddle through tranquil waters, you're enveloped by the ever-changing tapestry of nature—towering cliffs, lush forests, cascading waterfalls, and secluded coves. Coastal exploration by kayak allows you to venture into hidden corners that are often inaccessible by larger vessels, granting you the freedom to chart your own course and discover the untamed beauty of Alaska's shores.

Alaska's fjords and inlets are a testament to the powerful forces that have shaped the land. Glacial activity has carved deep channels into the coastline, creating a network of waterways that beckon kayakers to traverse their depths. Kayaking through fjords offers a sense of serenity as you glide along mirrored surfaces, the reflections of snow-capped peaks and verdant forests creating a mesmerizing panorama. Each paddle stroke becomes a rhythmic dance that propels you deeper into the heart of this majestic landscape.

One of the greatest thrills of kayaking in Alaska is the potential for encounters with marine life. As you paddle along the coast, you might spot seals sunbathing on rocky outcroppings or sea otters floating effortlessly on their backs. Whales, the gentle giants of the sea, breach and spout in the distance, their presence a reminder of the vastness of the ocean. These encounters are humbling reminders that you are a guest in the realm of these creatures, witnessing their lives in their natural habitat.

Alaska's coastline is adorned with a multitude of islands and shores waiting to be explored. Kayaking allows you to venture to places where human presence is minimal, where the rhythms of nature dictate the pace of life. You might discover secluded beaches where eagles perch and waves gently lap the shores, or you might navigate through labyrinthine channels that weave between islands, offering glimpses of untouched wilderness around every corner.

Kayaking in Alaska is not just about peaceful paddling; it's also an opportunity to experience the thrill of navigating tidal currents and rapids. The tides in Alaska can be dramatic, creating powerful currents that add an element of excitement to your journey. Skilled kayakers can harness these currents to their advantage, riding the tide like a natural roller coaster. Navigating through these dynamic waters offers a taste of adventure and a chance to test your skills against the forces of nature.

Kayaking in Alaska is a symphony that engages all your senses. The rhythmic splash of your paddle in the water, the salty scent of the sea breeze, the distant call of seabirds, and the cool touch of the water against your skin—all combine to create an immersive experience that

connects you with the environment. Each stroke of the paddle becomes a meditation, a chance to be present in the moment and fully absorb the beauty around you.

Kayaking along Alaska's coast offers a deeply personal connection with nature. As you paddle through the waters, you become attuned to the nuances of the environment—the subtle shifts in the weather, the ebb and flow of the tides, and the behaviors of the wildlife. This connection is a reminder that you are part of a larger ecosystem, a participant in the intricate web of life that defines these coastal landscapes.

For photographers, kayaking in Alaska is a dream come true. The unique vantage point of a kayak allows you to capture perspectives that are impossible to achieve from land or larger vessels. The juxtaposition of water and land, the interplay of light and shadow, and the reflections in the water create endless opportunities for striking images. Each photograph becomes a visual story that transports viewers to the heart of Alaska's wilderness.

ompleting a kayaking adventure along Alaska's coast is a testament to your own abilities and esilience. Navigating through diverse conditions, from calm waters to challenging currents, equires determination, skill, and adaptability. The sense of accomplishment that comes with uccessfully completing a journey—whether it's a day trip or a multi-day expedition—is a eminder of your capacity to embrace challenges and thrive in the face of adversity.

/hile kayaking allows you to access remote and pristine areas, it also comes with a esponsibility to practice ethical and responsible wilderness exploration. Respecting the nvironment, adhering to Leave No Trace principles, and following guidelines set by experts nd local authorities are essential components of responsible kayaking. By minimizing your npact, you contribute to the conservation of Alaska's natural beauty for generations to come.

ayaking adventures along Alaska's coast are not just about the physical act of paddling; they're journey of discovery and self-exploration. As you navigate the waters, you're also navigating he depths of your own thoughts and emotions. The solitude and quietude of the sea offer a pace for introspection, a chance to disconnect from the noise of modern life and reconnect vith the essence of your own being.

)escribing the experience of kayaking along Alaska's coast is a challenge, for words often fall hort of capturing the fullness of the experience. It's a journey that transcends language, a onnection that is felt deep within the soul. It's a reminder that, in the vastness of the natural vorld, you are a small yet integral part of a grand tapestry that has been woven through the ges.

n conclusion, kayaking adventures along Alaska's coast offer a transformative journey into the heart of nature's splendor. It's a chance to paddle through fjords, navigate tidal currents, and explore remote shores while immersing yourself in the beauty and tranquility of the wilderness. From encounters with marine life to the sense of accomplishment that comes with each stroke

of the paddle, kayaking in Alaska is an invitation to embrace adventure, connect with nature, and embark on a voyage of self-discovery. As you navigate the waters, you become a witness to the timeless dance between land and sea, a participant in the symphony of the wild, and a guardian of the delicate ecosystems that make Alaska's coast a haven for explorers and adventurers.

Great Alaskan Lumberjack Show: Entertaining Performance

In the heart of Alaska's rugged landscapes, where towering forests and untamed wilderness dominate the horizon, there exists a unique form of entertainment that pays homage to the region's rich history and culture—the Great Alaskan Lumberjack Show. This captivating performance is more than just a spectacle; it's a celebration of the spirit and grit that defined the lives of lumberjacks who forged their paths in this wild land. With a combination of skill, humor, and storytelling, the show brings to life the legacy of lumberjacks, their daring feats, and the camaraderie that bound them together.

The Great Alaskan Lumberjack Show is a tribute to the men and women who played a pivotal role in shaping the history of Alaska. In the late 19th and early 20th centuries, lumberjacks were the unsung heroes who harvested timber from the vast forests, often facing harsh conditions and dangerous challenges. The show's creators recognized the importance of preserving this heritage and devised a performance that not only entertains but also educates visitors about the vital role lumberjacks played in the development of the region.

At the heart of the Great Alaskan Lumberjack Show is a display of incredible skill and athleticism. Lumberjacks were known for their mastery of various tasks, from felling towering trees to precision axe throwing. The performers in the show demonstrate these skills with a level of precision and flair that captivates audiences of all ages. From the art of log rolling to the finesse of cross-cut sawing, each competition showcases the determination and dedication required to excel in the world of lumberjacking.

The Great Alaskan Lumberjack Show is a feast for the senses as performers engage in a series of timber sports events. These events, which originated from the practices of lumberjacks, showcase feats of strength, agility, and coordination. Axe throwing, underhand chopping, standing block chop, and springboard chop are just a few of the thrilling disciplines that bring the world of timber sports to life. The suspense of each event, as performers compete head-to-

head in a test of skill, adds an element of excitement that keeps audiences on the edge of their seats.

Beyond the skill and competition, the Great Alaskan Lumberjack Show is infused with humor and entertainment. The lumberjacks who participate in the show are not only talented athletes but also charismatic performers who engage the audience with their wit and comedic timing. Their banter, playful interactions, and humorous commentary create a lively atmosphere that resonates with visitors of all ages. The laughter that fills the air is a testament to the show's ability to captivate hearts and minds.

Interwoven within the performances are historical narratives that provide insight into the lives of lumberjacks and the challenges they faced. Through storytelling, the show transports audiences back in time, offering glimpses into the grit and determination required to thrive in

Alaska's wilderness. These narratives pay homage to the legacy of lumberjacks while highlighting the resilience and camaraderie that characterized their way of life.

The Great Alaskan Lumberjack Show also underscores the cultural significance of lumberjacks in Alaska's history. Lumberjacks were not merely workers; they were symbols of resilience, adaptability, and the pursuit of adventure. Their stories are woven into the fabric of Alaska's identity, reflecting the spirit of exploration and survival that defines the state. The show serves as a bridge between the past and the present, connecting modern audiences with the heritage of those who came before.

One of the distinctive aspects of the Great Alaskan Lumberjack Show is its interactive nature. Audience members are often invited to participate in the show, whether it's cheering for their favorite lumberjack or trying their hand at log rolling. This engagement adds a layer of immersion that transforms spectators into active participants, creating a sense of community and shared experience. The cheers and applause that resound from the audience contribute to the electric energy of the show.

While the Great Alaskan Lumberjack Show is undeniably entertaining, it also offers educational value by shedding light on a lesser-known aspect of Alaska's history. The show's performances are an opportunity for visitors to learn about the challenges, skills, and customs of lumberjacks who navigated the rugged terrain and harnessed the resources of the land. This educational component enriches the experience, allowing audiences to gain a deeper appreciation for the hardships and triumphs of those who contributed to Alaska's development.

The Great Alaskan Lumberjack Show caters to audiences of all ages, making it a popular choice for families seeking wholesome and engaging entertainment. Children are captivated by the displays of strength and skill, while parents and grandparents relish the nostalgic elements that transport them to an era of exploration and adventure. The show's ability to resonate with multiple generations creates a shared experience that fosters connection and camaraderie.

In a world driven by modern technology and rapid change, the Great Alaskan Lumberjack Show serves as a guardian of tradition. It honors a way of life that was defined by hard work, resourcefulness, and a deep connection to the land. By preserving and presenting this tradition through entertaining performances, the show ensures that the legacy of lumberjacks remains alive and accessible to present and future generations.

For visitors to Alaska, the Great Alaskan Lumberjack Show offers an authentic and immersive experience that captures the spirit of the Last Frontier. It's an opportunity to step into a world where axes and saws were the tools of the trade, where competition was fierce yet camaraderie prevailed, and where the wilderness served as both workplace and playground. The show encapsulates the essence of Alaska's history and landscape, providing a unique window into the past while offering modern audiences an unforgettable journey of entertainment.

In conclusion, the Great Alaskan Lumberjack Show is more than just an entertaining performance; it's a celebration of resilience, skill, and camaraderie. Through timber sports, comedy, historical narratives, and interactive engagement, the show transports audiences to a time when lumberjacks were the backbone of Alaska's development. It's a tribute to those who embraced the challenges of the wilderness and left an indelible mark on the state's history. The show's ability to entertain, educate, and inspire ensures that the legacy of lumberjacks continues to thrive, reminding us of the enduring spirit that defines Alaska's identity.

Tongass Historical Museum: Preserving Local History

Nestled in the heart of Ketchikan, Alaska, lies a treasure trove of stories, artifacts, and memories—the Tongass Historical Museum. This unassuming building holds within its walls a rich tapestry of local history, a testament to the people, cultures, and events that have shaped the region over the centuries. Stepping into the Tongass Historical Museum is like embarking on a journey through time, a chance to immerse oneself in the past and gain a deeper understanding of the unique heritage that defines Ketchikan and its surrounding areas.

The Tongass Historical Museum serves as a bridge between the present and the past, offering visitors a rare glimpse into the lives of those who came before. Through carefully curated exhibits, photographs, documents, and artifacts, the museum weaves a narrative that spans centuries. From the Indigenous peoples who first inhabited the area to the intrepid pioneers who settled along the waterfront, the museum's collections illuminate the stories of individuals and communities that have left an indelible mark on Ketchikan's history.

One of the hallmarks of the Tongass Historical Museum is its celebration of cultural diversity. Alaska's history is a tapestry woven with threads from various cultures, including Indigenous Tlingit, Haida, and Tsimshian communities, as well as the influences of European explorers, Russian traders, and American settlers. The museum's exhibits showcase the unique traditions, art forms, and way of life of these diverse groups, fostering an appreciation for the cultural mosaic that shapes Ketchikan's identity.

The museum's collection of Tlingit and Haida artifacts is a window into the worldviews and artistic expressions of Alaska's Indigenous peoples. From intricately carved totem poles that stand as testament to ancestral stories to intricately woven baskets that blend beauty and functionality, these artifacts embody the rich heritage of the region's First Nations. The museum's commitment to preserving and sharing these treasures honors the legacy of the Tlingit and Haida peoples and ensures that their traditions continue to thrive.

Ketchikan's history is closely intertwined with its maritime heritage. The Tongass Historical Museum pays homage to the brave souls who ventured into the rugged landscapes, establishing settlements and livelihoods along the waterfront. Exhibits dedicated to pioneer life offer a glimpse into the challenges and triumphs of those who carved out a new existence in a land of endless possibilities and hardships. The maritime history of Ketchikan is also celebrated, with displays that highlight the importance of fishing, logging, and boatbuilding in shaping the community.

The late 19th and early 20th centuries saw a flurry of activity in Alaska due to the Klondike Gold Rush. The museum's exhibits transport visitors back to this transformative period, when gold fever gripped the nation and fortune seekers flocked to the Last Frontier in search of riches. The stories of prospectors, entrepreneurs, and dreamers come to life through photographs, personal accounts, and artifacts, offering a vivid portrayal of a time when the promise of gold lured adventurers to Alaska's rugged landscapes.

The Tongass Historical Museum captures the essence of the Alaskan way of life—characterized by self-reliance, resilience, and a deep connection to the land and sea. Through displays of tools, equipment, and household items used by early settlers, the museum paints a picture of the resourcefulness required to thrive in a challenging environment. From canneries and logging camps to the development of infrastructure and transportation, the exhibits illustrate the evolution of Ketchikan as a vibrant and thriving community.

One of the invaluable roles of the Tongass Historical Museum is its ability to shift perspectives and challenge assumptions. By presenting the complexities of history, the museum encourages visitors to consider multiple viewpoints and engage in thoughtful reflection. The stories of both triumph and adversity, the intersections of cultures, and the dynamics of societal change prompt visitors to question, learn, and broaden their understanding of the past and its relevance to the present.

The Tongass Historical Museum is not merely a repository of artifacts; it's a dynamic hub of community engagement. Through educational programs, workshops, lectures, and special events, the museum fosters a sense of connection between past and present. It encourages intergenerational dialogue, invites residents to share their own stories, and facilitates conversations that contribute to a deeper appreciation for Ketchikan's history and the bonds that tie the community together.

The Tongass Historical Museum's mission extends beyond the present moment—it's about preserving heritage for future generations. Through meticulous conservation efforts and thoughtful curation, the museum ensures that the stories of Ketchikan's past remain accessible and relevant for years to come. The preservation of artifacts, photographs, and documents safeguards the memory of those who came before, allowing their experiences to continue to inspire and inform.

Stepping into the Tongass Historical Museum is an invitation to reflect on the interconnectedness of time, culture, and place. As visitors explore the exhibits, they encounter stories that resonate with the universal themes of human experience—perseverance, innovation, adaptation, and community. The museum's role as a repository of collective memory encourages visitors to consider their own place within this continuum and to recognize the significance of individual stories in shaping the broader narrative.

In conclusion, the Tongass Historical Museum is a living legacy that honors the past, educates the present, and inspires the future. Through its exhibits, artifacts, and narratives, the museum offers a window into the multi-faceted history of Ketchikan and its people. It reminds us that history is not a static record but a vibrant tapestry that weaves together diverse threads of experience. As visitors traverse the museum's halls, they embark on a journey of discovery— one that deepens their connection to the past and fosters a greater appreciation for the vibrant tapestry of Alaska's history.

Whale-Watching Tours: Discovering Marine Marvels

In the pristine waters of Alaska's coastal realms, a remarkable spectacle unfolds—a dance of giants beneath the waves. Whale-watching tours offer a front-row seat to one of nature's most awe-inspiring performances, where the mighty creatures of the sea breach, spout, and glide through the ocean's expanse. As the salty breeze caresses your skin and the cry of seabirds fills the air, you become a witness to a timeless symphony of life, a journey into the heart of the marine world that captivates, educates, and transforms.

Whale-watching tours in Alaska unveil a symphony of giants that grace the ocean's surface. Humpback whales, orcas, gray whales, and minke whales are just a few of the majestic creatures that call these waters home. Their sheer size and graceful movements inspire wonder, their behaviors a reminder of the intricate lives that unfold beneath the waves. As you set sail on a whale-watching expedition, you embark on a quest to encounter these marine marvels in their natural habitat.

Among the stars of Alaska's whale-watching tours are humpback whales, renowned for their acrobatics and charismatic behaviors. Witnessing a humpback breach—leaping out of the water and crashing back with a tremendous splash—is a sight that elicits gasps of amazement. These displays are not only captivating to watch but also carry deeper meanings, from communication to courtship. The distinctive patterns on the underside of their flukes serve as unique identifiers, a reminder of the individuality of each whale.

Orcas, also known as killer whales, are apex predators of the ocean, exuding an aura of power and mystery. Their sleek black-and-white bodies glide through the water with precision and grace. Orcas are known for their complex social structures and intricate communication systems, which vary between different pods and regions. Observing these intelligent creatures navigate the waters in coordinated groups is a testament to the bonds that tie their communities together.

Gray whales embark on one of the longest migrations of any mammal, traveling thousands of miles between their feeding grounds in Alaska and their breeding grounds in Baja California. Witnessing the annual migration of gray whales is a humbling experience that underscores the endurance and resilience of these marine giants. The sight of a mother and calf swimming in tandem speaks to the delicate balance of life in the ocean and the connection between generations.

Minke whales, with their elusive nature, add an air of mystery to Alaska's waters. Despite their relatively small size compared to other whale species, minke whales possess a sense of curiosity that often leads them to approach boats. These enigmatic creatures provide opportunities for up-close encounters, allowing passengers on whale-watching tours to observe their behaviors and movements in more detail.

Whale-watching tours in Alaska offer more than just a visual spectacle; they are educational expeditions that provide insight into the complex marine ecosystems. Expert naturalists and marine biologists often accompany these tours, sharing their knowledge about the biology, behaviors, and conservation efforts related to the whales and the surrounding environment. These guided experiences transform the tour into a learning opportunity, fostering a deeper understanding of the interconnected web of life in the ocean.

Whale-watching tours play a crucial role in promoting eco-tourism and conservation efforts. By offering visitors the chance to observe marine life in their natural habitats, these tours foster a sense of appreciation and connection to the ocean's wonders. This connection, in turn, nurtures a desire to protect and preserve these delicate ecosystems. Responsible whale-watching practices, such as maintaining a respectful distance from the animals and adhering to guidelines that minimize disturbance, contribute to the well-being of marine species.

On a whale-watching tour, you become privy to a diverse array of behaviors that illuminate the lives of these ocean inhabitants. Breaching, where whales launch themselves out of the water, is not only a spectacular display but also a way to shed parasites and communicate with others. Tail slapping, where a whale strikes the water's surface with its fluke, creates a resounding sound that carries underwater. Spouting, or blowing, reveals the presence of a whale as it exhales through its blowhole, sending a misty plume into the air.

Whale-watching tours often align with the migratory and feeding patterns of these marine creatures. During the summer months, nutrient-rich waters attract humpback whales to Alaska's coast to feed on krill and small fish. The spectacle of a humpback whale lunging through a swarm of prey, mouth agape, is a testament to the intricacies of the marine food chain. Observing these behaviors allows passengers to witness the delicate balance that sustains life in the ocean.

Whales are known for their complex vocalizations and communication strategies. Humpback whales, for instance, produce a variety of sounds, from haunting songs that can last for hours to social calls that convey information to other members of their pod. Orcas have distinct dialects that vary among different groups, contributing to their intricate social structure. Whale-watching tours often feature hydrophones that allow passengers to listen to the mesmerizing melodies and conversations of these underwater symphonies.

Whale-watching tours offer a profound connection with the natural world that is difficult to replicate elsewhere. The vastness of the ocean, the mystery of the depths, and the humbling presence of these marine giants combine to create an experience that transcends words. As you watch a whale breach, dive, or spout, you become part of a shared moment—a fleeting intersection of human and animal worlds that evokes a sense of wonder and humility.

Participating in whale-watching tours also holds the potential to ignite a passion for conservation. Witnessing these magnificent creatures thriving in their natural habitats underscores the importance of safeguarding the oceans and the fragile ecosystems they support. It serves as a reminder that the choices we make on land have a direct impact on the well-being of marine life. Whale-watching tours cultivate a sense of responsibility and stewardship that extends beyond the tour itself.

In conclusion, whale-watching tours offer an unparalleled opportunity to witness the magic of marine life in Alaska's waters. From the awe-inspiring breaches to the intricate social behaviors these tours provide a window into the lives of whales that captivates the imagination and tugs at the heartstrings. The experience is a symphony of senses—of salty air, the rush of excitement, the sight of majestic creatures, and the knowledge that you are witnessing nature's marvels. It's a memory of a lifetime, a journey into the heart of the ocean that leaves an indelible mark on your soul and a renewed appreciation for the magnificence of the natural world.

Ketchikan: A Blend of History and Nature

Nestled along the southeastern coast of Alaska, Ketchikan stands as a vibrant testament to the rich tapestry of history, culture, and natural beauty that defines the Last Frontier. This picturesque port city, embraced by the Tongass National Forest and kissed by the waters of the Inside Passage, offers visitors an immersive experience that seamlessly weaves together the allure of its indigenous heritage, the legacy of the salmon industry, and the breathtaking landscapes that surround it.

Ketchikan's story begins with the Tlingit people, whose roots in the region stretch back for centuries. These indigenous inhabitants, with a deep connection to the land and sea, have left their mark on Ketchikan's cultural landscape. Totem poles, carved with intricate designs that carry stories of generations past, grace the city and serve as a vivid reminder of the Tlingit's artistic and spiritual legacy. The Totem Heritage Center stands as a treasure trove of these masterful creations, offering insights into the traditions and narratives that have shaped the lives of the Tlingit and other native communities.

Saxman Native Village, just a short drive from Ketchikan, offers an immersive journey into the heart of Tlingit culture. This living cultural village welcomes visitors with open arms, inviting them to witness traditional Tlingit dances, observe intricate totem pole carvings in progress, and engage with artisans who are preserving and sharing their heritage. As you walk through Saxman, the resonance of drums and the swaying movements of dancers create an enchanting atmosphere that transports you to a realm where past and present seamlessly coexist.

Salmon, often referred to as the lifeblood of Alaska, holds a special place in Ketchikan's history. The city's heritage is intertwined with the ebb and flow of salmon runs that have sustained generations of residents. Visitors to Ketchikan have the opportunity to delve into this legacy at the Southeast Alaska Discovery Center, where exhibits explore the intricate life cycle of salmon and their ecological importance to the region. Witnessing the annual salmon runs and learning about their role in the ecosystem offers a newfound appreciation for the delicate balance of nature.

Creek Street, with its charming wooden buildings perched above Ketchikan Creek, exudes the nostalgic charm of a bygone era. Once a red-light district during the Gold Rush era, this historic boardwalk now hosts an array of shops, galleries, and museums. Wandering along Creek Street provides a glimpse into Ketchikan's past, as well as stunning views of the creek and the fish ladder where salmon navigate their way upstream.

Beyond its cultural treasures, Ketchikan embraces its natural surroundings with open arms. The Tongass National Forest, the largest national forest in the United States, envelops the city in a blanket of towering trees, lush foliage, and serene landscapes. Kayakers and hikers are beckoned by the siren call of Misty Fjords National Monument, where mist-shrouded cliffs, cascading waterfalls, and secluded coves create an otherworldly tableau. The majesty of the outdoors is a testament to Alaska's unyielding beauty, inviting exploration and introspection.

Ketchikan's proximity to both the water and the wilderness lends itself to a plethora of outdoor adventures. Guided kayaking tours allow you to paddle through tranquil waters while absorbing the grandeur of the Alaskan landscapes. Wildlife enthusiasts can embark on whale-watching excursions, where encounters with humpback whales, orcas, and seals are not uncommon. For those seeking a more hands-on experience, sportfishing trips provide the chance to reel in some of Alaska's prized catches, including salmon and halibut.

A visit to Ketchikan isn't complete without savoring the flavors of the region. Seafood takes center stage, with freshly caught salmon and halibut gracing the menus of local restaurants. Indulge in the culinary offerings while engaging with the warmth and hospitality of Ketchikan's residents. The community's spirit is palpable, whether you're perusing local art galleries, enjoying a performance by a Tlingit dance group, or simply engaging in conversation with those who call this place home.

In conclusion, Ketchikan stands as a microcosm of Alaska's splendor, where the pages of history intertwine with the vibrant pulse of nature. From its indigenous heritage to the legacy of salmon, the city invites visitors to immerse themselves in a journey that awakens the senses and stirs the soul. Ketchikan's harmonious blend of history, culture, and natural beauty paints a canvas that remains etched in the hearts of those fortunate enough to experience its wonders.

Attractions and Activities

Sitka, a coastal gem nestled in the heart of Alaska's Inside Passage, seamlessly blends its rich history with its awe-inspiring natural surroundings. This unique combination creates a tapestry of attractions and activities that offer visitors a multifaceted experience. Here are five of the best attractions and activities in Sitka, where history, culture, and nature converge:

1. Sitka National Historical Park: A Journey Through Time

Sitka National Historical Park, often referred to as Totem Park, encapsulates the essence of Sitka's cultural heritage. The park is home to a stunning collection of intricately carved totem poles, each telling a story of the indigenous Tlingit people. These towering works of art stand as testaments to the cultural legacy of the region. The park also features walking trails that wind through lush forests and along the coast, offering opportunities to witness wildlife and immerse yourself in the tranquility of nature.

2. Russian Bishop's House: A Glimpse into Sitka's Colonial Past

The Russian Bishop's House stands as a well-preserved relic of Sitka's colonial history. Constructed in the early 19th century, this elegant building served as the residence for Russian Orthodox bishops. Today, it operates as a museum that transports visitors back in time, offering insights into Sitka's role as the Russian colonial capital. The Russian Bishop's House showcases period furnishings, exhibits on Russian-Alaskan history, and a garden that evokes the essence of the past.

3. Alaska Raptor Center: A Haven for Birds of Prey

Nestled in the heart of Sitka, the Alaska Raptor Center is a sanctuary dedicated to the rehabilitation and conservation of injured birds of prey. Visitors have the opportunity to witness these magnificent creatures up close and learn about the center's efforts to protect and rehabilitate them. The center's captivating educational programs shed light on the critical role these birds play in Alaska's ecosystems and inspire a deeper appreciation for their importance.

4. Sitka Sound Science Center: Exploring Marine Ecology

For those intrigued by marine life and ecosystems, the Sitka Sound Science Center is a must-visit destination. This dynamic facility offers interactive exhibits that delve into the unique marine ecology of the region. Visitors can learn about the delicate balance of coastal ecosystems, witness marine creatures in touch tanks, and gain insights into the ongoing research efforts to understand and conserve Sitka's natural wonders.

5. Wildlife Tours and Outdoor Adventures: Embracing Nature

Sitka's pristine landscapes and abundant wildlife invite visitors to embark on a myriad of outdoor adventures. From guided kayaking tours that navigate serene waterways to whale-watching excursions that unveil the majesty of humpback whales breaching the surface, there's no shortage of opportunities to connect with nature. Hiking trails, such as the Gavan Hill Trail, offer breathtaking vistas and encounters with indigenous flora and fauna.

In conclusion, Sitka's blend of history and nature creates a harmonious tapestry of attractions and activities that cater to a diverse range of interests. Whether you're captivated by indigenous culture, intrigued by colonial history, fascinated by birds of prey, curious about marine ecology, or simply yearning to immerse yourself in Alaska's breathtaking landscapes, Sitka offers a wealth of experiences that resonate with the soul and leave a lasting impression.

Sitka National Historical Park: A Journey Through Time

Nestled on the western coast of Baranof Island in Alaska's Inside Passage, Sitka National Historical Park stands as a testament to the rich cultural heritage and natural beauty that define the Last Frontier. This captivating park, often lovingly referred to as Totem Park, seamlessly weaves together the threads of indigenous history, the splendor of pristine landscapes, and the allure of captivating artistry. As you step into the embrace of Sitka National Historical Park, you embark on a journey through time—an exploration of the stories, traditions, and connections that have shaped the tapestry of Sitka's past and present.

At the heart of Sitka National Historical Park lies a vibrant celebration of the Tlingit people, the indigenous inhabitants of the region. The Tlingit have deep roots in the lands surrounding Sitka, and their history is etched into every corner of the park. One of the most iconic elements of Totem Park is its collection of intricately carved totem poles. These towering works of art serve as storytellers, each pole telling tales of clan lineage, legends, and communal bonds.

As you walk along the park's pathways, you're invited to explore a diverse array of totem poles. The Tlingit and Haida poles, crafted with remarkable skill and adorned with mesmerizing designs, offer a window into the culture's artistic brilliance. The totem poles are more than mere sculptures; they are living expressions of heritage, identity, and the passage of time.

The Totem Walk within Sitka National Historical Park is a journey of discovery that introduces visitors to the significance of each totem pole. As you stroll through the forested pathways, ou'll encounter plaques and interpretive signs that provide context for the totem poles you encounter. These insights delve into the stories behind the carvings, the symbolism of the figures depicted, and the cultural narratives that have been passed down through generations.

The Totem Walk is a bridge that spans the realms of history and modernity. It connects visitors to the Tlingit's reverence for nature, their deep connection to the land and sea, and their belief in the intertwining of the spiritual and physical worlds. Each step reveals the layers of meaning embedded in the totem poles, inviting you to witness the essence of the Tlingit way of life.

At the heart of Sitka National Historical Park, the Naa Kahidi Community House stands as a living testament to the vitality of Tlingit culture. This clan house is an embodiment of Tlingit architecture and craftsmanship, constructed with traditional methods and adorned with intricate carvings. The clan house serves as a gathering space for ceremonies, cultural events, and educational programs that honor the Tlingit heritage.

Inside the clan house, the atmosphere is steeped in authenticity and reverence. The air is filled with the resonance of drumbeats and traditional songs, transporting visitors into a realm where the past is alive and the present is enriched by the echoes of history. The clan house serves as a vessel for storytelling, a space where the Tlingit narrative is shared with visitors from around the world.

Sitka National Historical Park stands as a testament to the commitment to preserving cultural heritage and natural beauty. The park's conservation efforts extend beyond totem poles and clan houses, encompassing the surrounding landscapes and ecosystems. The coastal rainforest, tidal flats, and estuary habitats create a canvas upon which the interplay between land and sea unfolds.

The park's role as a refuge for both cultural heritage and ecological diversity highlights the interconnectedness of human history and the natural world. The preservation of these spaces serves as an affirmation of the respect and reverence that the Tlingit and subsequent generations have shown toward the land that sustains them.

Sitka National Historical Park isn't just a repository of history; it's a bridge that connects people from different walks of life. Through cultural exchange programs, interpretive exhibits, and guided tours, the park invites visitors to embark on a journey of understanding and empathy.

The stories of the Tlingit people resonate with universal themes of identity, community, and the pursuit of harmony with the environment.

Visitors are encouraged to engage with the narratives of the Tlingit, to appreciate the intricacies of their artistry, and to gain insights into their profound relationship with the natural world. In doing so, a sense of interconnectedness emerges—a recognition that the lessons of history have the power to shape our collective future.

Sitka National Historical Park embodies the spirit of Alaska—an untamed and breathtaking realm where history, culture, and nature intertwine. Through the totem poles, clan houses, and landscapes, the park imparts lessons of respect for traditions, the importance of stewardship, and the boundless beauty that arises from the intersection of human creativity and the wonders of the natural world.

As you stand within the embrace of Totem Park, you're not merely a spectator; you're a participant in a journey through time. With each step, you honor the legacy of the Tlingit, celebrate the wisdom of the past, and carry forth the lessons of cultural appreciation and environmental preservation. Sitka National Historical Park stands as a living testament to the idea that history isn't confined to the pages of textbooks—it's alive, vibrant, and waiting to be discovered in the very landscapes that have borne witness to its unfolding.

Russian Bishop's House: A Glimpse into Sitka's Colonial Past

Perched on the shores of Sitka, Alaska, the Russian Bishop's House stands as a stately and enduring relic of a bygone era—a tangible link to the colonial history that has left an indelible mark on this picturesque coastal town. With its elegant architecture, fascinating exhibits, and immersive historical ambiance, the Russian Bishop's House offers visitors a captivating journey back in time, providing a window into the complexities of Sitka's colonial past and the convergence of cultures that shaped its destiny.

In the early 19th century, the Russian-American Company, a powerful trading enterprise under the patronage of the Russian Imperial Crown, sought to expand its influence and control over the lucrative fur trade in the North Pacific region. Sitka, known then as New Archangel, became the capital of Russian America—a strategic outpost that facilitated trade with indigenous peoples and European powers.

The Russian Bishop's House, built between 1841 and 1843, served as the residence of the Russian Orthodox bishops who oversaw the spiritual and administrative affairs of the Russian settlements in Alaska. As a testament to the influence of the Russian Orthodox Church in the region, the house stands as a physical representation of the ambitions, challenges, and cultural intersections that characterized this colonial period.

The Russian Bishop's House is a remarkable example of Russian colonial architecture, distinguished by its graceful lines, prominent roofline, and distinctive onion domes—a hallmark of Russian Orthodox design. The building's exterior is a captivating blend of Russian and Alaskan materials, featuring local red cedar and Sitka spruce. As you approach the house, its graceful façade and intricate woodwork offer a glimpse into the craftsmanship of a bygone era.

Stepping inside, you're transported to a world that reverberates with history. The interior has been meticulously restored to capture the ambiance of the 19th century, with period furnishings, religious artifacts, and vivid exhibits that bring the colonial past to life. Each room tells a story—a narrative of the Russian Orthodox Church's presence, the relationships forged with indigenous communities, and the challenges faced by both settlers and native peoples in this remote corner of the world.

The Russian Bishop's House embodies the multifaceted interactions that characterized colonial Sitka. While the Russian-American Company aimed to establish a fur trading empire, the Russian Orthodox Church sought to spread its faith and cultural norms among the indigenous peoples. This convergence of interests and ideologies had profound impacts on both the local communities and the European settlers.

The house offers insights into the cultural exchanges that took place within its walls. As the residence of the bishops, it became a center for religious gatherings, educational pursuits, and interactions with native Alaskans. These interactions, often marked by mutual curiosity and respect, fostered a complex web of human connections that transcended language and cultural barriers.

The exhibits within the Russian Bishop's House serve as portals that transport visitors to a time when Sitka was at the crossroads of global powers and indigenous civilizations. Artifacts, paintings, and religious items on display offer glimpses into the daily lives of the Russian Orthodox clergy and the native Alaskans. The spiritual significance of these objects, coupled with their historical context, provides a layered understanding of the challenges and triumphs of the colonial period.

One of the highlights of the house is the chapel—a sacred space that encapsulates the spiritual aspirations of the Russian Orthodox Church. The chapel's richly adorned interior, adorned with icons and religious art, echoes with the echoes of prayers offered by generations past. It stands as a testament to the enduring nature of faith and its role in shaping history.

The preservation of the Russian Bishop's House is a labor of love that speaks to the importance of honoring history. The dedicated efforts to restore and maintain the building ensure that future generations can continue to engage with the stories it holds. Educational programs, guided tours, and interpretive exhibits offer visitors the chance to deepen their understanding of the colonial era and its impact on Sitka's identity.

Through the lens of the Russian Bishop's House, visitors gain a nuanced perspective on the dynamics of colonialism—a phenomenon that shaped the course of human history, often leaving behind complex legacies that continue to influence contemporary society. The house serves as a space for reflection, prompting dialogue about cultural exchange, identity, and the narratives that weave individuals and communities together.

As you explore the Russian Bishop's House, you're reminded that the history contained within its walls is not confined to the past—it reverberates with relevance today. The stories of resilience, adaptation, and coexistence offer lessons that resonate in our interconnected world. The house stands as a monument to the ability of human beings to forge connections amidst differences and to navigate the challenges of unfamiliar landscapes.

In conclusion, the Russian Bishop's House is more than an architectural gem; it's a portal to the past—a testament to the multifaceted interactions that have shaped Sitka's history. Through its exhibits, artifacts, and evocative atmosphere, the house invites visitors to step into the shoes of those who once called it home. It celebrates the complexities of colonial encounters, fosters appreciation for the architectural heritage that endures, and offers a space for contemplation about the echoes of the past that continue to resonate in the present.

Alaska Raptor Center: A Haven for Birds of Prey

Nestled within the captivating landscapes of Sitka, Alaska, lies a sanctuary of healing and hope—the Alaska Raptor Center. This haven for birds of prey stands as a testament to the commitment of dedicated individuals who work tirelessly to rehabilitate injured raptors, educate the public, and advocate for the conservation of these majestic creatures. With its mission rooted in compassion, education, and the preservation of avian diversity, the Alaska Raptor Center offers visitors a unique opportunity to connect with these remarkable birds, gain insights into their vital role in ecosystems, and witness the transformative power of human care.

Birds of prey, also known as raptors, occupy a special place in the intricate web of ecosystems. These magnificent creatures, which include eagles, owls, hawks, and falcons, serve as apex predators, playing a crucial role in maintaining the balance of nature. From controlling rodent populations to shaping the behavior of their prey, raptors contribute to the health and sustainability of ecosystems worldwide.

However, the lives of these birds are not without challenges. Injuries caused by accidents, collisions with vehicles, or encounters with human-made hazards can leave raptors vulnerable and in need of assistance. This is where the Alaska Raptor Center steps in—a place of refuge that offers a second chance at life for these awe-inspiring avian hunters.

Founded in 1980, the Alaska Raptor Center's mission revolves around the rehabilitation, education, and conservation of birds of prey. The center's staff and volunteers are dedicated to providing expert care for injured raptors, nursing them back to health, and preparing them for their eventual return to the wild whenever possible. The journey from admission to release is a collaborative effort that involves medical attention, rehabilitation facilities, and an unwavering commitment to the well-being of each individual bird.

At the center's clinic, injured raptors receive specialized care tailored to their unique needs. From setting broken bones to treating infections, the staff employs a combination of veterinary expertise and a deep understanding of raptor behavior to ensure the best possible outcome for each patient. As the birds progress in their recovery, they are gradually reintroduced to natural behaviors that are essential for their survival in the wild.

Beyond its role as a rehabilitation center, the Alaska Raptor Center serves as an educational hub—a place where visitors can connect with the world of raptors and gain a deeper appreciation for their ecological significance. Guided tours, interactive exhibits, and captivating educational programs offer a window into the lives of these birds and the challenges they face.

The center's educational initiatives are designed to spark curiosity and instill a sense of stewardship for the natural world. Visitors are invited to witness live raptor presentations, where the grace and power of these birds are on full display. The up-close encounters foster empathy and understanding, encouraging visitors to consider the importance of preserving habitats, minimizing human impact, and coexisting harmoniously with the creatures that share our planet.

The Alaska Raptor Center's impact extends beyond its sanctuary gates. The center is a staunch advocate for raptor conservation, championing efforts to protect habitats, raise awareness about threats to raptors, and promote responsible human behavior in their shared environments. Through community engagement, public programs, and partnerships with like-minded organizations, the center amplifies the message of raptor conservation and the need to ensure a sustainable future for these vital predators.

In addition to its rehabilitation and education efforts, the Alaska Raptor Center contributes to scientific research and data collection that inform conservation strategies. By studying raptor behavior, migration patterns, and the impact of human activities on their populations, the

center plays a critical role in expanding our understanding of these magnificent creatures. The knowledge gained from these studies is essential for shaping effective conservation policies and safeguarding the future of raptors in the wild.

The stories of raptors that find their way to the Alaska Raptor Center are stories of resilience, determination, and the transformative power of human care. Through skilled rehabilitation, these birds are given a second chance—a chance to once again soar through the skies, hunt for prey, and contribute to the delicate balance of ecosystems. The release of rehabilitated raptors back into their natural habitats is a poignant reminder of the impact that compassion and expertise can have on the lives of individual animals and the broader environment.

The Alaska Raptor Center's work serves as a call to action—a reminder that the well-being of raptors is intertwined with the health of our planet. As visitors witness the dedication of the center's staff, the resilience of rehabilitated birds, and the majesty of raptors in flight, they are encouraged to consider their role in the conservation of these creatures.

Support for the Alaska Raptor Center takes many forms, from financial contributions that fuel rehabilitation efforts to responsible behavior that minimizes human impact on raptor habitats. By connecting with the center's mission, visitors become ambassadors for raptor conservation, sharing the knowledge they've gained and inspiring others to take part in the collective effort to safeguard the future of these magnificent birds.

In conclusion, the Alaska Raptor Center stands as a beacon of hope—a place where the synergy of rehabilitation, education, advocacy, and research converges to create a haven for birds of prey. The center's impact transcends its physical boundaries, reaching into the hearts of those who are touched by the stories of recovery and release. Through its transformative work, the center reminds us of the profound interconnectedness of all living beings and the responsibility we share to preserve the diversity and vitality of our natural world.

Sitka Sound Science Center: Exploring Marine Ecology

Nestled on the shores of Sitka, Alaska, a place of wonder and discovery beckons—a place where the mysteries of marine ecology are unveiled, and the intricate relationships between land, sea, and life are illuminated. This place is the Sitka Sound Science Center, a beacon of knowledge and exploration that invites visitors to delve into the depths of marine ecosystems, gain insights into the delicate balance of coastal habitats, and forge connections between the natural world and human existence. Through its engaging exhibits, interactive programs, and commitment to

research, the center provides a gateway to understanding the vital role that marine environments play in shaping the planet's biodiversity and sustainability.

coastal environments are among the Earth's most dynamic and complex ecosystems, where the boundaries between land and sea blur and intertwine. The Sitka Sound Science Center is strategically located at this intersection, offering a unique vantage point to explore the diverse interactions that shape coastal life. This nexus of marine and terrestrial realms creates a tapestry of biological diversity, ecological processes, and environmental dynamics that the center aims to uncover and share.

One of the core missions of the Sitka Sound Science Center is to educate and inspire visitors, both young and old, about the wonders of marine ecology. The center achieves this goal through a variety of engaging and immersive experiences. Interactive exhibits draw visitors into the world of marine organisms, unveiling the hidden intricacies of underwater life. Touch tanks, filled with creatures ranging from tide pool inhabitants to marine invertebrates, encourage tactile exploration and foster a sense of connection to marine environments.

Guided tours and educational programs provide deeper insights into the center's work and the broader significance of marine ecosystems. Visitors have the opportunity to learn about local species, understand the interplay of environmental factors, and witness the vital role that healthy oceans play in maintaining the balance of life on Earth.

Marine ecology is a multidimensional field, encompassing a range of subjects from the smallest microorganisms to the largest marine mammals. The Sitka Sound Science Center serves as a hub for unlocking these marine mysteries through research, data collection, and scientific exploration.

The center's scientists and researchers engage in studies that contribute to our understanding of marine ecosystems, their responses to changing conditions, and the impact of human activities on marine life. By monitoring water quality, tracking species populations, and investigating ecological interactions, the center sheds light on the intricate web of life that thrives beneath the waves.

Estuaries, where freshwater from rivers meets saltwater from the sea, are some of the most productive and biodiverse ecosystems on Earth. The Sitka Sound Science Center's location on the edge of the Sitka Sound Estuary provides an ideal opportunity to study and appreciate the unique characteristics of this critical habitat.

Estuaries serve as nurseries for countless marine species, offering shelter, food, and ideal conditions for growth. The center's research focuses on understanding the dynamics of estuarine ecosystems, tracking migratory patterns of fish, and unraveling the complex relationships that support a multitude of species—from salmon to shorebirds.

Central to the ecological narrative of the Pacific Northwest is the iconic salmon, a keystone species that plays a pivotal role in the region's ecosystems. The Sitka Sound Science Center places a special emphasis on the life cycle of salmon, from their journey as eggs in freshwater streams to their return as fully grown adults.

Through interpretive displays, visitors learn about the intricate stages of salmon development and the challenges they face in navigating their way through the complex web of freshwater and marine environments. Understanding the salmon's journey provides insights into the broader connections between ecosystems, species interactions, and the cycles that sustain life in the North Pacific.

The Sitka Sound Science Center's impact extends beyond its physical exhibits and educational programs—it's deeply rooted in the local community. By fostering partnerships with schools, organizations, and indigenous communities, the center nurtures a sense of stewardship and environmental responsibility.

Through community engagement initiatives, the center empowers individuals to take an active role in the conservation of marine environments. Workshops, seminars, and collaborative projects promote awareness and sustainable practices, ensuring that the lessons learned within the center's walls resonate beyond its boundaries.

The Sitka Sound Science Center's work is a call to conservation—a reminder of the urgent need to protect and preserve our marine ecosystems. As visitors explore the intricacies of marine life they become advocates for the oceans, inspired to make choices that minimize human impact and promote sustainability.

Support for the center's mission takes many forms, from volunteering and participating in citizen science projects to promoting responsible fishing practices and advocating for marine conservation policies. Each act contributes to the broader effort to ensure the health and longevity of our oceans, safeguarding the delicate balance of life that thrives within them.

In conclusion, the Sitka Sound Science Center serves as a window to the wonder of marine ecology—a world of interconnectedness, complexity, and beauty that shapes our planet's future. Through its exhibits, programs, and research, the center invites us to explore the realms of underwater life, gain insights into the delicate balance of ecosystems, and recognize our role as stewards of the oceans. As we stand on the shores of Sitka, gazing out at the vast expanse of the Pacific, the center reminds us that the mysteries of the deep are within our reach, waiting to be uncovered, appreciated, and conserved for generations to come.

Wildlife Tours and Outdoor Adventures: Embracing Nature

In the heart of Alaska's untamed landscapes, where snow-capped peaks touch the sky and pristine waters stretch to the horizon, a world of wonder and wilderness awaits. Alaska's rugged beauty is a canvas upon which nature paints its most awe-inspiring scenes, and for those who seek to immerse themselves in the splendor of the wild, wildlife tours and outdoor adventures offer a gateway to an unparalleled connection with the natural world. From majestic mountains to serene fjords, from elusive wildlife to vibrant flora, these experiences invite us to embrace the essence of nature and foster a profound appreciation for the intricate ecosystems that shape the Last Frontier.

Alaska's allure lies in its wild heart—a place where nature reigns supreme and humans are but visitors in the grand theater of life. Wildlife tours and outdoor adventures provide a chance to heed the call of the wild, stepping beyond the boundaries of modernity and embracing the rhythms of the natural world. Whether it's the ethereal dance of the Northern Lights or the enchanting melodies of birdsong at dawn, these experiences invite us to engage with the primal forces that have shaped the Earth for millennia.

Alaska's landscapes are as diverse as they are breathtaking. From the towering glaciers of Glacier Bay to the expansive tundra of Denali National Park, every corner of the state boasts its own unique character. Wildlife tours and outdoor adventures serve as a conduit for exploration, guiding us through a symphony of landscapes that range from lush rainforests to rugged coastlines.

Alaska is a haven for wildlife, offering encounters with creatures that embody the essence of the untamed. Brown bears amble along the shores, bald eagles soar through the skies, and humpback whales breach the surface with breathtaking grace. Wildlife tours provide opportunities to witness these animals in their natural habitats, offering a glimpse into their behaviors, interactions, and survival strategies.

Outdoor adventures in Alaska are a thrilling invitation to push boundaries, embrace challenges, and forge memories that last a lifetime. Whether it's kayaking through icy fjords, hiking along pristine trails, or embarking on a dog sledding expedition, these activities offer a tangible connection to the wild spirit of the land. The rush of adrenaline that comes from conquering a mountain peak or navigating a rushing river is a reminder of our own capacity for resilience and determination.

Alaska's natural beauty is interwoven with the cultural heritage of indigenous peoples who have called this land home for centuries. Outdoor adventures often offer the opportunity to engage with local communities, learning about their traditions, stories, and deep connections to the land. Whether it's participating in a traditional ceremony or listening to ancestral tales around a campfire, these interactions add a layer of cultural enrichment to the outdoor experience.

The wilderness of Alaska is a classroom like no other, teaching us lessons about adaptation, interconnectedness, and the delicate balance of life. Observing how plants and animals thrive in harsh conditions inspires a newfound appreciation for resilience and ingenuity. Witnessing predator-prey dynamics in action underscores the importance of maintaining ecological equilibrium. As we navigate the natural world, we become students of its wisdom, learning valuable insights that can be applied to our own lives.

Wildlife tours and outdoor adventures hold within them the potential to spark a passion for conservation. As we witness the wonders of nature, we also come face to face with the fragility of these ecosystems. The shrinking glaciers, changing migration patterns, and dwindling habitats become more than statistics—they become urgent calls to action. The immersive experiences of these adventures forge a bond between participants and the natural world, motivating us to protect and preserve these environments for future generations.

With the privilege of experiencing Alaska's wilderness comes a responsibility to tread lightly and minimize our impact. Outdoor ethics and Leave No Trace principles become guiding principles as we navigate these delicate ecosystems. The goal is to ensure that our presence leaves behind no trace of our passage, allowing these landscapes to remain unspoiled and inviting for both present and future generations.

In the wilderness, the noise of the modern world recedes, and a profound silence takes its place. This silence is not empty; it's a canvas upon which introspection and connection can flourish. Away from the distractions of screens and schedules, the mind finds clarity and space to reflect. This solitude becomes a conduit for self-discovery, mindfulness, and a deep sense of being part of something far greater than ourselves.

In conclusion, wildlife tours and outdoor adventures in Alaska offer more than just experiences; they provide a transformative journey that enriches the soul and broadens our perspectives. These encounters with nature's beauty, power, and complexity leave an indelible mark, instilling a deep reverence for the planet's wild places and a commitment to their protection. As we venture into the wilderness, we're reminded that we are not separate from nature but an integral part of it—a realization that fosters a profound sense of responsibility and stewardship. In the wild landscapes of Alaska, we find not only breathtaking vistas but also a deeper understanding of our place in the intricate web of life.

Anchorage: Alaska's Urban Hub

Nestled in the heart of the Last Frontier, Anchorage stands as a captivating urban hub amidst Alaska's untamed wilderness. While not a traditional port of call for most cruise ships, Anchorage is often the gateway to a wide array of Alaskan adventures. With a unique blend of urban amenities and access to pristine nature, this vibrant city offers visitors an opportunity to delve into the diverse facets of Alaskan culture, history, wildlife, and breathtaking landscapes. Anchorage's intriguing juxtaposition of modernity and wilderness beckons travelers to explore its bustling streets and embark on transformative journeys into the surrounding wilds.

Anchorage's history is rich and varied, reflecting the interplay of native cultures, explorers, and settlers. Indigenous peoples, including the Dena'ina Athabascans, have called this region home for thousands of years. The establishment of the Alaska Railroad in the early 20th century played a pivotal role in the city's growth, transforming it from a tent city to a thriving urban center. Anchorage's strategic location made it an important military base during World War II, further influencing its development. Today, the city stands as a testament to resilience, adaptation, and the spirit of the Alaskan frontier.

Anchorage offers a myriad of attractions that showcase its unique blend of urban amenities and Alaskan heritage. The Anchorage Museum serves as a cultural anchor, delving into the history, art, and science of the region. Its exhibits celebrate the indigenous cultures of Alaska, the state's history of exploration, and its vibrant contemporary art scene. Visitors can immerse themselves in immersive displays that showcase the challenges and triumphs of life in this northern expanse.

Downtown Anchorage presents an eclectic array of shops, galleries, and restaurants, where visitors can savor Alaskan cuisine, shop for native art and crafts, and connect with the local community. The Alaska Native Heritage Center offers an immersive experience that introduces visitors to the cultures, traditions, and languages of Alaska's indigenous peoples, providing a deeper understanding of the land's rich heritage.

What sets Anchorage apart from many other cities is its unparalleled access to the wild landscapes that define Alaska. The city's location between the Chugach Mountains and the shores of Cook Inlet ensures that outdoor adventures are just a stone's throw away. Kincaid Park, a sprawling urban park, offers a network of trails for hiking, biking, and wildlife viewing. During the winter months, it transforms into a wonderland for cross-country skiing and snowshoeing.

Chugach State Park, spanning half a million acres, envelopes Anchorage in a tapestry of natural wonders. From the Flattop Mountain Trail offering panoramic views of the city and surrounding mountains to the Eagle River Nature Center, where hikers can explore scenic alpine and forested trails, Chugach State Park presents an open invitation to explore Alaska's untouched wilderness.

Anchorage boasts an intriguing coexistence of urban development and wildlife. The city's residents often find themselves sharing their surroundings with moose, bald eagles, and even the occasional bear. Kincaid Park and the Tony Knowles Coastal Trail are popular places to spot moose grazing amid a backdrop of natural beauty. Additionally, the Alaska Wildlife Conservation Center, located just outside the city, provides a haven for orphaned and injured wildlife, offering visitors a unique opportunity to observe bears, bison, caribou, and more in a naturalistic environment.

Anchorage's dining scene reflects the state's diverse culinary offerings. From freshly caught seafood to locally sourced game meats, the city's restaurants provide a taste of Alaskan flavors. Seafood enthusiasts can indulge in king crab, salmon, and halibut, often sourced directly from the waters of Cook Inlet. Innovative chefs incorporate these local ingredients into modern dishes that celebrate the region's bounty. Anchorage's breweries and distilleries further contribute to its culinary landscape, offering a taste of locally crafted beers and spirits.

Anchorage's calendar is dotted with festivals and events that celebrate the unique character of Alaska. The Fur Rendezvous, an annual winter carnival, features dog sledding races, snow sculpting competitions, and a vibrant atmosphere that brings the community together during the colder months. The Anchorage International Film Festival showcases a diverse array of films, while the summer Solstice Festival marks the longest day of the year with music, food, and cultural festivities.

Anchorage's location within the auroral oval makes it a prime location for witnessing the captivating dance of the Northern Lights. During the winter months, the city's proximity to the Arctic Circle increases the chances of seeing this breathtaking natural phenomenon. As the night sky comes alive with shimmering colors, visitors can embark on guided tours or venture to nearby dark-sky locations to witness the magic of the aurora borealis.

While not a traditional port of call for cruise ships, Anchorage's significance as a gateway to Alaskan adventures cannot be overstated. From Anchorage, travelers can embark on journeys to Denali National Park, where they can witness North America's tallest peak, Denali (formerly Mount McKinley), in all its glory. The city also serves as a starting point for exploring the Kenai Peninsula's stunning landscapes, including the Kenai Fjords National Park, home to awe-inspiring glaciers and marine life.

conclusion, Anchorage serves as a vibrant urban hub that bridges the gap between Alaska's untamed wilderness and modern amenities. Its unique blend of cultural attractions, access to

outdoor adventures, and proximity to breathtaking natural wonders make it a perfect pre- or post-cruise destination. Anchorage's dynamic character encapsulates the essence of the Last Frontier, offering travelers a chance to explore the diverse facets of Alaska's culture, history, and captivating landscapes in a city that serves as a portal to the wild and awe-inspiring realms beyond its limits.

Best Attractions and Activities in Anchorage: Alaska's Urban Hub

Anchorage, Alaska's urban hub, offers a captivating blend of urban amenities and access to the stunning natural beauty that defines the state. From cultural attractions to outdoor adventures, the city presents a wealth of experiences that capture the essence of the Last Frontier. Here are five of the best attractions and activities that visitors can enjoy in Anchorage:

1. Anchorage Museum: A Cultural Anchorage

The Anchorage Museum serves as a cultural hub, offering visitors a comprehensive insight into Alaska's history, art, and science. The museum's exhibits span a wide range of topics, from indigenous cultures and the state's history of exploration to contemporary art and science exhibits. The immersive displays provide a deep dive into Alaska's rich heritage, allowing visitors to understand the challenges and triumphs of life in this unique region.

2. Tony Knowles Coastal Trail: Scenic Exploration

The Tony Knowles Coastal Trail is a beloved recreational trail that offers breathtaking views of the city's skyline, the Chugach Mountains, and the waters of Cook Inlet. The 11-mile trail winds along the coastline, making it perfect for walking, jogging, biking, and rollerblading. As you traverse the trail, keep an eye out for local wildlife, including moose and bald eagles.

3. Alaska Wildlife Conservation Center: Wildlife Encounters

Located just outside Anchorage, the Alaska Wildlife Conservation Center provides a unique opportunity to observe native wildlife up close. The center is home to orphaned and injured animals, including bears, bison, moose, and caribou. Visitors can take guided tours to learn

about the animals' stories and conservation efforts while enjoying the picturesque backdrop o the surrounding Chugach Mountains.

4. Chugach State Park: Outdoor Adventures

Chugach State Park, one of the largest state parks in the United States, envelops Anchorage in pristine wilderness playground. With numerous trails for hiking, biking, and wildlife viewing, th park offers endless opportunities for outdoor adventures. Flattop Mountain Trail, a popular hike, rewards hikers with panoramic views of the city and surrounding landscapes. Eagle River Nature Center provides access to alpine and forested trails for those seeking a deeper immersion in nature.

5. Alaska Native Heritage Center: Cultural Immersion

The Alaska Native Heritage Center offers a rich cultural experience that introduces visitors to the diverse cultures, traditions, and languages of Alaska's indigenous peoples. Through engaging exhibits, live performances, and interactive demonstrations, visitors gain a deeper understanding of native art, music, storytelling, and daily life. The center's immersive approach allows for meaningful connections and insights into the land's original inhabitants.

From cultural exploration to encounters with wildlife and outdoor escapades, these five attractions and activities in Anchorage showcase the city's ability to provide a well-rounded Alaskan experience. Anchorage's unique blend of urban amenities and access to untouched wilderness offers a captivating journey that encapsulates the spirit of the Last Frontier. Whether you're strolling along the coastal trail, delving into indigenous cultures, or observing majestic wildlife, Anchorage invites you to embark on a transformative adventure that showcases the diverse and awe-inspiring facets of Alaska.

Anchorage Museum: A Cultural Anchorage

Nestled within the heart of Anchorage, Alaska, the Anchorage Museum stands as a beacon of culture, history, and art, inviting visitors to embark on a captivating journey through the diverse tapestry of the Last Frontier. This cultural institution is more than just a museum; it is a dynamic hub that engages, educates, and immerses visitors in the stories that have shaped Alaska's past, present, and future. From indigenous heritage to exploratory endeavors, from contemporary art

to scientific exploration, the Anchorage Museum offers a multifaceted experience that captures the essence of Alaska's rich and intricate identity.

At the heart of the Anchorage Museum's narrative lies a deep respect for and celebration of Alaska's indigenous cultures. The museum provides a platform for indigenous voices, traditions, and stories to take center stage. Exhibits highlight the rich diversity of native communities across the state, including the Athabascan, Yup'ik, Inupiaq, and Tlingit peoples. Through artifacts, art, and interactive displays, visitors gain insight into traditional practices, spiritual beliefs, and the profound connection between Alaska's indigenous communities and the land they call home.

Alaska's history is deeply intertwined with exploration and pioneering spirit. The Anchorage Museum pays homage to the explorers, adventurers, and settlers who have braved the challenges of the Last Frontier. Visitors can trace the footsteps of intrepid explorers who navigated treacherous terrains, crossed unforgiving seas, and discovered new horizons. The museum's exhibits shed light on the early days of Alaska's development, from the arrival of Russian fur traders to the Klondike Gold Rush that forever altered the region's landscape and character.

The Anchorage Museum serves as a canvas that showcases the creative pulse of Alaska's art scene. Its galleries feature an eclectic array of art forms, from traditional indigenous works to contemporary pieces that reflect the state's modern aesthetic. Paintings, sculptures, textiles, and multimedia installations capture the beauty, challenges, and inspiration drawn from Alaska's landscapes and cultures. This convergence of artistic expression provides visitors with a unique lens through which to understand the multidimensional nature of the Last Frontier.

Alaska's rugged landscapes and pristine wilderness have long captivated the curiosity of scientists and researchers. The Anchorage Museum pays homage to this spirit of inquiry by offering exhibits that delve into the scientific exploration of the region's ecosystems, wildlife, and geological wonders. Visitors can uncover the mysteries of glaciers, learn about the unique adaptations of Arctic animals, and gain insights into the environmental changes that impact Alaska's delicate balance.

The Alaska Native Heritage Center, a part of the Anchorage Museum, provides a unique opportunity to experience the cultures, traditions, and languages of Alaska's indigenous peoples in a deeply immersive manner. Through interactive exhibits, demonstrations, and live performances, visitors gain a firsthand understanding of native artistry, storytelling, music, and daily life. This cultural immersion fosters connections between visitors and Alaska's original inhabitants, deepening their appreciation for the heritage that has shaped the state's identity.

Beyond its exhibits, the Anchorage Museum is a center of learning that encourages visitors of all ages to engage with the rich narratives of Alaska. The museum offers educational programs, workshops, and lectures that foster a deeper understanding of Alaska's history, culture, and environment. From hands-on activities for children to thought-provoking discussions for adults, the museum promotes lifelong learning and exploration.

The Anchorage Museum functions as a gathering space that brings together residents and visitors alike. Cultural events, performances, and festivals held at the museum serve as a reflection of Anchorage's vibrant community spirit. The museum's role as a cultural anchor extends beyond its physical walls, radiating its influence throughout the city and fostering a sense of belonging and interconnectedness.

As a cultural institution, the Anchorage Museum serves as an anchor for Alaska's multifaceted identity. It preserves the legacy of indigenous cultures, honors the pioneering endeavors that have shaped the state, celebrates artistic expression, and fosters a deeper connection to Alaska's natural wonders. Through its exhibits, programs, and immersive experiences, the museum invites visitors to not only explore Alaska's past but also engage with its present and future.

In conclusion, the Anchorage Museum stands as a cultural anchorage that offers a portal into the heart and soul of Alaska. By weaving together indigenous heritage, exploration narratives, artistic expression, scientific discovery, and community engagement, the museum provides a holistic understanding of the state's diverse and intricate identity. As visitors journey through its halls, they are invited to immerse themselves in the stories, experiences, and creativity that define the Last Frontier, leaving with a deeper appreciation for the tapestry of cultures, histories, and landscapes that make Alaska an enduring source of inspiration and wonder.

Tony Knowles Coastal Trail: Scenic Exploration

In the heart of Anchorage, Alaska's bustling urban hub, lies a hidden gem that offers an escape into the natural beauty that defines the Last Frontier. The Tony Knowles Coastal Trail is a picturesque pathway that winds along the coastline, offering visitors an unparalleled opportunity to immerse themselves in stunning landscapes, breathe in the crisp Alaskan air, and witness a harmonious convergence of urbanity and wilderness. As a beacon of scenic exploration, the trail weaves together breathtaking views, wildlife encounters, and a sense of tranquility that beckons both locals and visitors to embark on a transformative journey through Anchorage's natural wonders.

Stretching for approximately 11 miles, the Tony Knowles Coastal Trail serves as a testament to Anchorage's commitment to preserving its natural landscapes and providing access to outdoor

recreational opportunities. Named after former Alaska Governor Tony Knowles, the trail embodies his vision of connecting the city's urban core with the untouched beauty of the surrounding environment. As visitors traverse the trail, they witness the seamless fusion of urban amenities with the awe-inspiring vistas that define Alaska.

One of the trail's most captivating features is its ability to offer panoramic views that extend beyond Anchorage's skyline. From various vantage points, visitors are treated to unobstructed vistas of the city's skyscrapers juxtaposed against the majestic Chugach Mountains. The sparkling waters of Cook Inlet provide a serene backdrop, and on clear days, the sightlines stretch to include the snow-capped peaks of the Alaska Range. These sweeping views serve as a constant reminder of the city's unique location, nestled between rugged mountains and the expanse of the sea.

While Anchorage may be an urban center, the Tony Knowles Coastal Trail allows for intimate wildlife encounters that highlight the area's wild side. Moose, with their imposing antlers, are often spotted along the trail, gracefully navigating through meadows and wooded areas. Bald eagles, Alaska's iconic national bird, soar overhead, adding a touch of majesty to the landscape. The trail's proximity to the water also provides opportunities to spot marine life, from seals to migratory birds that frequent the inlet's shores.

The Tony Knowles Coastal Trail is a dynamic entity that evolves with the changing seasons. In the warmer months, the trail comes alive with vibrant wildflowers that dot the landscape, creating a kaleidoscope of colors against the backdrop of lush greenery. Summer also brings extended daylight hours, allowing for leisurely strolls, invigorating runs, and relaxing picnics that stretch well into the evening.

As autumn arrives, the trail transforms into a canvas of fiery hues as the leaves change color, painting the scenery with rich reds, oranges, and golds. The air becomes crisper, and the trail's ambiance takes on a sense of tranquility that complements the changing season.

In winter, a blanket of snow envelops the landscape, creating a serene and ethereal atmosphere. The trail becomes a favorite for cross-country skiing and snowshoeing enthusiasts who seek solace in the pristine wilderness amid the hushed quietude of the season.

The Tony Knowles Coastal Trail isn't just a path; it's a journey of discovery that introduces visitors to several notable points of interest. Earthquake Park, for instance, offers a poignant reminder of the 1964 Good Friday Earthquake, which drastically altered the landscape and shaped the course of the city's development. Interpretive signs along the trail provide insight into the geological and historical significance of the area.

Point Woronzof provides a picturesque viewpoint from which visitors can gaze across the waters of Cook Inlet and witness the majestic sweep of the Alaska Range on the horizon. Beluga Point

offers another vantage point for observing marine life, with the opportunity to catch sight of beluga whales during their migratory season.

The Tony Knowles Coastal Trail is designed to be accessible and inclusive, inviting visitors of all ages and abilities to experience its beauty. The paved path is well-maintained and suitable for walking, jogging, running, biking, and even rollerblading. Benches and picnic areas along the way provide opportunities to rest, reflect, and soak in the surrounding scenery. The trail's gentle gradient ensures that it can be enjoyed by individuals of varying fitness levels, making it a beloved destination for families, solo adventurers, and outdoor enthusiasts.

Beyond its role as a pathway for scenic exploration, the Tony Knowles Coastal Trail serves as a shared space that fosters a sense of community. Locals and visitors alike come together to enjoy the trail's beauty, often greeting each other with smiles and friendly gestures as they pass by. The trail's popularity has also led to the organization of various community events, from charity walks to fun runs, which contribute to the sense of camaraderie and shared appreciation for the natural wonders that Anchorage offers.

The Tony Knowles Coastal Trail transcends its physical attributes to become a symbol of Anchorage's connection to the natural world. It stands as a reminder that within the heart of a bustling urban center lies the opportunity for transformative journeys into pristine wilderness. As visitors follow the trail's meandering path, they are invited to explore, reflect, and connect with the landscapes that have shaped Alaska's identity. The trail's scenic splendor, wildlife encounters, and panoramic views converge to create an experience that captures the essence of Alaska's natural soul, leaving an indelible mark on those who embark on its transformative journey.

Alaska Wildlife Conservation Center: Wildlife Encounters

Nestled in the heart of the Last Frontier, the Alaska Wildlife Conservation Center (AWCC) stands as a haven for both animals and humans, offering a unique and transformative experience that idges the gap between conservation, education, and appreciation for the state's diverse ildlife. Situated amidst the breathtaking landscapes of the Chugach Mountains, the center rves as a sanctuary for orphaned, injured, and displaced animals, providing them with a cond chance at life while also granting visitors an up-close and personal connection to laska's remarkable fauna. The AWCC isn't just a place; it's a portal that invites guests to itness the majesty of bears, moose, caribou, and more, while fostering a deeper nderstanding of the importance of conservation efforts and the delicate balance between uman development and the wild.

ounded in 1993, the Alaska Wildlife Conservation Center was established with a clear mission: provide a safe haven for Alaska's injured and orphaned wildlife, with the ultimate goal of eleasing them back into the wild whenever possible. The center takes in animals that have een affected by various circumstances, including habitat loss, vehicle collisions, or bandonment. Through its rehabilitation efforts, the AWCC works tirelessly to ensure that hese animals can regain their health and independence, contributing to the preservation of laska's diverse wildlife populations.

he Alaska Wildlife Conservation Center is home to a diverse array of animals, each epresenting a unique facet of the state's wildlife. Visitors have the opportunity to encounter nimals that are emblematic of Alaska's natural landscapes and ecosystems. From majestic rown bears to graceful moose, and from swift wolves to iconic bald eagles, the center's esidents embody the spirit of the Last Frontier. Other inhabitants include musk oxen, wood ison, caribou, and more. Each animal serves as an ambassador for its species, offering a hance for visitors to learn about their behaviors, habitats, and the conservation challenges hey face.

he AWCC is more than just an animal sanctuary; it's an educational platform that fosters a eeper connection between visitors and Alaska's wildlife. Interpretive signs, guided tours, and ducational programs provide insights into the biology, ecology, and behavior of the center's nimal residents. Visitors can learn about the intricate interdependencies within Alaska's cosystems and gain a better understanding of how human activities can impact these delicate alances. Through these educational initiatives, the AWCC plays a crucial role in raising wareness about the importance of conservation efforts and responsible wildlife management.

he Alaska Wildlife Conservation Center operates with a strong commitment to animal welfare nd conservation ethics. The center's primary focus is on the well-being and long-term viability f the animals in its care. While the center offers an opportunity for visitors to view and learn bout wildlife up close, it goes beyond providing mere entertainment. It serves as a reminder hat wildlife tourism should prioritize the welfare and natural behaviors of the animals, and that esponsible conservation practices are paramount to ensuring the survival of Alaska's iconic pecies.

For photographers and wildlife enthusiasts, the Alaska Wildlife Conservation Center offers a unique opportunity to capture stunning images of animals against a backdrop of pristine Alaskan landscapes. The naturalistic enclosures and spacious habitats provide ample opportunities for close observation and intimate photography without disturbing the animals' natural behaviors. Capturing the raw beauty and majesty of these creatures in their habitats fosters a deeper appreciation for their significance within the ecosystem.

The Alaska Wildlife Conservation Center's offerings change with the seasons, providing visitors with an ever-evolving experience. Spring and summer bring the opportunity to witness animal exploring their spacious habitats, interacting with each other, and engaging in natural behaviors.

Fall introduces a unique perspective as the animals prepare for the onset of winter, displaying behaviors like antler shedding and increased foraging.

Throughout the year, the center hosts a variety of educational programs, workshops, and events that further connect visitors to Alaska's wildlife. From behind-the-scenes tours to wildlife-focused lectures, these programs provide a deeper understanding of the animals' lives, the challenges they face, and the conservation efforts that are essential for their survival.

The Alaska Wildlife Conservation Center's impact extends beyond its immediate boundaries. By fostering a connection between visitors and Alaska's wildlife, the center contributes to the broader mission of conservation awareness and advocacy. The stories of the animals that have found refuge at the center serve as powerful narratives that highlight the delicate balance between human development and the preservation of natural habitats.

Through its efforts, the AWCC inspires individuals to become stewards of the environment, encouraging them to support wildlife conservation initiatives and make choices that positively impact the natural world. Ultimately, the center's legacy lies in its ability to instill a sense of responsibility and appreciation for Alaska's unique wildlife, leaving an indelible mark on the hearts and minds of those who are fortunate enough to witness the majesty of its animal residents.

In conclusion, the Alaska Wildlife Conservation Center stands as a testament to the symbiotic relationship between humanity and the natural world. By providing a safe haven for injured and orphaned animals, the center not only saves lives but also creates opportunities for meaningful encounters and educational insights. As visitors walk the paths of the AWCC, they gain a deeper understanding of Alaska's biodiversity, the challenges facing its wildlife, and the vital role that conservation efforts play in securing a future where humans and animals can coexist harmoniously within the awe-inspiring landscapes of the Last Frontier.

Chugach State Park: Outdoor Adventures

Nestled in the rugged embrace of the Chugach Mountains, Chugach State Park stands as an untamed expanse of wilderness that beckons adventurers and nature enthusiasts to embark on a journey of outdoor exploration. As Alaska's largest state park and a sanctuary of unspoiled landscapes, Chugach captures the essence of the Last Frontier, offering a tapestry of diverse ecosystems, towering peaks, shimmering lakes, and abundant wildlife. From exhilarating hikes to tranquil lakeside moments, the park's vastness provides a canvas for a wide spectrum of

outdoor adventures that awaken the senses, invigorate the spirit, and forge lasting connections to the raw and untamed beauty of Alaska's wilderness.

Encompassing over half a million acres, Chugach State Park stretches from the outskirts of Anchorage to the remote edges of the Chugach Mountains. This expansive wilderness showcases the remarkable diversity of Alaska's landscapes, ranging from coastal forests and alpine meadows to rugged peaks and icy glaciers. The park's untouched beauty serves as a refuge for a variety of plant and animal species, making it a vital haven for conservation efforts and a living testament to Alaska's natural splendor.

Chugach State Park boasts an extensive network of hiking trails that cater to adventurers of all levels. From novice hikers seeking leisurely strolls to seasoned trekkers seeking challenging ascents, the park's trails offer a range of options to suit every preference. Flattop Mountain Trail is a perennial favorite, offering a relatively short but steep hike that rewards hikers with panoramic views of Anchorage, the Alaska Range, and the Cook Inlet. For those seeking a more secluded experience, trails like Wolverine Peak and Bird Ridge offer rugged terrain and breathtaking vistas that immerse hikers in the untamed beauty of the Chugach.

Chugach State Park is a haven for backcountry enthusiasts who crave a deeper connection to nature. The park's vastness ensures that even beyond the well-trodden trailheads, there are opportunities for solitude and exploration. Adventurers equipped with the necessary skills and gear can venture into the heart of the park, where pristine alpine meadows, hidden lakes, and dramatic valleys await discovery. Backpacking, camping, and exploring off-the-beaten-path areas allow for an authentic wilderness experience that fosters a sense of self-reliance and an intimate connection to the land.

For those seeking the thrill of conquering towering summits, the Chugach Mountains provide a playground of high-altitude adventures. Peaks like Mount Baldy, Eagle Peak, and Mount Eklutna challenge climbers with varying degrees of technical difficulty, offering routes that range from steep ascents to technical climbs that require specialized skills and equipment. These alpine pursuits reward climbers not only with breathtaking views from their summits but also with a profound sense of accomplishment and communion with the rugged landscape.

Chugach State Park teems with a rich array of wildlife, reflecting the diverse ecosystems that call the park home. From the elusive Dall sheep that dot the high cliffs to the moose that meander through lush meadows, encounters with Alaska's iconic animals are a common occurrence for park visitors. Black and brown bears roam the forests, and marmots dart across rocky slopes. Birdwatchers can delight in spotting eagles soaring overhead and ptarmigans blending seamlessly with their alpine surroundings. The park's living symphony of nature invites visitors to witness these creatures in their natural habitats, reminding us of the delicate balance that exists between the human world and the wild.

Chugach State Park isn't just a realm of mountains and forests; it also encompasses an aquatic wonderland that invites visitors to engage with its pristine waters. The park is home to numerous lakes and streams that offer opportunities for fishing, kayaking, canoeing, and paddleboarding. Eklutna Lake, a glacial-fed jewel, beckons with crystal-clear waters that reflect the towering peaks surrounding it. The chance to cast a line and experience the serenity of the water adds yet another layer of diversity to the park's outdoor offerings.

Chugach State Park's allure extends to the winter months, transforming its landscapes into a winter wonderland that offers a unique array of recreational opportunities. The snow-covered trails become pathways for cross-country skiing and snowshoeing, allowing adventurers to navigate through serene forests and over frozen lakes. Backcountry skiers and snowboarders can access remote slopes for thrilling descents, while snowmobilers can explore the park's snow-blanketed expanses.

Chugach State Park holds cultural significance for Alaska's indigenous communities, who have long held a deep connection to the land. The park contains archaeological sites, traditional use areas, and historical landmarks that reflect the stories of the Dena'ina Athabascan people, whose heritage is woven into the fabric of the Chugach. Visitors are encouraged to tread lightly and respect the cultural heritage of the land, recognizing the importance of preserving its legacy for future generations.

Chugach State Park isn't merely a collection of trails and mountains; it's a gateway that unveils the very essence of Alaska. It invites individuals to step beyond the confines of urbanity and immerse themselves in the untamed beauty of the Last Frontier. The park's landscapes, from rugged peaks to serene lakeshores, serve as a canvas for personal discovery and a connection to the land's enduring spirit. As visitors embark on outdoor adventures, they are met with challenges that cultivate resilience, moments of awe that inspire reverence, and encounters with nature that awaken a sense of humility.

Chugach State Park's preservation is a collective responsibility that falls upon visitors, park rangers, and the broader community. Responsible recreation, Leave No Trace principles, and a commitment to conservation are essential to ensuring that the park's pristine beauty remains unspoiled for generations to come. The park's delicate ecosystems and the habitats of its inhabitants rely on these efforts to thrive amid the ever-changing world.

In conclusion, Chugach State Park stands as an embodiment of Alaska's wild and untamed soul. Its vast landscapes, diverse ecosystems, and outdoor adventures offer a kaleidoscope of experiences that tap into the primal connection between humans and nature. From conquering mountain peaks to meandering along tranquil lakeshores, every step within the park is an opportunity for discovery, contemplation, and connection. Through its trails and vistas, Chugach State Park unveils the true essence of the Last Frontier, inviting individuals to immerse

themselves in the transformative power of the outdoors and forge an unbreakable bond with the raw and majestic beauty of Alaska's wilderness.

Alaska Native Heritage Center: Cultural Immersion

In the heart of the Last Frontier, where the ancient rhythms of indigenous cultures resonate with the modern world, the Alaska Native Heritage Center stands as a living testament to the rich tapestry of Alaska's original inhabitants. This immersive cultural destination beckons visitors to step into a world where traditions, stories, and artistry come alive, offering a unique opportunity to engage with the diverse indigenous peoples that have called this land home for millennia. Through interactive exhibits, captivating performances, and authentic demonstrations, the center invites individuals to embark on a transformative journey of cultural immersion, fostering a deep understanding of Alaska's indigenous heritage and the enduring spirit that shapes its identity.

The Alaska Native Heritage Center serves as a bridge that spans time, connecting the present to the ancient legacies of Alaska's indigenous peoples. The center's mission is to celebrate and honor the diverse cultures, languages, and traditions of these communities, while also raising awareness about the challenges they face and the resilience they demonstrate. With indigenous Alaskan communities representing numerous distinct cultures, including the Athabascan, Inupiaq, Yup'ik, and Tlingit, the center offers a space where their stories can be shared, their voices heard, and their contributions celebrated.

At the core of the Alaska Native Heritage Center's immersive experience are its interactive exhibits and authentic demonstrations. Visitors have the opportunity to witness traditional practices, engage with native artistry, and participate in activities that provide insight into daily life in indigenous communities. From the art of building traditional dwellings to the crafting of intricate masks and regalia, the center's workshops and demonstrations offer a hands-on experience that bridges the gap between the past and the present.

Oral traditions have long been central to indigenous cultures, serving as vessels that carry knowledge, history, and wisdom from one generation to the next. The Alaska Native Heritage Center honors this tradition by hosting storytelling sessions that provide a window into the worldviews, beliefs, and narratives that have guided indigenous communities for centuries. These storytelling sessions serve as a reminder of the power of spoken word, and they foster a deeper connection between visitors and the enduring legacies of Alaska's native peoples.

The Alaska Native Heritage Center features diverse cultural zones that showcase the unique identities of different indigenous groups across Alaska. Each zone provides visitors with an immersive experience that highlights the distinct traditions, languages, and art forms of its respective community. Through exhibits, artifacts, and demonstrations, visitors can gain an understanding of the nuanced ways in which Alaska's native cultures have thrived in harmony with their environments.

Performance is an integral part of indigenous cultures, serving as a means of celebration, expression, and connection to the spiritual realm. At the Alaska Native Heritage Center, visitors are treated to captivating dance performances and musical displays that draw from the traditions of various native groups. These performances not only entertain but also offer a glimpse into the significance of dance and music within indigenous communities, reflecting their connections to nature, ancestral spirits, and communal bonds.

Languages are a cornerstone of culture, serving as carriers of unique worldviews, philosophies, and ways of being. Many indigenous languages around the world, including those in Alaska, are at risk of fading into obscurity. The Alaska Native Heritage Center plays a crucial role in language revitalization efforts by incorporating indigenous languages into its exhibits, programs, and presentations. This emphasis on language preservation not only safeguards an integral aspect of indigenous identity but also underscores the center's commitment to cultural continuity.

The Alaska Native Heritage Center is not a static institution; it is a dynamic space that fosters connections between visitors, indigenous communities, and cultural practitioners. The center collaborates with native elders, artisans, and storytellers who share their knowledge and expertise, ensuring that the cultural experiences offered are authentic and rooted in tradition. This collaboration provides visitors with a genuine connection to Alaska's indigenous cultures and an opportunity to learn directly from those who hold the key to preserving their heritage.

he Alaska Native Heritage Center serves as a bridge that connects people from all walks of life, ostering mutual understanding and respect between indigenous and non-indigenous ndividuals. Through cultural exchange, visitors can dispel misconceptions, challenge tereotypes, and forge connections that transcend cultural boundaries. By engaging with ndigenous cultures in a respectful and meaningful manner, visitors contribute to the center's roader mission of promoting unity, empathy, and appreciation for Alaska's diverse tapestry.

he Alaska Native Heritage Center not only showcases the traditions of the past but also mpowers indigenous youth to explore their own cultural identities and express themselves reatively. The center provides a platform for young artists, dancers, and musicians to share heir talents and perspectives, helping to ensure that indigenous cultures remain vibrant and elevant to future generations. This encouragement of cultural expression contributes to the enter's mission of fostering a sense of pride and belonging among Alaska's indigenous ommunities.

n essence, the Alaska Native Heritage Center is more than a museum; it's a living legacy that mbodies the resilience, creativity, and vitality of Alaska's indigenous peoples. As visitors step nto its grounds, they embark on a journey of discovery that transcends time and space. They re invited to learn, engage, and connect with the diverse cultures that have shaped Alaska's istory and continue to shape its future. By immersing themselves in the traditions, stories, and rtistry of native communities, visitors leave with a deeper appreciation for the rich tapestry of Alaska's indigenous heritage and a renewed sense of their own place within the broader human xperience.

Glacier Bay: A Natural Wonder of Majestic Ice and Timeless Beauty

Amid the untouched wilderness of Alaska lies a place of awe-inspiring grandeur, a realm where owering glaciers flow like rivers of ice into turquoise waters, and the rhythm of nature's ncient processes plays out before your eyes. Glacier Bay National Park and Preserve, a JNESCO World Heritage Site, is a testament to the raw power and exquisite beauty of Earth's lacial landscapes. With its dramatic fjords, calving glaciers, and abundant wildlife, Glacier Bay s a natural wonder that beckons adventurers, scientists, and nature enthusiasts to experience he sublime dance of ice, water, and time.

he story of Glacier Bay is intricately woven with the history of Earth's geology. Approximately 200 years ago, a massive glacier known as the Grand Pacific Glacier extended to the present-day mouth of the bay. As this glacier began to retreat, it unveiled a succession of smaller glaciers, each contributing to the formation of the bay's iconic fjords and inlets. Today, Glacier Bay showcases the effects of glacial erosion and the sculpting power of ice over millennia.

Glacier Bay is not a static landscape; it's a living canvas where glaciers continue to shape the terrain. The glaciers here are known as tidewater glaciers, meaning they flow directly into the ocean. Witnessing the calving process, where massive chunks of ice break off and crash into the water, is a breathtaking spectacle. This dynamic dance between ice and water constantly reshapes the bay, carving fjords, islands, and coastal features.

The frigid waters of Glacier Bay are teeming with life, drawing an array of marine species to its depths. Humpback whales breach the surface, orcas glide through the waters, and sea lions bask on icebergs. The nutrient-rich environment supports a variety of fish, from salmon to halibut. Bird enthusiasts are treated to the sight of bald eagles soaring overhead, while seabirds such as puffins and cormorants inhabit the rocky shores and cliffs.

Glacier Bay stands as a tangible testament to the impact of climate change. The glaciers here have been retreating since the early 18th century, with some retreating as much as 65 miles. This rapid retreat is a stark reminder of the Earth's changing climate. Scientists study Glacier Bay to better understand the dynamics of glacial retreat and its implications for global sea level rise. The park serves as an environmental barometer, reminding us of the urgency to address climate change.

Designated as a national monument in 1925 and later as a national park, Glacier Bay's preservation efforts are fueled by a commitment to understanding and protecting this unique ecosystem. Researchers study the park's glacial processes, marine life, and ecosystem dynamics, contributing to the broader body of scientific knowledge. As visitors explore the park, they become part of ongoing research efforts that seek to conserve and safeguard this pristine wilderness.

Experiencing Glacier Bay is often done through organized cruises that navigate the icy waters, allowing passengers to witness the grandeur of the glaciers and the wildlife that calls the region home. Park rangers provide informative commentary, offering insights into the geology, biology, and history of the area. Visitors can explore the tidewater glaciers by kayak, observing the ice up close and listening to the echoes of calving ice.

Before it became a national park, Glacier Bay was home to indigenous Tlingit and Huna people who shared a deep connection with the land and water. Their presence is still felt in the region, and visitors can learn about their rich cultural heritage through guided tours and interactions with local communities. The park's visitor center also provides information about the region's human history and the role of indigenous cultures.

Preserving Glacier Bay's pristine environment while allowing visitors to experience its majesty is a delicate balancing act. The National Park Service and cruise operators collaborate to ensure sustainable tourism practices. Visitor numbers are regulated, and strict guidelines are in place to minimize impacts on the delicate ecosystem. This approach ensures that future generations can continue to marvel at the wonders of Glacier Bay.

Glacier Bay is more than a visual spectacle; it's a place of reflection and contemplation. The towering glaciers, serene fjords, and pristine waters inspire a sense of humility and awe. The grandeur of nature's power and the eons-long processes that have shaped the land prompt introspection about our place in the world and our responsibility to protect it.

In conclusion, Glacier Bay is a natural wonder that defies description. It's a living testament to the Earth's geological history, a canvas where ice and water engage in an eternal dance, and a sanctuary for diverse marine and avian life. Beyond its breathtaking landscapes, Glacier Bay serves as a beacon of environmental awareness and a call to action against climate change. Whether observed from a cruise ship, explored by kayak, or appreciated through scientific

research, Glacier Bay continues to captivate hearts and minds, reminding us of the timeless beauty and fragility of our planet.

Attractions and Activities

Glacier Bay National Park is a treasure trove of natural wonders, offering a plethora of attractions and activities that immerse visitors in the breathtaking beauty and dynamic processes of glacial landscapes. From witnessing calving glaciers to observing diverse wildlife, each experience in Glacier Bay is a testament to the power of nature and the importance of preserving this pristine wilderness. Here are five of the best attractions and activities that await you in Glacier Bay:

1. Margerie Glacier: Witnessing Calving Majesty

Margerie Glacier is one of the most iconic and awe-inspiring attractions in Glacier Bay. This tidewater glacier spans 21 miles long and is known for its dramatic calving events, where massive chunks of ice break off and crash into the sea with a thunderous roar. Observing these calving events from the deck of a cruise ship is a breathtaking spectacle, offering a rare glimpse into the dynamic processes of glacial movement. The sheer size and power of Margerie Glacier leave a lasting impression on all who witness its majesty.

2. John Hopkins Inlet: Birdwatching and Glacial Beauty

John Hopkins Inlet offers a unique blend of natural wonders. The inlet is surrounded by towering cliffs, ice-covered mountains, and glaciers that spill into the water. Its sheltered waters are a haven for diverse marine life, making it an excellent location for wildlife spotting. Birdwatchers are treated to the sight of seabird colonies, including puffins and cormorants, perched on rocky ledges. The pristine beauty of John Hopkins Inlet, combined with the opportunity to observe wildlife in their natural habitat, makes it a must-visit attraction.

3. Bartlett Cove: Visitor Center and Nature Trails

Bartlett Cove serves as the gateway to Glacier Bay National Park and Preserve. It's home to the Glacier Bay Visitor Center, where you can learn about the park's history, ecosystems, and ongoing research efforts. The visitor center offers interactive exhibits, ranger-led programs, and

guided walks that provide insights into the park's natural and cultural heritage. Additionally, Bartlett Cove features nature trails that wind through lush forests and offer opportunities for birdwatching and enjoying serene landscapes.

4. Kayaking: Immersive Exploration

Kayaking in Glacier Bay offers a unique and intimate way to explore its landscapes and wildlife. Paddling through the calm waters of the bay allows you to get up close to glaciers, icebergs, and marine life. The tranquility of kayaking also enhances the sense of connection with nature, providing a serene experience that complements the grandeur of the glaciers. Guided kayaking tours are available for visitors of all skill levels, ensuring a safe and educational adventure.

5. Whale Watching: Majestic Marine Encounters

Glacier Bay is a prime location for whale watching, as its nutrient-rich waters attract humpback whales, orcas, and other marine mammals. The sight of a humpback whale breaching the surface or a pod of orcas gracefully gliding through the water is a captivating experience that highlights the rich biodiversity of the region. Many cruise operators offer whale watching excursions that provide the opportunity to witness these majestic creatures in their natural habitat, creating memories that last a lifetime.

In conclusion, Glacier Bay National Park offers a diverse range of attractions and activities that allow visitors to immerse themselves in the wonders of a natural landscape shaped by glacial forces. From witnessing the dramatic calving of glaciers to observing marine life and exploring serene coves by kayak, each experience in Glacier Bay is an invitation to connect with nature's raw beauty and ponder the intricate processes that have shaped the region over millennia. Whether you're a wildlife enthusiast, a nature lover, or simply seeking to be humbled by the grandeur of the wilderness, Glacier Bay has something to offer that will leave an indelible mark on your heart and soul.

Margerie Glacier: Witnessing the Majestic Drama of Glacial Calving

Amid the grandeur of Glacier Bay National Park, one natural wonder stands out with its awe-inspiring presence and dramatic displays of power: the Margerie Glacier. Nestled within the

heart of this pristine wilderness, Margerie Glacier has captured the imagination of travelers and scientists alike. Its towering ice walls, vivid blue hues, and thunderous calving events create a mesmerizing spectacle that is both a testament to the Earth's geological processes and a stark reminder of the ongoing impact of climate change. In this exploration, we delve deep into the majesty of Margerie Glacier, revealing the intricate dance of ice and water that has shaped this remarkable landscape.

Margerie Glacier is a tidewater glacier, a type that flows directly into the sea. The glacier's story is a narrative of time and transformation, shaped over centuries by the forces of nature. As the Earth's climate cooled, massive ice sheets carved valleys and fjords, laying the groundwork for the creation of Glacier Bay. As the climate warmed, these ice sheets retreated, revealing a succession of smaller glaciers, including Margerie Glacier, which continue to shape the bay's rugged terrain.

At the heart of Margerie Glacier's allure lies the mesmerizing phenomenon of calving. Calving is the process by which chunks of ice break off from the glacier's edge and crash into the sea below. This spectacle is a symphony of sound and motion, as massive icebergs are born from the glacier's frozen embrace. The resulting echoes of calving thunder across the bay, reverberating through the air as a reminder of the glacier's dynamic nature.

Margerie Glacier's interaction with its environment is a powerful display of nature's creative forces. As the glacier advances, it carries debris and rocks from the mountainsides it grinds against, creating a moraine—a ridge of rock and sediment—along its edge. This moraine acts as a dam, preventing seawater from eroding the glacier's base. However, as the glacier's ice extends into the water, it becomes susceptible to the erosive power of the ocean. The interaction between ice, water, and rock shapes the glacier's unique features, creating cavernous ice formations and imposing ice walls.

One of Margerie Glacier's most captivating features is its vibrant blue hue. The color arises from the unique properties of ice and the way it interacts with light. As ice compacts over time, air bubbles are trapped within its crystalline structure. When light enters the ice, it encounters these air bubbles and is scattered, resulting in the brilliant blue color that defines the glacier's façade. The play of light on the ice's surface creates a mesmerizing visual effect, evoking a sense of wonder and intrigue.

While the timeless beauty of Margerie Glacier is undeniable, its very existence serves as a visual reminder of the profound impacts of climate change. Glacier Bay itself is a result of glacial retreat over the past 200 years. Margerie Glacier, like many glaciers around the world, has been retreating due to rising temperatures, resulting in significant changes to the bay's landscape. Witnessing the glacier's retreat is a somber reminder of the urgent need to address climate change and protect these fragile environments.

Visiting Margerie Glacier is an experience that engages all the senses. Many visitors have the opportunity to witness the glacier's magnificence from the deck of a cruise ship. As the ship approaches the glacier, a hushed awe falls over the passengers. The air is charged with anticipation as everyone watches for signs of calving—large chunks of ice breaking off the glacier and plunging into the water below. Cameras click, capturing these fleeting moments of raw beauty and power.

Calving events are the highlight of any visit to Margerie Glacier. As chunks of ice fracture and tumble into the sea, they create a symphony of sound. The cracks and booms reverberate across the water, punctuating the silence with a thunderous chorus. The icebergs that result from calving float in the water, their jagged edges reflecting the sunlight. The spectacle is both humbling and humbling and invigorating, a reminder of nature's unrelenting creative forces.

The ethereal beauty of Margerie Glacier comes with the responsibility to protect and preserve it for future generations. The National Park Service and various organizations work diligently to ensure that Glacier Bay remains a sanctuary of natural wonder. Measures are in place to manage visitor impact, minimize pollution, and promote sustainable tourism practices. The preservation of Margerie Glacier is intertwined with the broader effort to mitigate the impacts of climate change and raise awareness about the fragile balance of our planet's ecosystems.

Margerie Glacier invites us to step into a story that spans eons—a story of ice ages and warming periods, of geological upheavals and quiet retreats. It's a story that reminds us of the impermanence of even the most monumental landscapes and the urgency of our role in feguarding the Earth's delicate balance. Margerie Glacier's majestic calving events, its vivid blue hues, and its enduring presence serve as a timeless testament to the Earth's geological history, the power of glacial forces, and the profound impact of humanity on the natural world.

In conclusion, Margerie Glacier is a natural wonder that captures the essence of Earth's dynamic processes. Its towering ice walls and thunderous calving events offer a glimpse into the raw power of nature, while its vivid blue hues and serene surroundings evoke a sense of wonder and reverence. Witnessing the majesty of Margerie Glacier is an opportunity to connect with the beauty of the natural world and reflect on the intricate interplay of ice, water, and time. As we stand in the presence of this glacial masterpiece, we are reminded of our role as stewards of the Earth and the imperative to preserve the splendor that defines Glacier Bay National Park.

John Hopkins Inlet: A Symphony of Glacial Beauty and Avian Wonders

Nestled within the pristine expanse of Glacier Bay National Park, the John Hopkins Inlet stands as a testament to the captivating beauty and intricate interconnectedness of Earth's natural wonders. This hidden gem within the larger glacial tapestry of Glacier Bay offers visitors a unique blend of breathtaking glacial landscapes and a thriving avian sanctuary. From the towering cliffs to the vibrant ecosystems that flourish in its waters, John Hopkins Inlet presents an opportunity to immerse oneself in a world where glacial beauty and avian splendor converge.

John Hopkins Inlet is a testament to the immense power of glacial erosion and the transformative effects of ice on the landscape. The inlet was carved over millennia by the relentless movement of glaciers, creating a dramatic fjord surrounded by towering cliffs and rocky shores. The towering mountains that flank the inlet bear the marks of glacial activity, their rugged faces revealing the unmistakable imprint of ice's inexorable advance and retreat.

At the head of the inlet lies its icy crown jewel—the John Hopkins Glacier. This tidewater glacier flows from the heights of the Fairweather Range, its ice plunging into the sea with an air of majestic grandeur. The glacier's icy blue hues and intricate patterns evoke a sense of reverence inviting visitors to contemplate the incredible forces that shape our planet's landscapes. The glacier's advance and retreat offer an ever-changing panorama, providing insights into the ebb and flow of Earth's glacial rhythms.

Similar to its counterpart, the Margerie Glacier, the John Hopkins Glacier showcases the mesmerizing phenomenon of calving. As enormous icebergs break away from the glacier's face they plunge into the frigid waters below with a resounding splash. The resulting spectacle is a symphony of sound and motion, a natural performance that echoes across the inlet and reverberates in the hearts of those fortunate enough to witness it. These calving events offer a tangible reminder of the glacier's ceaseless movement and the ongoing processes that shape the world around us.

While the glaciers are the stars of the show, John Hopkins Inlet also serves as a vibrant theater for avian life. The towering cliffs provide nesting sites for a diverse array of seabirds, creating a bustling colony of activity that fills the skies and the waters below. Bird enthusiasts are treated to the sight of puffins, kittiwakes, and cormorants, each species leaving its mark on the tapestry of avian diversity. The cliffs echo with the calls of these winged inhabitants, creating an auditory experience that complements the visual splendor.

John Hopkins Inlet is not only a place of breathtaking beauty; it's also a thriving ecosystem that sustains a delicate balance of life. The nutrient-rich waters support a variety of marine species, from fish to marine mammals. As the glacier feeds into the inlet, it releases minerals that provide sustenance for phytoplankton, the base of the marine food chain. This intricate web of life is a reminder of the interconnectedness of all living things and the vital role that glaciers play in shaping ecosystems.

Like all glaciers, the John Hopkins Glacier is not immune to the impacts of climate change. Rising temperatures have led to the glacier's retreat, altering the landscape and affecting the delicate ecosystems that depend on its presence. The sight of retreating glaciers serves as a stark reminder of the urgent need to address climate change and protect these fragile environments. The conservation efforts within Glacier Bay National Park strive to safeguard this unique ecosystem and educate visitors about the importance of preserving our natural heritage.

Exploring John Hopkins Inlet is a voyage of discovery that offers a multisensory experience. Many visitors have the opportunity to witness the inlet's grandeur from the deck of a cruise ship, sailing past the towering cliffs and gazing in awe at the glacier's frozen façade. The crisp air is filled with the mingling scents of saltwater and ancient ice, creating an atmosphere of purity and reverence. As visitors navigate the inlet's waters, they become part of a narrative that stretches back through time, connecting them with the ancient forces that have shaped this majestic landscape.

John Hopkins Inlet is a place that inspires introspection and contemplation. Its towering cliffs, pristine waters, and majestic glaciers evoke a sense of timelessness, inviting visitors to pause and reflect on the grandeur of the natural world. In a society marked by constant movement and noise, the tranquil serenity of the inlet offers a space for quiet appreciation and connection. As you stand in the presence of this glacial masterpiece, you are reminded of the fleeting beauty of our planet and the responsibility we share in preserving it for generations to come.

In the end, John Hopkins Inlet is more than a geological formation or a habitat for birds—it's a living testament to the ever-changing narrative of our planet. It tells a story of relentless glacial movement, avian resilience, and the interplay of time and nature's creative forces. As visitors stand before the towering glaciers and witness the avian ballet in the skies, they become part of this ongoing story. With every calving event and every bird's call, John Hopkins Inlet reminds us of the enduring beauty of our world and the imperative to cherish and protect it.

In conclusion, John Hopkins Inlet is a symphony of glacial beauty and avian wonders that invites us to explore the intricate dance between ice and life. Its towering cliffs, vibrant ecosystems, and majestic glacier provide a canvas for reflection, contemplation, and connection with the natural world. As visitors navigate its waters and witness its dynamic processes, they become witnesses to the ongoing narrative of Earth's geological history and the delicate balance of its

ecosystems. John Hopkins Inlet leaves an indelible mark on the heart, a reminder of the awe-inspiring beauty that can be found at the intersection of ice and life.

Bartlett Cove: Where Nature and History Converge

Nestled within the pristine embrace of Glacier Bay National Park and Preserve, Bartlett Cove is more than just a geographical location—it's a gateway to the heart of the natural world and a repository of human history. As visitors step onto its shores, they are greeted by a serene cove, towering trees, and the gentle lapping of the waves. Yet, beyond its natural beauty, Bartlett Cove offers a wealth of experiences that invite exploration, learning, and a deep connection with the wilderness. From the Glacier Bay Visitor Center to the intricate network of nature trails, Bartlett Cove is a place where nature and history converge to create an immersive and transformative journey.

As visitors arrive at Bartlett Cove, they are greeted by a tranquil inlet surrounded by dense forests and the majestic mountains that characterize Glacier Bay National Park. The cove's serene waters mirror the changing moods of the sky, reflecting the towering trees that line its shores. This initial encounter with Bartlett Cove serves as an introduction to the park's rugged beauty and the sense of quietude that pervades the wilderness.

The Glacier Bay Visitor Center serves as the focal point of exploration in Bartlett Cove. This center is not just a building; it's a treasure trove of knowledge and a portal to the wonders of the park. Inside, visitors can find interactive exhibits that delve into the geological history of the region, the intricate ecosystems that thrive within it, and the ongoing research efforts that aim to preserve its natural splendor. Park rangers are on hand to answer questions, provide insights, and offer educational programs that illuminate the park's significance and the challenges it faces.

Bartlett Cove is a place where the natural world intersects with human history. Before becoming a national park, these lands were home to indigenous Tlingit and Huna people, whose deep connection with the land and water shaped their cultures and traditions. The visitor center provides an opportunity to learn about their rich history, offering insights into their relationship with the environment and the legacy they left behind. Through exhibits and guided tours, visitors can gain a deeper appreciation for the indigenous cultures that have thrived in these lands for generations.

One of the most captivating aspects of Bartlett Cove is the intricate network of nature trails that wind through its lush forests and meandering shores. These trails offer a unique perspective of

the park's ecosystems and provide opportunities for close encounters with the natural world. The Forest Trail immerses visitors in the temperate rainforest, where towering trees, moss-covered rocks, and the songs of birds create a serene ambiance. The Bartlett River Trail follows the river's course, leading to tranquil viewpoints and opportunities for birdwatching. Each trail tells a different story, unveiling the park's secrets and inviting visitors to become active participants in its narrative.

Bartlett Cove is an ideal starting point for aquatic exploration, with its calm waters providing a safe haven for kayakers and canoeists. Paddling through the cove's serene waters offers a unique perspective of the landscape, allowing visitors to glide past lush shores and observe marine life from a different vantage point. The quiet rhythm of paddling enhances the sense of connection with the surroundings, offering an intimate experience that complements the grandeur of the mountains and forests

Bartlett Cove is a haven for birdwatchers, with its diverse habitats attracting a rich array of avian species. The cove's forests are alive with the melodies of songbirds, while the shoreline and waters host a variety of seabirds and waterfowl. From bald eagles soaring overhead to the haunting calls of loons echoing across the cove, Bartlett Cove provides an auditory and visual symphony for those who appreciate the beauty of birds in their natural habitat.

For those seeking a deeper connection with the wilderness, Bartlett Cove offers opportunities for camping and overnight stays. The park's campgrounds provide a rustic experience, allowing visitors to immerse themselves in the rhythms of the natural world. Falling asleep to the sounds of rustling leaves and waking up to the calls of birds offers a unique perspective of the park's nocturnal and early morning activities. Camping under the starlit sky fosters a sense of humility and wonder, reminding visitors of their place within the vastness of the cosmos.

Bartlett Cove serves as a microcosm of the broader conservation efforts within Glacier Bay National Park and Preserve. The National Park Service, in collaboration with various organizations, works diligently to preserve the delicate balance of the park's ecosystems while offering visitors the opportunity to engage with its beauty. Sustainable tourism practices are in place to minimize human impact, and educational programs inspire a sense of stewardship and responsibility for the park's future.

In the heart of Bartlett Cove, visitors are presented with a canvas of nature's gifts—a symphony of forests, mountains, waters, and the legacies of indigenous cultures. As one walks along the nature trails, watches the sun set over the cove, or listens to the tales of park rangers at the visitor center, a sense of awe and wonder takes root. Bartlett Cove invites self-discovery and reflection, allowing visitors to connect with their inner selves as they connect with the wilderness.

In essence, Bartlett Cove is a place of stories. It's a place where the stories of glaciers, forests, indigenous peoples, and the Earth's geological history converge. As visitors explore its landscapes, engage with its history, and breathe in its serenity, they become part of the ongoing narrative that defines this special place. Each footstep on the trails, each paddle stroke on the cove, and each moment of reflection adds a new chapter to the legacy of Bartlett Cove.

In conclusion, Bartlett Cove is more than a visitor destination—it's a threshold into the world of Glacier Bay National Park and Preserve. It's a place where history is preserved, where ecosystems flourish, and where human curiosity is nurtured. From the Glacier Bay Visitor Center to the inviting nature trails, Bartlett Cove invites visitors to step beyond the ordinary and embrace the extraordinary. It's a space where nature and history come together to create an immersive experience that leaves a lasting imprint on the heart and soul. As visitors depart from its shores, they carry with them not just memories, but a deeper connection to the natural world and a renewed commitment to its preservation.

Kayaking: Immersive Exploration of Nature's Majesty

In the realm of outdoor adventures, kayaking stands as a quintessential activity that offers a unique and intimate connection with the natural world. From tranquil lakes to winding rivers and rugged coastlines, kayaking allows enthusiasts to traverse waterways and immerse themselves in landscapes that often remain hidden from the beaten path. Among the many locations that beckon kayakers, few places rival the allure of Glacier Bay National Park and Preserve in Alaska. This remote and breathtaking destination offers kayaking enthusiasts an unparalleled opportunity to engage with the pristine wilderness, witness majestic glaciers, and connect with the rhythm of nature. In this exploration, we embark on a journey into the world of kayaking—an immersive experience that allows adventurers to explore the grandeur of Glacier Bay like never before.

Kayaking is more than just a mode of transportation on water; it's an art that combines skill, strength, and serenity. The gentle dip of the paddle, the rhythm of the strokes, and the glide of the kayak over the water create a meditative experience that fosters a deep connection with the environment. As kayakers propel themselves forward, they become attuned to the subtleties of the water's currents, the call of distant birds, and the embrace of the landscape. Kayaking transforms the act of movement into a sensory journey, where each stroke brings adventurers closer to the heart of the wilderness.

Nestled within the expansive landscapes of Glacier Bay National Park, kayakers are welcomed by an environment that seems almost untouched by time. The glacier-carved fjords, towering

mountains, and pristine waters create a paradise for those seeking to explore nature's beauty in its purest form. The tranquil waters of the bay offer a canvas for kayakers to embark on their journey of discovery, whether they are beginners seeking serene exploration or experienced paddlers craving a thrilling adventure.

One of the most exhilarating experiences Glacier Bay offers kayakers is the opportunity to paddle among glaciers. Imagine the sensation of gliding through crystal-clear waters, with towering ice walls on either side. As the kayak navigates through icy passages, paddlers can observe the intricate details of the glacier's surface, the brilliant shades of blue, and the crevasses that create a labyrinth of frozen artistry. Paddling near these natural giants evokes a sense of humility and awe, as adventurers are reminded of the immensity and power of nature.

Kayakers in Glacier Bay are often treated to intimate wildlife encounters that are not easily accessible through other means of exploration. The quiet and unobtrusive nature of kayaking allows adventurers to approach wildlife without causing disturbance. From humpback whales breaching the surface to sea otters lounging on kelp beds, the waters of Glacier Bay teem with

e. The rhythmic sound of paddles becomes a symphony that harmonizes with the calls of seabirds and the whispers of the breeze.

For kayakers, every day in Glacier Bay is a canvas of opportunity, stretching from the golden hues of sunrise to the tranquil beauty of sunset. The day begins with the anticipation of exploration as kayakers set out on calm waters, the first rays of light casting a warm glow on the landscape. As the sun climbs higher, its light dances on the water's surface, illuminating hidden coves and revealing the secrets of the shoreline. Each stroke of the paddle takes adventurers deeper into the heart of the wilderness, where the beauty of the land and the tranquility of the water become companions on the journey.

One of the most cherished aspects of kayaking in Glacier Bay is the sense of solitude it offers. Unlike larger vessels, kayaks allow for intimate access to hidden coves, quiet bays, and secluded shores. Paddlers can venture into nooks and crannies that are off the beaten path, forging their own routes through the waterways. This solitude not only fosters a connection with the environment but also provides a space for introspection and contemplation. The rhythmic motion of paddling becomes a form of meditation, allowing kayakers to disconnect from the demands of modern life and immerse themselves in the present moment.

Glacier Bay's kayaking experiences cater to a wide range of skill levels and preferences. For those new to kayaking, guided tours offer an opportunity to learn the basics while exploring the bay's highlights under the guidance of experienced instructors. These tours provide insight into the ecosystem, glacial dynamics, and the park's history, enhancing the journey with a depth of knowledge. Experienced kayakers can opt for more challenging routes, venturing into remote areas where the raw beauty of Glacier Bay is at its most untouched. Multi-day kayaking

expeditions allow adventurers to camp along the shoreline, forging a deep connection with the landscape over an extended period.

With the privilege of kayaking in Glacier Bay comes the responsibility to protect and preserve its delicate ecosystems. The National Park Service and local operators collaborate to ensure that kayaking is conducted in an environmentally responsible manner. Guidelines are in place to minimize human impact, protect wildlife habitats, and prevent pollution. Kayakers are encouraged to leave no trace, practicing a "pack it in, pack it out" approach to waste management. By embracing these principles, kayakers become active participants in the park's conservation efforts.

As kayakers paddle through Glacier Bay's serene waters, their journey is punctuated by moments of wonder and discovery. The sight of a seal peeking curiously above the surface, the sound of a distant waterfall cascading into the bay, and the reflection of snow-capped mountains on tranquil waters become memories etched into their souls. These moments of connection with nature create a lifelong bond, a connection that draws adventurers back to the water time and again. The memories carved in water become a source of inspiration, reminding kayakers of the beauty and fragility of our planet.

Kayaking in Glacier Bay transcends the boundaries of adventure; it becomes a spiritual journey—an exploration of the self as much as the environment. The rhythmic paddling, the symphony of nature's sounds, and the embrace of solitude allow kayakers to tap into a profound sense of connectedness with the natural world. In the midst of this untouched wilderness, kayakers find themselves humbled by the grandeur of the glaciers, invigorated by the purity of the waters, and enriched by the stories whispered by the breeze. Through kayaking, adventurers become not just witnesses but active participants in the symphony of Glacier Bay, fostering a bond that lingers long after the paddles are stowed away.

Whale Watching: Embarking on Majestic Marine Encounters

In the realm of nature's wonders, few experiences match the awe and fascination of encountering whales in their natural habitat. Whale watching has evolved from a mere pastime into a profound and transformative adventure, allowing enthusiasts to witness the magnificence of these marine giants and gain a deeper appreciation for the intricacies of ocean ecosystems. Among the premier destinations for whale watching, few places rival the breathtaking beauty and diversity of Glacier Bay National Park in Alaska. As visitors set sail on its pristine waters, they

are granted a front-row seat to one of the most captivating displays in the natural world—the majestic dance of whales against the backdrop of glaciers and mountains. In this exploration, we delve into the world of whale watching—a voyage that invites us to connect with nature's grandeur, contemplate the mysteries of the ocean, and champion the preservation of these magnificent creatures.

Whales occupy a unique place in the human psyche—an embodiment of the vastness and mystery of the ocean. Their sheer size and grace inspire reverence, while their movements beneath the waves convey a sense of intelligence and wonder. For centuries, these marine mammals have captivated human imagination, from ancient maritime myths to modern conservation efforts. Whale watching offers an opportunity to go beyond the surface and witness these creatures in their element, forging a connection that transcends mere observation.

Glacier Bay National Park stands as a haven for marine life, attracting an array of whale species due to its nutrient-rich waters and diverse ecosystems. Humpback whales, orcas, minke whales, gray whales, and more grace the bay's waters with their presence. The park's location, nestled between the Fairweather Range and the Pacific Ocean, creates a unique confluence of conditions that sustains a bountiful marine food chain. As these species navigate the cold Alaskan waters, they provide visitors with a stunning spectacle of nature's biodiversity.

Among the charismatic cetaceans that inhabit Glacier Bay, humpback whales take center stage. These giants of the sea are renowned for their acrobatic displays, including breaching, tail slapping, and fluke waving. The sight of a humpback whale breaching—a massive body propelling itself out of the water and crashing back with a thunderous splash—is an indelible image that leaves observers in awe. The reasons behind these behaviors remain a subject of scientific inquiry, but the experience of witnessing such displays is universally captivating.

Orcas, often referred to as killer whales, are another iconic presence in Glacier Bay's waters. These apex predators are known for their intelligence, complex social structures, and diverse hunting techniques. The sight of an orca pod slicing through the water with coordinated precision is a reminder of the intricate dynamics of marine life. Orcas' distinctive black-and-white markings and their role as top predators in the ecosystem contribute to their allure and mystique.

Whale watching in Glacier Bay also highlights the fascinating phenomenon of migration. Many whale species undertake epic journeys spanning thousands of miles, driven by the quest for food, mating opportunities, and warmer waters for calving. Observing these majestic creatures as they traverse the oceans to reach their breeding or feeding grounds underscores the interconnectedness of global ecosystems. It's a reminder that the health of these distant habitats impacts the well-being of the whales that rely on them.

Whales hold profound cultural significance in indigenous traditions, particularly for the Tlingit and Huna people who have called the region home for generations. These communities have deep-rooted connections with the marine environment, and whales are often depicted in their art, stories, and oral histories. Observing whales in Glacier Bay carries echoes of these cultural connections, as visitors witness not only the natural beauty of the animals but also the intertwined relationship between indigenous cultures and the ocean.

Whale watching, when conducted responsibly, can serve as a powerful tool for ecotourism and conservation. By fostering an appreciation for whales and the marine environments they inhabit, it encourages visitors to become advocates for ocean preservation. Many tour operators in Glacier Bay adhere to strict guidelines to minimize disturbance to the animals, maintaining a safe and respectful distance while providing informative narratives that enhance the experience. As visitors gain a deeper understanding of these creatures, they are more likely to support conservation efforts aimed at protecting their habitats and mitigating threats.

Whale watching in Glacier Bay is a spectacle of oceanic elegance. As visitors set sail on the calm waters, anticipation hangs in the air. The first sighting of a spout—a column of water vapor rising from the surface—elicits a collective gasp, a moment of shared wonder that transcends language and background. Binoculars and cameras are poised, ready to capture the breathtaking moments that unfold as whales breach, flukes emerge from the water, and dorsal fins slice through the surface.

One of the most captivating aspects of whale watching is the opportunity to hear the enchanting songs of certain whale species, most famously the humpback whale. These songs are complex and hauntingly beautiful, with intricate patterns and melodies that resonate through the water. The purpose of these songs remains a mystery, whether they are for mating, communication, or other functions. Regardless of their purpose, the experience of listening to a whale's song adds a layer of depth to the encounter, immersing observers in the auditory tapestry of the ocean.

While the experience of whale watching is undeniably captivating, it's important to acknowledge the challenges that whales face in the modern world. Whales are vulnerable to a range of threats, including ship strikes, entanglement in fishing gear, habitat degradation, and climate change. Conservation efforts are crucial to ensure the survival of these majestic creatures and the preservation of their habitats. By engaging in responsible whale watching and supporting organizations dedicated to marine conservation, visitors become allies in the fight to protect the giants of the sea.

Whale watching in Glacier Bay leaves an enduring imprint on the hearts of those fortunate enough to witness these majestic marine creatures. The experience becomes a touchstone—a reminder of the delicate balance of the ocean, the mysteries that still await discovery, and the responsibility to be stewards of the natural world. As observers return from their encounters,

they carry with them a profound connection to the whales, the oceans, and the interconnected web of life that sustains us all.

Whale watching in Glacier Bay is more than a pastime; it's a symphony of wonder that resonates in the soul. The sight of a whale's fluke disappearing into the depths, the sound of its breath echoing across the water, and the knowledge of the epic journeys these creatures undertake create a tapestry of awe. Through whale watching, adventurers become witnesses to the rhythms of the ocean, the mysteries of marine life, and the timeless beauty of the natural world. It's an invitation to explore, contemplate, and ultimately celebrate the magnificence of Earth's oceans and the creatures that call them home.

Icy Strait Point: Immerse Yourself in an Authentic Alaskan Experience

Nestled within the pristine wilderness of Hoonah, Alaska, Icy Strait Point beckons travelers with the promise of an unparalleled and authentic Alaskan experience. This unique destination stands as a testament to the harmonious relationship between nature and culture, offering visitors a chance to engage with the region's rich history, indigenous heritage, and awe-inspiring landscapes. Far from the bustling crowds of traditional ports, Icy Strait Point provides a tranquil haven where nature's wonders and cultural immersion converge. This exploration delves into the depths of Icy Strait Point, revealing its indigenous roots, sustainable practices, wildlife encounters, adventure offerings, and the transformative journey it offers to those seeking an intimate and genuine connection with the Last Frontier.

At the heart of Icy Strait Point lies a profound connection to the indigenous Tlingit people, who have inhabited the region for thousands of years. The Huna Tlingit, in particular, have deep ties to the land, sea, and forests that encompass the area. Icy Strait Point is owned and operated by Huna Totem Corporation, a Tlingit-owned organization that embraces the principles of sustainability, preservation of heritage, and sharing the cultural legacy with visitors. Exploring the grounds, visitors encounter art installations, totem poles, and interpretive displays that tell the stories of the Tlingit people and their profound relationship with the natural world.

Icy Strait Point offers a range of authentic cultural experiences that allow visitors to connect with the Tlingit culture on a personal level. The Native Heritage Center showcases traditional dance performances, storytelling, and art demonstrations that provide insight into the spiritual significance of rituals and practices. The experience extends beyond observation, as visitors can actively participate in activities like beading, wood carving, and blanket weaving, gaining firsthand knowledge of ancient skills passed down through generations.

The surrounding waters of Icy Strait Point are a thriving ecosystem where marine life thrives. Whale watching tours are a highlight, offering the chance to witness humpback whales breaching, tail slapping, and feeding in their natural habitat. The nutrient-rich waters attract various marine species, including orcas, sea lions, seals, and porpoises, creating an unforgettable marine safari. Guided by expert naturalists, visitors gain insights into the behavior and biology of these magnificent creatures while fostering a deeper appreciation for the delicate balance of Alaska's ecosystem.

For those seeking more adventurous pursuits, Icy Strait Point provides an array of activities that highlight the rugged beauty of Alaska's wilderness. Zip-lining through the treetops offers a unique vantage point, allowing you to soar above the verdant landscape while admiring the expansive views of the sea. Guided ATV tours venture into the heart of the forest, granting access to hidden trails and panoramic vistas. Kayaking in the sheltered waters of Port Frederick offers a serene way to connect with the surrounding nature while observing wildlife up close.

Icy Strait Point is a model for sustainable tourism, prioritizing the preservation of natural resources and the minimization of environmental impact. From the construction of the port to the operations of its attractions, sustainability is at the forefront. The restoration of a salmon cannery into a cultural center exemplifies the dedication to preserving historical structures while offering educational opportunities. Additionally, the region's commitment to wildlife conservation ensures that encounters with animals are respectful and nonintrusive, maintaining the well-being of the ecosystem.

The culinary experiences at Icy Strait Point celebrate the bounty of Alaska's land and sea. The restored cannery houses restaurants that showcase fresh and locally sourced ingredients, including seafood harvested from the surrounding waters. Visitors can savor Alaskan king crab, wild salmon, and other delicacies while admiring sweeping views of the landscape. Participating in culinary demonstrations and tastings provides insights into the traditional and contemporary flavors of Alaska, enriching the cultural experience.

More than a mere destination, Icy Strait Point offers a transformative journey that transcends tourism and delves into the soul of Alaska. The preservation of heritage, celebration of culture, and the embrace of sustainable practices align to create an environment where visitors are not only awed by the landscapes but also enriched by the authentic interactions and educational experiences. The quiet moments spent in the shadow of towering totem poles, the exchanges with Tlingit artisans, and the awe-inspiring encounters with wildlife collectively shape a narrative of connection, reverence, and understanding.

In conclusion, Icy Strait Point stands as a living testament to the delicate harmony between nature and culture. It invites travelers to step beyond the surface of Alaska's landscapes and delve into the heart of its indigenous roots, rich heritage, and thriving ecosystems. The authenticity of the experiences offered, the commitment to sustainability, and the opportunity for personal transformation make Icy Strait Point not just a port of call but a gateway to a deeper appreciation of the intricate tapestry that defines the Last Frontier.

Attractions and Activities

y Strait Point offers a plethora of attractions and activities that provide an authentic and
nmersive Alaskan experience. Here are five of the best attractions and activities that showcase
ie essence of this unique destination:

Whale Watching Tour: Witness Marine Giants

mbark on a whale watching tour that takes you into the pristine waters surrounding Icy Strait
oint. This activity offers an unparalleled opportunity to witness humpback whales in their
atural habitat, breaching and feeding. Knowledgeable naturalists provide insights into the
ehavior and biology of these magnificent creatures while highlighting the delicate balance of
laska's marine ecosystem. The experience of encountering these marine giants up close is
oth awe-inspiring and humbling, leaving an indelible mark on your Alaskan journey.

Native Heritage Center: Immerse in Tlingit Culture

xplore the Native Heritage Center, where the rich Tlingit culture comes to life through
iteractive exhibits, storytelling, and traditional performances. Engage in activities like beading,
ood carving, and blanket weaving, gaining firsthand experience of skills passed down through
enerations. Totem poles and art installations reveal the deep spiritual connection between the
lingit people and the natural world. The center serves as a bridge between the past and
resent, offering a profound understanding of the indigenous roots that define Icy Strait Point.

Zip-lining Adventure: Soar Above the Wilderness

or an adrenaline-fueled adventure, embark on a zip-lining experience that allows you to soar
bove the lush Alaskan wilderness. Zip-lining through the treetops provides a unique

erspective, offering sweeping views of the landscape, the sea, and the surrounding mountains.
he rush of the wind against your face, combined with the breathtaking vistas, creates an
xhilarating experience that connects you with the natural beauty of the region in an
nforgettable way.

ATV Exploration: Traverse Hidden Trails

enture deep into the heart of the Alaskan forest with a guided ATV tour. Traverse hidden trails
nd rugged terrain as you journey through the wilderness. This activity allows you to connect

with nature on a more intimate level, as you navigate through towering trees and enjoy panoramic views of the landscape. The experienced guides provide insights into the local flora fauna, and the importance of preserving these pristine ecosystems.

5. Port Frederick Kayaking: Serene Wilderness Encounter

Embark on a kayaking adventure in the sheltered waters of Port Frederick. Paddle through cal waters surrounded by breathtaking landscapes, including lush forests and majestic mountains The tranquility of kayaking allows you to observe wildlife up close without disturbing their natural behaviors. Keep an eye out for marine life, such as sea otters, seals, and eagles, while relishing the serene beauty of Alaska's wilderness.

These attractions and activities at Icy Strait Point encapsulate the essence of an authentic Alaskan experience. Whether you're seeking encounters with wildlife, cultural immersion, adrenaline-fueled adventures, or serene explorations of nature, Icy Strait Point offers a diverse range of opportunities to connect with the region's rich heritage and awe-inspiring landscapes Each experience adds depth to your understanding of Alaska's intricate tapestry, making your journey a truly transformative one.

Whale Watching Tour: Immerse Yourself in the Majesty of Marine Giants

In the vast expanse of the ocean, a dance of giants unfolds beneath the surface. Humpback whales, the magnificent leviathans of the deep, breach and frolic in their natural habitat, captivating the hearts and imaginations of those fortunate enough to witness their graceful performances. Embarking on a whale watching tour is an invitation to partake in one of nature's

most awe-inspiring spectacles—a journey that transcends the ordinary and plunges you into the realm of marine giants. In no place is this experience more remarkable than in the pristine waters surrounding Icy Strait Point, where humpback whales converge to feed, play, and captivate onlookers in an encounter that resonates deeply with the essence of the Last Frontier.

The experience of witnessing humpback whales in the wild is akin to attending a grand symphony, where the rhythms of the ocean, the crescendo of waves, and the harmony of nature's creatures merge into a magnificent composition. The symphony begins with the distinctive sound of the humpback's exhalation—the blow, followed by the dramatic pause as the majestic flukes rise above the water's surface, revealing the sheer power and elegance of these marine giants.

Humpback whales are renowned for their incredible migratory journeys, covering thousands of miles between their feeding and breeding grounds. The Alaskan waters serve as a vital feeding ground for these cetaceans, as they gorge themselves on krill and small fish to build the reserves needed for their migration to tropical breeding areas. Icy Strait Point is strategically located along the migratory route, making it an ideal destination for witnessing the majestic humpbacks as they engage in behaviors that have captivated human curiosity for centuries.

Whale watching tours at Icy Strait Point are led by expert naturalists who possess an intimate understanding of the whales' behaviors, migration patterns, and social dynamics. These knowledgeable guides transform the experience into an educational and immersive journey. They share insights into the biology of the humpbacks, explaining how to identify individual whales based on unique markings and patterns on their flukes. As you cruise the waters, these guides provide a rich narrative that unveils the secret lives of the marine giants, enhancing your connection with these majestic creatures.

Humpback whales are known for their acrobatic displays that include breaching, tail slapping, and spy hopping. Breaching, in which a whale propels its massive body out of the water and crashes back with a resounding splash, remains one of the most iconic behaviors. The reasons behind breaching are still debated by researchers—whether it's for communication, play, or simply a display of strength. Tail slapping, where the tail fin is rhythmically slapped against the water's surface, is another mesmerizing behavior often interpreted as a form of communication.

One of the most remarkable aspects of humpback whales is their intricate and hauntingly beautiful songs. Male humpbacks are known for their complex songs, which are composed of a sequence of sounds that can last for hours. These songs are believed to serve various purposes, from attracting potential mates to establishing territory. Each season, the song evolves, adding new layers and variations—a phenomenon that remains one of the great mysteries of the animal kingdom. While onboard a whale watching tour, hydrophones may be deployed into the water, allowing you to listen to the ethereal melodies of the humpbacks as they echo through the depths.

Responsible whale watching is grounded in principles of conservation and ethics. The well-being of the whales and the preservation of their natural behaviors are paramount. Whale watching operators at Icy Strait Point adhere to strict guidelines that maintain a safe distance from the animals, avoiding any disturbance to their activities. This approach ensures that the interactions are respectful, nonintrusive, and in harmony with the ecological balance of the marine environment.

Embarking on a whale watching tour transcends mere observation; it fosters a profound connection with the natural world. The sight of a humpback whale breaching, the echo of its song, and the ripple of its flukes against the water's surface create memories that linger long after the tour concludes. Witnessing these marine giants in their habitat prompts contemplation of the intricate interconnectedness of life on Earth, as well as the importance of preserving these ecosystems for future generations.

The legacy of the humpback whales extends beyond their majestic presence—it is woven into the fabric of cultural mythology, scientific exploration, and the shared wonderment of humanity. Witnessing them in their natural environment evokes a sense of humility and reverence, urging us to protect and conserve the oceans they call home. The impact of a whale watching tour at Icy Strait Point lingers as a transformative journey, where the vastness of the ocean and the grace of the humpbacks intertwine to remind us of the beauty and fragility of our planet.

In conclusion, a whale watching tour is an invitation to immerse yourself in the majesty of marine giants, a voyage that transcends the ordinary and delves into the extraordinary realm of humpback whales. Icy Strait Point, with its strategic location and expert naturalists, offers a unique vantage point for this awe-inspiring encounter. As you witness the breaching, tail slapping, and melodic songs of these cetaceans, you become part of a symphony that celebrates the timeless connection between humanity and the oceans, leaving you forever transformed by the beauty and wonder of the marine world.

Native Heritage Center: A Portal to Tlingit Culture and Legacy

In the heart of the Alaskan wilderness, nestled within the tranquil embrace of Icy Strait Point, lies a cultural haven that serves as a bridge between the past and the present. The Native Heritage Center stands as a testament to the enduring spirit of the Tlingit people, preserving and sharing their rich cultural heritage with visitors from around the world. This immersive center not only showcases the artistry, traditions, and history of the Tlingit people but also

fosters a deep connection between generations and cultivates a profound understanding of the intricate tapestry that defines Alaskan indigenous cultures.

The Native Heritage Center invites visitors to step into the heart of Tlingit traditions, where stories are told through intricate totem poles, handcrafted artifacts, and mesmerizing dance performances. Each element within the center resonates with the spirit of the Tlingit people, reflecting their deep connection to the land, sea, and sky. Totem poles, intricately carved with symbols and stories, stand as silent witnesses to centuries of heritage and wisdom, embodying the Tlingit philosophy of unity between humans and the natural world.

At the Native Heritage Center, art is not a relic of the past; it is a living expression that continues to evolve and thrive. Visitors are invited to engage in hands-on art demonstrations and workshops, where skilled artisans share their expertise in beadwork, wood carving, and other traditional crafts. These interactive experiences provide a rare opportunity to delve into the techniques that have been passed down through generations, bridging the gap between ancient customs and contemporary expression.

A highlight of the Native Heritage Center is its vibrant dance performances, where the Tlingit culture comes alive through rhythmic movements, intricate regalia, and mesmerizing storytelling. Traditional dances are more than mere entertainment—they are conduits for passing down narratives, legends, and historical events. The performances celebrate the interconnectedness of the Tlingit people with the world around them, creating a visceral connection between performers and audience members.

The Native Heritage Center serves as a platform for cultural exchange, fostering understanding and appreciation among diverse communities. It opens a window into the Tlingit way of life, allowing visitors to grasp the deep respect for nature, the reverence for ancestors, and the close-knit communal bonds that define Tlingit society. Through personal interactions, visitors gain insights into the values, rituals, and beliefs that have shaped the Tlingit worldview.

For the Tlingit people, the Native Heritage Center represents more than a physical space—it symbolizes the revitalization of cultural identity. It stands as a testament to the resilience of a community that has weathered challenges and adversity, yet remains committed to preserving its heritage for future generations. The center serves as a hub for fostering a sense of pride and belonging, ensuring that the traditions of the Tlingit people remain vibrant and relevant in a rapidly changing world.

The Native Heritage Center operates on the principle that culture is not static; it evolves while staying rooted in its origins. By preserving and perpetuating traditional practices, the center provides a foundation upon which new generations can build their own expressions of identity. It instills a sense of responsibility and stewardship among young Tlingit individuals, empowering them to become custodians of their cultural legacy.

One of the core principles of the Native Heritage Center is ethical tourism—a commitment to upholding the integrity of the Tlingit culture and ensuring that interactions are respectful and mutually beneficial. Visitors are encouraged to approach the center with an open heart and a willingness to learn, understanding that the Tlingit culture is not a commodity but a living, breathing entity that deserves reverence and respect.

A visit to the Native Heritage Center is not merely a tour; it is a transformative journey that transcends geographical distances and temporal boundaries. It is an encounter that imparts wisdom, fosters understanding, and kindles empathy. The totem poles speak of ancient stories, the dance performances resonate with ancestral voices, and the workshops offer a tangible connection to the past. As visitors leave the center, they carry with them not only cherished memories but also a profound appreciation for the diversity of human culture and the enduring legacy of the Tlingit people.

The Native Heritage Center stands as a beacon of cultural continuity, ensuring that the Tlingit people's ancestral wisdom remains alive and relevant in the modern world. It provides a sanctuary where traditions are celebrated, stories are shared, and the essence of Tlingit culture is captured for posterity. More than a physical space, the center is a sanctuary of the soul—a place where past and present intersect, where stories are woven into existence, and where the Tlingit people's legacy continues to flourish.

In conclusion, the Native Heritage Center is a testament to the resilience, vitality, and enduring spirit of the Tlingit people. It is a portal through which visitors can step into the heart of Tlingit culture, immersing themselves in traditions, stories, and artistry that have transcended time. The center's commitment to cultural preservation, ethical tourism, and intergenerational exchange ensures that the flame of Tlingit heritage burns brightly, illuminating the path for all who seek to understand, appreciate, and celebrate the rich tapestry of Alaska's indigenous cultures.

Zip-lining Adventure: Soaring Through the Alaskan Wilderness

In the heart of Alaska's untamed wilderness, an exhilarating adventure awaits—one that defies gravity and offers a unique perspective of the landscape that stretches before you. The art of zip-lining has evolved from a daredevil's dream into an accessible and thrilling outdoor activity that allows participants to experience the natural world from an entirely new vantage point. At Icy Strait Point, nestled within the serene embrace of nature, the zip-lining adventure takes on a

distinct character, offering an opportunity to soar above the wilderness, witness panoramic views, and create memories that linger long after the exhilaration has subsided.

p-lining is more than a recreational pursuit; it's an invitation to elevate your senses, defy gravity, and immerse yourself in an experience that seamlessly blends adrenaline with awe. The journey begins as you ascend to the launch platform, anticipation building with each step. The moment your feet leave the platform, you're suspended in mid-air, the wind rushing past your face, and the landscape unfolding beneath you in a breathtaking panorama.

s you zip along the cable, the symphony of sights and sensations unfolds around you. The beauty of the wilderness comes alive in new and unexpected ways—the rustling leaves, the scent of pine, and the distant calls of wildlife create an immersive sensory experience. The vastness of the Alaskan wilderness stretches out before you, revealing mountains, valleys, and shimmering waters that paint a landscape both majestic and serene.

ne of the most remarkable aspects of zip-lining is the perspective it provides—a bird's-eye view of the world below. The treetops become your playground as you traverse the canopy, gaining an intimate understanding of the complex ecosystems that thrive in these heights. Observing the interconnectedness of plant life, the shimmering rivers, and the undulating terrain from this vantage point offers a profound appreciation for the delicate balance of nature.

While the thrill of zip-lining is undeniable, there's a paradoxical tranquility that accompanies the experience. The rush of adrenaline is accompanied by moments of serene contemplation as you glide through the air. The rhythmic motion becomes a meditation, allowing you to connect with the environment and find solace in the embrace of nature.

ip-lining adventures at Icy Strait Point adhere to principles of environmental stewardship, ensuring that the experience is not only thrilling but also respectful of the natural surroundings. The platforms and cables are strategically positioned to minimize impact on the ecosystem, preserving the delicate balance of the wilderness. The adventure serves as a model for responsible adventure tourism, encouraging participants to engage with nature while safeguarding its integrity.

ip-lining is often a personal triumph—an opportunity to conquer fears, push boundaries, and discover newfound courage. Stepping off the platform requires a leap of faith, a willingness to embrace the unknown and overcome doubts. The sense of accomplishment that follows is a reminder of the power of stepping outside your comfort zone and embracing the challenges that life presents.

Zip-lining often becomes a shared experience that forges bonds and creates lasting memories. The camaraderie that forms among participants as they embark on this adventure together is palpable. Laughter, encouragement, and the collective celebration of conquering fears foster a sense of connection that transcends the exhilaration of the moment.

The impact of a zip-lining adventure extends beyond the immediate thrill—it's a journey that leaves an indelible mark on the soul. The rush of wind, the panoramic views, and the intimate connection with the wilderness become a part of you, shaping your perspective and rekindling a sense of wonder for the natural world. The transformative power of the experience is a testament to the human spirit's capacity for exploration and discovery.

Zip-lining is a journey beyond physical boundaries—it's a metaphorical leap into the unknown that mirrors life's many adventures. The courage to step off the platform, the exhilaration of the ride, and the triumph of reaching the end resonate with the broader journey of personal growth and exploration. It's a reminder that embracing the unknown and pushing past limitations can lead to profound moments of self-discovery.

The zip-lining adventure at Icy Strait Point serves as a reminder of the importance of preserving the wild landscapes that provide the backdrop for these exhilarating experiences. It fosters a connection between participants and the environment, inspiring a desire to protect the natural world for future generations. This connection, born from the rush of zip-lining, can lead to a deeper commitment to conservation and environmental stewardship.

In conclusion, a zip-lining adventure at Icy Strait Point is more than a thrilling experience; it's a journey that transcends the confines of gravity and offers a fresh perspective on the world. The rush of wind, the panoramic views, and the sense of accomplishment combine to create a transformative encounter that lingers long after the adventure concludes. It's a testament to the human spirit's capacity for exploration, the bonds that form through shared experiences, and the profound impact that nature's beauty can have on the soul.

ATV Exploration: Unveiling the Wilderness through Hidden Trails

In the heart of Alaska's rugged landscapes, where towering mountains meet dense forests and crystalline waters, an adventure of exploration and discovery awaits. ATV (All-Terrain Vehicle) exploration is a gateway to traverse hidden trails that wind through the wilderness, unveiling the raw beauty and untamed majesty of the Last Frontier. At Icy Strait Point, nestled within the embrace of nature's grandeur, the ATV adventure takes on a unique character, offering participants an opportunity to connect with the land, navigate through hidden paths, and create memories that resonate long after the engines have quieted.

ATV exploration is more than an outdoor activity; it's an invitation to embrace the wilderness with open arms. As participants gear up and embark on their ATVs, a sense of anticipation fills the air. The roar of the engine becomes a symphony that echoes the heartbeat of the land, a rhythmic pulse that draws adventurers into the heart of the untamed.

The trail ahead unfolds like a story waiting to be told, each turn revealing a new facet of the landscape's character. From densely wooded areas to open meadows, the diversity of terrains mirrors the complexity of the Alaskan wilderness. The rhythmic bounce of the ATV over rocky terrain and the gust of wind against your face become tactile reminders of your immersion in nature.

One of the most enchanting aspects of ATV exploration is the discovery of hidden gems that lie beyond the beaten path. The trails wind through pristine landscapes that may have remained untouched for generations. As you navigate through secluded trails, you encounter breathtaking vistas, secret viewpoints, and pristine waterways that are inaccessible by conventional means. These hidden treasures become a part of your personal journey, etching their beauty into your memory.

ATV exploration offers an intimate connection with the land that few other activities provide. The sensation of guiding the ATV through the wilderness—whether crossing streams, ascending hills, or navigating twists and turns—forges a deep bond between participant and environment. The land becomes your partner in adventure, guiding your journey and offering challenges that evoke a sense of accomplishment.

As you traverse hidden trails, the landscape becomes a living classroom that imparts insights into ecology, biodiversity, and the delicate balance of the ecosystem. Expert guides offer commentary on the flora, fauna, and geological formations that shape the land. You gain an appreciation for the resilience of life in the wilderness and the interconnectedness of all living beings.

The Alaskan wilderness is not only a natural wonder; it's also a canvas of cultural and historical significance. ATV exploration often weaves stories of indigenous peoples, explorers, and pioneers who have left their marks on the land. These narratives add depth to the adventure, transforming it into a multi-layered experience that connects you with the heritage and stories of those who have walked the same trails.

ATV exploration transcends physical boundaries—it's an invitation to explore remote and inaccessible areas that are otherwise beyond reach. The vehicles provide access to landscapes that remain largely untouched, allowing you to immerse yourself in the unspoiled beauty of Alaska's wilderness. This sense of exploration echoes the spirit of the early pioneers who ventured into the unknown, seeking to understand and connect with the land.

Icy Strait Point's ATV exploration adventures are guided by principles of environmental stewardship. Trails are carefully selected to minimize impact on the environment, ensuring that the natural integrity of the landscape remains preserved. ATV exploration is a model for responsible adventure tourism, striking a balance between satisfying the human desire for adventure while safeguarding the delicate ecosystems that sustain life.

ATV exploration is more than just a physical journey; it's a path of personal growth and self-discovery. Conquering challenging terrains, navigating obstacles, and pushing the boundaries of your comfort zone foster a sense of accomplishment and empowerment. The adventure becomes a mirror for life's challenges, reminding you of your resilience and capacity to overcome obstacles.

ATV exploration often becomes a shared experience that fosters bonds and creates lasting memories. The camaraderie that forms among participants as they navigate through hidden trails is palpable. Laughter, encouragement, and the collective celebration of challenges overcome forge connections that transcend the adventure itself.

In conclusion, ATV exploration is a journey that transcends the bounds of the ordinary and the familiar. It's an opportunity to immerse yourself in the wilderness, to traverse hidden trails that reveal the intricacies of the land's character. The rhythm of the engine, the varied terrains, and the shared experiences all culminate in a transformative encounter that lingers long after the adventure concludes. ATV exploration is a reminder that nature's beauty is best experienced up close, and that the wilderness is a canvas of stories waiting to be discovered. It's an ode to exploration, a celebration of nature's grandeur, and a testament to the resilience of the human spirit.

Port Frederick Kayaking: Paddling Through Serenity and Splendor

In the embrace of Alaska's majestic landscapes, where mountains meet the sea and untamed wilderness flourishes, an enchanting adventure awaits—one that allows you to connect intimately with nature and experience the serenity of the wild. Kayaking at Port Frederick offers a serene wilderness encounter that transcends the ordinary and immerses you in a world of natural beauty and tranquility. Amidst the pristine waters and the breathtaking vistas of Icy Strait Point, kayaking becomes a journey of discovery, a connection with marine life, and an opportunity to create memories that echo long after the gentle ripples have faded.

Kayaking is more than a recreational pursuit; it's an invitation to paddle through the symphony of nature's serenity. As you glide across the calm waters of Port Frederick, the rhythmic motion of the paddle becomes a soothing cadence, in harmony with the gentle lap of water against the kayak's hull. The tranquility is palpable, and you become an integral part of the serene composition that unfolds around you.

The panoramic views that greet you while kayaking in Port Frederick are nothing short of awe-inspiring. Towering mountains, verdant forests, and the vast expanse of the sea converge to create a breathtaking tableau of natural beauty. The juxtaposition of earth, water, and sky offers a profound appreciation for the delicate balance of the ecosystem and the grandeur of the Alaskan wilderness.

Kayaking in Port Frederick is an opportunity to enter the realm of marine life, observing creatures in their natural habitat without disrupting their activities. The sheltered waters teem with life—sea otters playfully float on their backs, harbor seals curiously peer from the water's surface, and eagles soar overhead, scanning the waters for a potential meal. The kayak becomes a window to the ocean's wonders, allowing you to witness the daily rituals of these majestic creatures.

One of the remarkable aspects of kayaking is the silent mode of transportation it offers. Unlike motorized vessels, kayaks glide through the water with minimal disturbance, allowing for nonintrusive encounters with wildlife. This quiet approach enables you to observe marine life exhibiting their natural behaviors, from foraging to resting, providing a glimpse into the intricate web of life beneath the waves.

While kayaking offers moments of tranquility, it is also an active endeavor that engages both body and mind. The rhythmic paddling engages your muscles as you navigate the waters, creating a sense of oneness with the environment. The act of paddling becomes a form of meditation, allowing you to be fully present in the moment and attuned to the world around you.

Guided kayaking expeditions at Port Frederick are led by local experts who possess intimate knowledge of the ecosystem, marine life, and the history of the region. These guides enrich the experience with commentary on the flora and fauna, sharing stories of the land's indigenous peoples, and providing insights into the delicate balance of the environment. Their expertise adds depth to the adventure, transforming it into an educational and enlightening journey.

Kayaking adventures at Icy Strait Point adhere to principles of environmental respect and stewardship. Routes are carefully planned to minimize impact on sensitive ecosystems, ensuring that the natural balance remains undisturbed. The commitment to preserving the wilderness ensures that kayaking participants become ambassadors for responsible adventure tourism, fostering a deeper understanding of the delicate ecosystems they explore.

The waters of Port Frederick are not just a canvas of natural beauty; they are also steeped in cultural and historical significance. Indigenous peoples have navigated these waters for generations, and the sea holds stories of their traditions, livelihoods, and encounters with the wilderness. As you paddle through these waters, you connect with a legacy that extends beyond the present moment, feeling the echoes of those who have come before.

Kayaking at Port Frederick offers more than just physical activity—it provides a transformative connection with nature's healing power. The rhythmic motion of the paddle, the gentle lapping of water, and the encompassing embrace of the landscape create a sense of calm and inner peace. The experience becomes a balm for the soul, washing away the stresses of modern life and inviting you to be fully present in the moment.

Kayaking adventures often become shared moments of camaraderie, forging connections and creating lasting memories. The experience of paddling together, observing marine life, and sharing in the wonders of the wilderness fosters a sense of unity among participants. Laughter, shared observations, and the collective awe of nature's beauty create bonds that transcend the adventure itself.

In conclusion, kayaking at Port Frederick is an invitation to immerse yourself in the serenity and splendor of the Alaskan wilderness. It's a journey that transcends the ordinary and offers a unique perspective of the natural world. The paddle becomes your connection to marine life, the waters become your canvas of exploration, and the memories become a lasting legacy. The experience serves as a reminder of the importance of environmental stewardship and the profound impact that responsible adventure tourism can have on fostering a deeper connection between humans and the natural world. Kayaking becomes a conduit for understanding, respect, and awe—an experience that echoes in the heart long after the kayak has been returned to the tranquil waters of Port Frederick.

Section 4: Cruise Ship Amenities and Features

Cabin Options in Alaska Cruise: A Home Away from Home at Sea

Embarking on an Alaska cruise is a journey of a lifetime, a chance to explore the pristine landscapes and breathtaking beauty of the Last Frontier. As you plan your cruise adventure, one of the key decisions you'll make is choosing the perfect cabin to call your home away from home during your voyage. From cozy interiors to luxurious suites, Alaska cruises offer a range of cabin options to suit every traveler's preferences and budget. Let's delve into the variety of cabin choices available, each promising comfort, convenience, and a front-row seat to the wonders of the Alaskan wilderness.

1. Interior Cabins: Cozy Retreats

Interior cabins are a popular choice for travelers seeking a comfortable and budget-friendly option. These cabins are located within the ship's interior, providing a peaceful and private retreat. While they may not offer windows or balconies, interior cabins are well-appointed with all the essential amenities to ensure a restful stay. They are ideal for those who plan to spend most of their time exploring the ship's facilities and enjoying the various activities and entertainment.

2. Oceanview Cabins: Views of the Sea

For those who appreciate natural light and glimpses of the sea, oceanview cabins are a wonderful choice. These cabins feature windows or portholes that allow you to admire the changing scenery and catch sight of passing wildlife from the comfort of your cabin. Oceanview cabins offer a balance between affordability and the joy of having a connection to the outside world, making them a popular choice for cruisers who want a touch of the maritime experience.

3. Balcony Cabins: Personal Outdoor Retreats

Balcony cabins take the cruising experience to the next level by providing your own private outdoor space. Step out onto your balcony to breathe in the fresh Alaskan air, watch for whale and eagles, and soak in the stunning views of glaciers and fjords. Balcony cabins offer a sense of intimacy and tranquility, making them an excellent choice for travelers who want to enjoy the scenery without leaving the comfort of their cabin.

4. Suites: Luxury and Elegance

If you're seeking the ultimate in luxury and space, suites are the epitome of elegance and comfort. Suites offer larger living areas, separate sleeping and sitting areas, and often come with enhanced amenities and personalized services. They may include private verandas, expansive windows, and even whirlpool tubs. Staying in a suite provides an indulgent experience that allows you to truly unwind and savor the cruise to the fullest.

5. Family Cabins: Spacious Accommodation

Many Alaska cruises offer family-friendly cabins designed to accommodate groups traveling together. These cabins often feature interconnected rooms, bunk beds, and extra space to ensure everyone's comfort. Traveling with family or a group of friends is made even more enjoyable when you can share the experience from the convenience of adjoining cabins.

6. Solo Traveler Cabins: Exclusive Comfort

Cruising solo doesn't mean sacrificing comfort or convenience. Many cruise lines offer solo traveler cabins designed specifically for individual travelers. These cabins are tailored to provide comfort and privacy for solo adventurers, often featuring reduced single supplement fees and dedicated communal spaces where solo travelers can connect with like-minded cruisers.

7. Accessible Cabins: Inclusive Accommodation

Cruise lines are increasingly mindful of providing accessible accommodations for travelers with mobility challenges or disabilities. Accessible cabins are designed to ensure comfort and convenience, with features such as wider doorways, roll-in showers, and other accessibility aids. These cabins are a testament to the commitment of cruise lines to making cruising accessible and inclusive for all passengers.

8. Spa Cabins: Wellness and Relaxation

For those seeking rejuvenation and wellness, some cruise lines offer spa cabins situated near onboard spa facilities. These cabins often come with additional amenities like complimentary spa treatments, access to relaxation areas, and special perks that enhance the overall wellness experience during your cruise.

In conclusion, the range of cabin options available on an Alaska cruise ensures that every traveler can find the perfect accommodation that suits their preferences and needs. Whether you're looking for affordability, panoramic views, private outdoor spaces, luxury amenities, or family-friendly features, there's a cabin type that will make your cruise experience exceptional. Your choice of cabin becomes not only your place of rest but also your haven of comfort as you embark on a voyage through the pristine wilderness and captivating landscapes of Alaska.

Onboard Entertainment: Elevating the Alaska Cruise Experience

An Alaska cruise is not just a journey; it's a multifaceted experience that encompasses exploration, relaxation, and enrichment. As you set sail through the breathtaking landscapes and glacial fjords, your adventure extends beyond the shores to the heart of the ship itself. Onboard entertainment is an integral part of the cruise experience, offering a diverse array of activities, performances, and experiences that captivate, delight, and enrich passengers of all ages. From Broadway-style shows to educational lectures, onboard entertainment transforms the cruise ship into a floating oasis of entertainment and culture, enhancing your journey through the Last Frontier.

1. Broadway-Quality Productions: Theatrical Marvels at Sea

One of the highlights of onboard entertainment is the Broadway-style productions that bring the magic of the stage to the open sea. Lavish sets, dazzling costumes, and talented performers come together to create captivating performances that rival those found in the world's most renowned theaters. From musical revues to full-scale productions of beloved classics, these shows transport audiences to a world of imagination and spectacle.

2. Live Music and Bands: Melodies That Set the Mood

Live music is the heartbeat of onboard entertainment, setting the rhythm and atmosphere throughout the ship. From upbeat poolside performances to elegant jazz ensembles in lounges, the sounds of live music create an ambiance that complements every moment of your cruise. Talented musicians and bands perform a diverse range of genres, ensuring that there's a musical backdrop to suit every taste.

3. Comedy and Variety Shows: Laughter on the High Seas

Laughter is universal, and onboard comedy and variety shows are designed to bring smiles to passengers' faces. Stand-up comedians, improv troupes, and variety acts take the stage, delivering doses of humor and entertainment that help create a lighthearted atmosphere. These performances provide a delightful way to unwind after a day of exploration.

4. Movie Nights: Cinematic Under the Stars

Under the starry Alaskan skies, passengers can enjoy open-air movie screenings on deck. From classic films to recent blockbusters, movie nights are a popular way to relax and enjoy entertainment in a unique outdoor setting. Snuggle up under warm blankets and savor popcorn as you watch movies with fellow cruisers against the backdrop of the sea.

5. Educational Lectures and Workshops: Enrichment at Sea

An Alaska cruise is not only about sightseeing; it's also an opportunity to learn and expand your horizons. Many cruise lines offer educational lectures and workshops on a variety of topics, from wildlife and ecology to history and culture. Experts in various fields provide insights that deepen your understanding of the regions you're visiting, making your cruise a journey of enrichment.

6. Culinary Demonstrations: A Feast for the Senses

For those with a passion for food and drink, culinary demonstrations are a treat for the senses. Experienced chefs showcase their skills, offering cooking tips, insights into local cuisine, and the opportunity to savor delectable creations. From interactive cooking classes to wine tastings, these demonstrations provide a hands-on way to immerse yourself in the culinary arts.

7. Dance Parties and Theme Nights: Celebrate in Style

Cruise ships come alive with energy during dance parties and theme nights. From elegant formal evenings to lively themed parties, passengers have the chance to dress up, dance, and celebrate in style. Whether you're showing off your moves on the dance floor or enjoying the glamour of a masquerade ball, these events add an element of festivity to your cruise.

8. Art Auctions and Galleries: Nurturing Creativity

Art lovers will find their niche in onboard art galleries and auctions. Curated collections of fine art, sculptures, and other creations are showcased, offering passengers the chance to appreciate and acquire unique pieces. Art auctions provide an interactive platform for acquiring artworks while learning about the artists and their inspirations.

9. Casino and Gaming: A Dash of Excitement

For those seeking a touch of excitement, onboard casinos offer a range of gaming options. From slot machines to card games, passengers can try their luck and enjoy the thrill of gaming while surrounded by the luxury and comfort of the ship.

10. Children and Family Activities: Enchanting Young Minds

Alaska cruises are family-friendly, with a host of activities designed to entertain and engage passengers of all ages. Children's clubs, arts and crafts sessions, storytelling, and age-appropriate entertainment ensure that young travelers have their own share of onboard fun and adventure.

In conclusion, onboard entertainment is an integral part of the Alaska cruise experience, enriching your journey with a diverse tapestry of activities and performances. From the enchantment of theatrical productions to the relaxation of live music, from laughter-inducing comedy shows to educational lectures, each element of entertainment adds layers of enjoyment to your voyage. Whether you're seeking relaxation, cultural enrichment, family fun, or simply the joy of being entertained, the onboard offerings ensure that every moment of your cruise is as memorable and fulfilling as the stunning landscapes that unfold beyond the ship's rails.

Culinary Odyssey: Dining Delights on Your Alaska Cruise

An Alaska cruise isn't just a journey through stunning landscapes; it's also a culinary adventure that tantalizes your taste buds with a diverse array of flavors, aromas, and dining experiences. From elegant dining rooms to casual cafes, the dining options onboard your cruise ship are designed to satisfy every palate and cater to every preference. As you traverse the serene waters and breathtaking fjords of Alaska, you'll also be embarking on a culinary journey that showcases the richness of regional ingredients, the creativity of culinary experts, and the joy of sharing meals with fellow passengers.

1. Main Dining Rooms: Elegance and Excellence

The main dining rooms onboard your Alaska cruise ship are the epitome of elegance and excellence. These grand spaces offer a range of delectable options for breakfast, lunch, and dinner. With diverse menus that showcase international cuisine and local specialties, the main dining rooms provide a gourmet experience that elevates every meal into a celebration of flavors and presentation.

2. Specialty Restaurants: Gastronomic Gems

For a dining experience that stands out, specialty restaurants are a must-visit. These upscale dining venues offer a curated menu that focuses on specific cuisines, themes, or culinary techniques. From gourmet steakhouses to Italian trattorias, each specialty restaurant presents a unique culinary narrative that transports you to a world of gastronomic delight.

3. Buffet and Casual Dining: Relaxed and Flavorful

Casual dining venues, including buffet options, provide a more relaxed atmosphere while still delivering a delicious array of choices. Cruise ship buffets offer a bounty of international dishes, from hearty breakfasts to flavorful lunches and themed dinners. The casual setting allows you to savor your meal at your own pace, making it a popular choice for families and those seeking a laid-back dining experience.

Room Service: Dining in Privacy

Enjoying a meal in the privacy of your cabin is a luxury that Alaska cruise lines offer through room service. Whether you're craving a morning coffee and pastry or a late-night snack, room service ensures that you can indulge in a culinary treat whenever the mood strikes. It's a perfect option for moments when you want to relax and enjoy the comfort of your cabin.

Alaskan Flavors: A Taste of the Region

An Alaska cruise wouldn't be complete without savoring the flavors of the region's bountiful harvest. Cruise lines often incorporate Alaskan seafood, such as succulent salmon, king crab, and halibut, into their menus. These local delicacies provide a true taste of Alaska and highlight the culinary riches of the area you're exploring.

Culinary Events and Demonstrations: Interactive Enchantment

Cruise ships often host culinary events and demonstrations that allow passengers to engage with the art of cooking and mixology. From cooking classes with expert chefs to wine tastings led by sommeliers, these experiences provide insights into the world of gastronomy and offer the chance to learn new skills while at sea.

Food Festivals and Themes: Celebrating Diversity

Throughout your cruise, you may have the opportunity to participate in food festivals and themed dining events that celebrate the diversity of global cuisine. From Mexican fiestas to Asian-inspired evenings, these themed events create an immersive experience where you can explore different cultures through their culinary traditions.

Customizable Dining: Personalized Pleasures

Cruise lines are increasingly attuned to individual dietary preferences and restrictions, offering customizable dining experiences. Vegetarian, vegan, gluten-free, and other dietary options are readily available, ensuring that every passenger can savor a delightful meal that caters to their needs and preferences.

9. Social Dining: Building Connections

Dining onboard an Alaska cruise isn't just about savoring exceptional cuisine; it's also about building connections and forging friendships. Many cruise lines offer communal dining options that allow passengers to share a table with fellow travelers. These shared meals provide an opportunity to exchange stories, connect with people from different parts of the world, and create lasting memories.

10. Children's Dining: Delights for Young Palates

Cruising with children is a family affair, and cruise lines ensure that young passengers have their own delightful dining experiences. Children's menus offer favorites that cater to young palates, ensuring that even the youngest cruisers can enjoy delicious meals tailored to their tastes.

In conclusion, dining and culinary experiences are an integral part of the Alaska cruise journey, enhancing your voyage through a symphony of flavors, presentations, and ambiance. Whether you're savoring gourmet cuisine in an elegant dining room, exploring specialty restaurants that transport you to distant lands, or enjoying casual bites with breathtaking views, every meal becomes a memorable event that contributes to the tapestry of your cruise experience. The diverse range of dining options ensures that each day brings a new culinary delight, each bite a celebration of the art of food, and each meal an opportunity to share stories and create connections with fellow passengers. An Alaska cruise is not just a feast for the eyes; it's a feast for the senses that nourishes both body and soul.

Made in the USA
Las Vegas, NV
02 January 2024

83780751R00105